MICROCONTROLLER AND EMBEDDED SYSTEM

MICROCONTROLLER AND EMBEDDED SYSTEM

For B.Tech. Sixth Semester course of GBTU Lucknow and MTU, Noida

(SECOND EDITION)

A. K. Singh
Dean (Academics) and HOD
Electronics and Communication Engineering
Goel Institute of Technology and Management
Lucknow (U.P.)

NEW AGE
UPTU

An Imprint of

NEW AGE INTERNATIONAL (P) LIMITED, PUBLISHERS
New Delhi • Bangalore • Chennai • Cochin • Guwahati
Hyderabad • Kolkata • Lucknow • Mumbai
Visit us at **www.newagepublishers.com**

Published by New Age International (P) Ltd., Publishers
First Edition: 2008
Second Edition: 2012

Branches:

- 37/10, 8th Cross (Near Hanuman Temple), Azad Nagar, Chamarajpet, **Bangalore**-560 018. Tel.: (080) 2675 6823, Telefax: 2675 6820, E-mail: bangalore@newagepublishers.com
- 26, Damodaran Street, T. Nagar, **Chennai**-600 017. Tel.: (044) 24353401, Telefax: 24351463 E-mail: chennai@newagepublishers.com
- CC-39/1016, Carrier Station Road, Ernakulam South, **Cochin**-682 016. Tel.: (0484) 2377004, Telefax: 4051303 E-mail: cochin@newagepublishers.com
- Hemsen Complex, Mohd. Shah Road, Paltan Bazar, Near Starline Hotel, **Guwahati**-781 008. Tel.: (0361) 2513881 Telefax: 2543669, E-mail: guwahati@newagepublishers.com
- 105, 1st Floor, Madhiray Kaveri Tower, 3-2-19, Azam Jahi Road, Nimboliadda, **Hyderabad**-500 027. Tel.: (040) 24652456, Telefax: 24652457, E-mail: hyderabad@newagepublishers.com
- RDB Chambers (Formerly Lotus Cinema)106A, 1st Floor, S.N. Banerjee Road, **Kolkata**-700 014. Tel.: (033) 22273773, Telefax: 22275247, E-mail: kolkata@newagepublishers.com
- 16-A, Jopling Road, **Lucknow**-226 001. Tel.: (0522) 2209578, 4045297, Telefax: 2204098 E-mail: lucknow@newagepublishers.com
- 142C, Victor House, Ground Floor, N.M. Joshi Marg, Lower Parel, **Mumbai**-400 013. Tel.: (022) 24927869 Telefax: 24915415, E-mail: mumbai@newagepublishers.com
- 22, Golden House, Daryaganj, **New Delhi**-110 002. Tel.: (011) 23262370, 23262368, Telefax: 43551305 E-mail: sales@newagepublishers.com

---

ISBN : 978-81-224-3360-9

₹ 200.00

C-11-12-6081

Printed in India at Ajit Printers, Delhi.
Typeset at Inhouse.

PUBLISHING FOR ONE WORLD
NEW AGE INTERNATIONAL (P) LIMITED, PUBLISHERS
4835/24, Ansari Road, Daryaganj, New Delhi-110002
Visit us at **www.newagepublishers.com**

Dedicated to
my parents and my teachers
who have helped shape me into who
I am today

Preface to the Second Edition

The increased uses of microcontroller in modern control engineering necessitate an indepth knowledge of the subject. There are lot of references available on microcontroller which discusses various topics separately. This comprehensive text fulfills the course requirement on the subject of microcontrollers for B. Tech. degree course in Electronics and Communication, Electronic and Instrumentation, Electronic Instrumentation and Control, Instrumentation and Control Engineering of U.P. Technical University, Lucknow and other technical universities. It will also serve as a useful reference book for competitive examinations.

Most of the materials in this book have been taken from book Microcontrollers "Features and Applications" co-authored with Dr. D.S. Yadav and upgraded. The book is divided into nine chapters. Each chapter begins with an introduction and ends with review questions and exercise problems. Chapter 1 provides an introduction to the microcontrollers history and detail features a microcontrollers could be, and detailed discussions on individual microcontrollers are contained in rest of the chapters. Chapter 2 introduces 8051 microcontrollers features, organization and instruction sets with examples. Chapter 3 deals with assembly language programming (8051) in detail. Chapter 4 discusses interrupt structure of 8051, serial communication as well as timer and counter operations with there applications. Chapters 5, 6 and 7 cover 8051 interfacing of microcontroller for real world applications and automations. Chapter 8 describes Intel 8096 microcontroller. Chapter 9 introduces Motorola MC68HC11 microcontrollers. There is also an appendix on Motorola MC68HC11 programming.

All the topics are illustrated with clear diagram and simple language is used throughout the text to facilitate easy understanding of the concepts. The author welcomes constructive suggestion and comments from the readers for the improvement of this book.

A.K. SINGH

Acknowledgements

This book is the result of the dedication and encouragement of many individuals. I would like to thank my family members especially wife Menka, daughter Omanshi and son Astitva for their patience and continuing support and parents for their blessings.

I am indebted to my teachers, friends and especially Manish Tiwari co-author of the book *Digital Principles—Switching Theory* for his valuable contribution and suggestion during the completion of this manuscript.

I thankfully acknowledge the contributions of various authors, data manuals, journals, reference manuals, etc. from where materials have been collected to enrich the contents of the book. Finally, I would like to thank New Age International (P) Limited, Publishers, especially the editorial team for their continuous support and encouragement to made the book a reality.

At last but not the least by the blessing of almighty and good fortune I get such a supporting and cooperative people around me who in one way or other help me to complete this project in time.

A.K. SINGH

SYLLABUS

B. Tech. Sixth Semester

EIC 601 MICROCONTROLLER (Theory Subjects) 310

Unit	Topic	Chapter/ Section	Proposed number of Lectures
I	Introduction, Microcontrollers and Embedded processors, Overview of the 8051, Inside the 8051, Addressing modes.	0.3, 1.1, 1.2, 2.1, 5.1-5.4,	6
II	Introduction to 8051 assembly programming, Assembling and running an 8051 program. The program counter and ROM space in the 8051, 8051 data types and directives, 8051 flag bits and the PSW register, 8051 register banks and stack, 8051 I/O programming, I/O bit manipulation programming.	2.2, 2.3, 2.4, 2.5, 2.6, 2.7, 4.1, 4.2	8
III	Programming the 8051 timers, Counter programming, Basics of serial communications, 8051 connection to RS-232, 8051 serial port programming assembly, 8051 interrupts, Programming timer interrupts, programming external hardware interrupts, programming the Serial communication interrupts, Interrupts priority in the 8051.	9.1, 9.2, 10.1, 10.2, 10.3, 11.1, 11.2, 11.3, 11.4, 11.5	10
IV	Interfacing with 8051: Memory address decoding 8031/51 interfacing with external ROM, 8051 data memory space, LCD, Keyboard, Parallel and Serial ADC, DAC interfacing, Sensor interfacing and Signal Conditioning, Stepper motor and DC motor.	14.2, 14.3, 14.4, 12.1, 12.2, 13.1, 13.2, 13.3, 17.2, 17.3	10
V	Programming the 8255 and Interfacing, Introduction to Intel 8096 and MC68HC11 microcontroller*.	15.1, 15.2, Text Book 2: Ch. 3 & 4	6

Contents

Contents

Chapter 1

Introduction to Microcontrollers

1.1 INTRODUCTION

Microcontrollers have only been with us for a few decades but their impact (direct or indirect) on our lives is profound. Usually these are supposed to be just *data processors performing exhaustive numeric operations*. But their presence is unnoticed at most of the places like

- *At supermarkets* in Cash Registers, Weighing Scales, etc.
- *At home* in Ovens, Washing Machines, Alarm Clocks, etc.
- *At play* in Toys, VCRs, Stereo Equipment, etc.
- *At office* in Typewriters, Photocopiers, Elevators, etc.
- *In industry* in Industrial Automation, safety systems, etc.
- *On roads* in Cars, Traffic Signals, etc.

What inside them makes these machines "smart"? The answer is microcontroller.

Creating applications for the microcontrollers is different than any other development job in electronics and computing. Before selecting a particular device for an application, it is important to understand what the different options and features are and what they can mean with regard to developing the application.

The purpose of this chapter is to introduce the concept of a microcontrollers, how it differ from microprocessors, different type of commercial microcontrollers available as well as their applications. The reminder of the book will go through and present different types of microcontrollers and also programming and interfacing techniques of microcontroller, mainly 8051, in detail.

1.2 EMBEDDED CONTROLLER

Simply an embedded controller is a controller that is embedded in a greater system. One can define an embedded controller as a controller (or computer) that is embedded into some device for some purpose other than to provide general purpose computing.

Is an embedded controller is the same as a microcontroller? The answer is definitely no. One can state devices such as 68000, 32032, x86, Z80, and so on that are used as embedded controllers but they aren't microcontrollers.

We might be correct by stating that an embedded controller controls something (for example controlling a device such as a microwave oven, car braking system or a cruise missile). An embedded controller may also embed the on-chip resources like a microcontroller. Microcontrollers and microprocessors are widely used in embedded systems. Though microcontrollers are preferred over microprocessors for embedded systems due to low power consumption.

1.3 MICROCONTROLLERS AND MICROPROCESSORS

A controller is used to control some process. At one time, controllers were built exclusively from logic components, and were usually large, heavy boxes. Later on, microprocessors were used and the entire controller could fit on a small circuit board. This is still common– one can find many controllers powered by one of the many common microprocessors (including Zilog Z80, Intel 8088, Motorola 6809, and others).

As the process of miniaturization continued, all of the components needed for a controller were built right onto one chip. A one chip computer, or microcontroller was born.

A CPU built into a single VLSI chip is called microprocessor. The simplified block diagram of the CPU is shown in the Fig. 1.1. It contains arithmetic and logic unit (ALU), Instruction decode and control unit, Instruction register, Program counter (PC), clock circuit (internal or external), reset circuit (internal or external) and registers. For example, Intel 8085 is 8-bit microprocessor and Intel 8086/8088 is 16-bit microprocessor.

Microprocessor is general-purpose digital computer central processing unit (CPU). The microprocessor is general-purpose device and additional external circuitry are added to make it microcomputer.

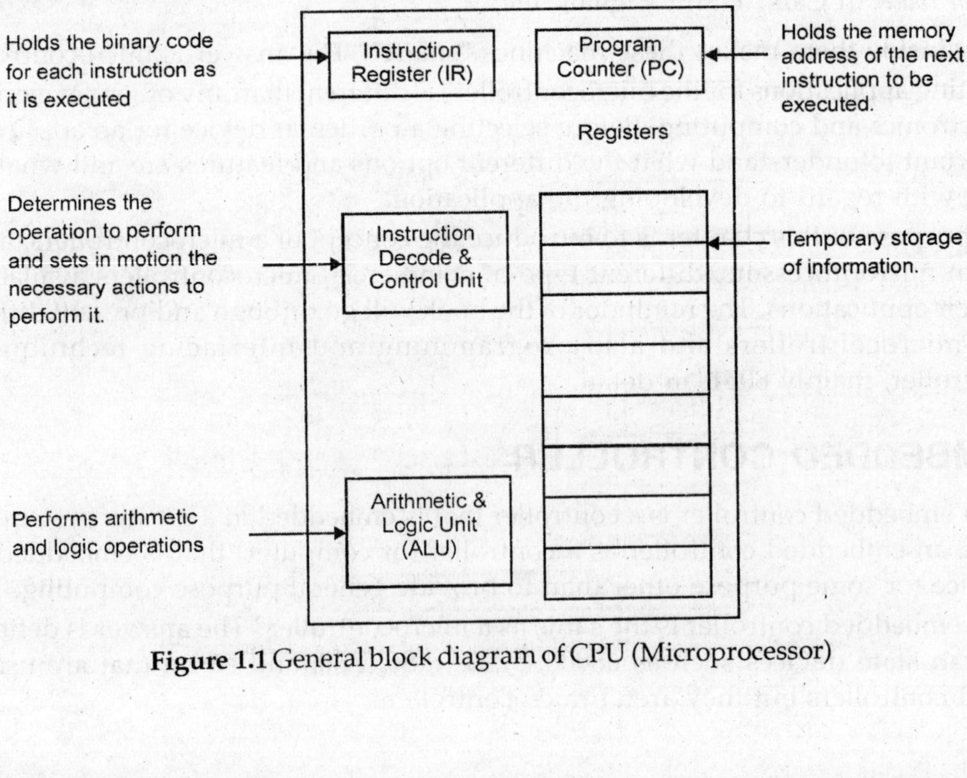

Figure 1.1 General block diagram of CPU (Microprocessor)

A digital computer having microprocessor as the CPU along with I/O devices and nemory is known as microcomputer. The block diagram in the Fig. 1.2 shows a nicrocomputer.

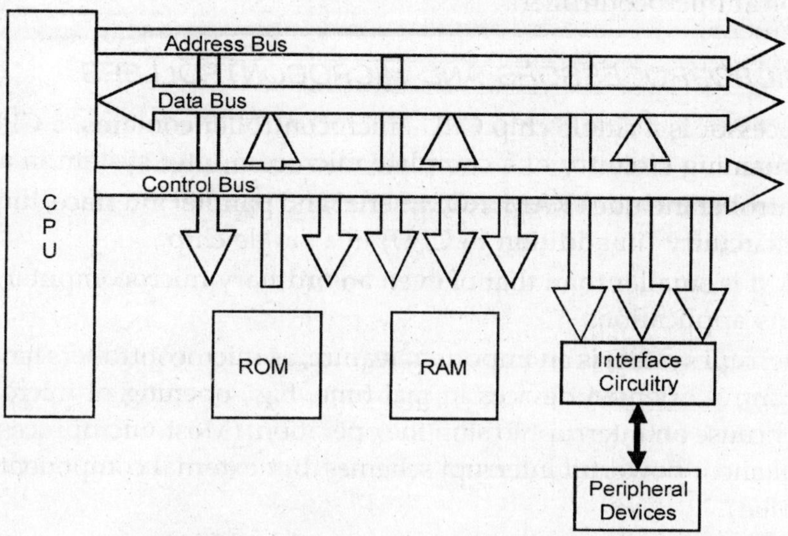

Figure 1.2 Microcomputer block diagram

A microcontroller is a highly integrated chip, which includes on single chip, all or nost of the parts needed for a controller. The microcontroller typically includes: CPU Central Processing Unit), RAM (Random Access Memory), EPROM/PROM/ROM Erasable Programmable Read Only Memory), I/O (input/output) – serial and parallel, imers, interrupt controller. For example, Intel 8051 is 8-bit microcontroller and Intel 096 is 16-bit microcontroller.

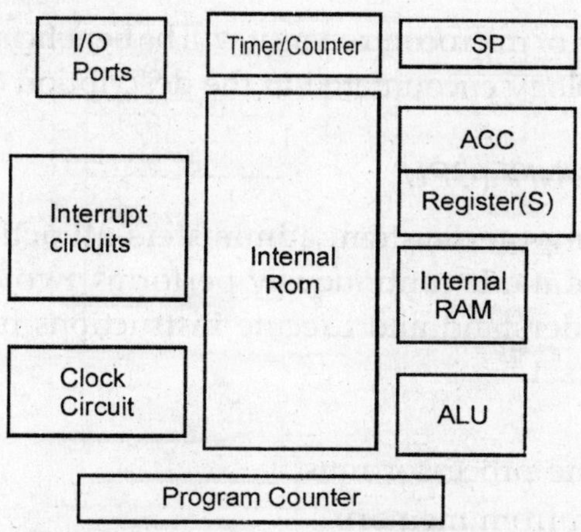

Figure 1.3 A block diagram of a microcontroller

By only including the features specific to the task (control), cost is relatively low. A typical microcontroller has bit manipulation instructions, easy and direct access to I/O (input/output), and quick and efficient interrupt processing. Figure 1.3 shows the block diagram of a typical microcontroller.

COMPARING MICROPROCESSORS AND MICROCONTROLLERS

- Microprocessor is a single chip CPU, microcontroller contains, a CPU and much of the remaining circuitry of a complete microcomputer system in a single chip.
- Microcontroller includes RAM, ROM, serial and parallel interface, timer, interrupt schedule circuitry (in addition to CPU) in a single chip.
  –RAM is smaller than that of even an ordinary microcomputer, but enough for its applications.
  –Interrupt system is an important feature, as microcontrollers have to respond to control oriented devices in real time. E.g., opening of microwave oven's door cause an interrupt to stop the operation. (Most microprocessors can also implement powerful interrupt schemes, but external components are usually needed).
- Microprocessors are most commonly used as the CPU in microcomputer systems. Microcontrollers are used in small, minimum component designs performing control-oriented activities.
- Microprocessor instruction sets are "processing intensive", implying powerful addressing modes with instructions catering to large volumes of data. Their instructions operate on nibbles, bytes, etc. Microcontrollers have instruction sets catering to the control of inputs and outputs. Their instructions operate also on a single bit. E.g., a motor may be turned ON and OFF by a 1-bit output port.

Before going in to details of microcontrollers it will be beneficial to go through common and frequently used terminology encountered in the description of microcontrollers.

CENTRAL PROCESSING UNIT (CPU)

CPU is the brain of the computer system, administers all activity in the system and performs all operations on data. It continuously performs two operations: *fetching* and *executing* instructions. It understand and execute instructions based on a set of binary codes called the instruction set.

Machine Cycle

To execute an instruction–the processor must:

1. Fetch the instruction from memory
2. Decode the instruction

3. Execute the instruction
4. Store the result back in the memory. These four steps refer to Machine Cycle.

Generally one machine cycle = X clock cycles ("X" depends on the particular instruction being executed). Shorter the clock cycle, lesser the time it takes to complete one machine cycle, so instructions are executed faster. Hence, faster the processor.

FETCHING AND EXECUTING AN INSTRUCTION

Fetching involves the following steps:

(a) Contents of PC are placed on address bus.

(b) READ signal is activated.

(c) Data (instruction opcode) are read from RAM and placed on data bus.

(d) Opcode is latched into the CPU's internal instruction register.

(e) PC is incremented to prepare for the next fetch from memory.

While execution involves decoding the opcode and generating control signals to gate internal registers in and out of the ALU and to signal the ALU to perform the specified operation.

THE BUSES: ADDRESS, DATA, AND CONTROL

A BUS is a collection of wires carrying information with a common purpose. For each *read* or *write* operation, the CPU specifies the location of the data or instruction by placing an address on the address bus, then activates a signal on the control bus indicating whether the operation is read or write.

–READ OPERATIONS retrieve a byte of data from memory at the location specified and place it on the **data bus**. CPU reads the data and places it in one of its internal registers.

–WRITE OPERATIONS put data from CPU on the data bus and store it in the location specified.

ADDRESS BUS carries the address of a specified location. For n address lines, 2^n locations can be accessed. E.g., A 16-bit address bus can access 2^{16} = 65,536 locations or 64K locations (2^{10} = 1024 = 1K, 2^6 = 64).

DATA BUS carries information between the CPU and memory or between the CPU and I/O devices.

CONTROL BUS carries control signals supplied by the CPU to synchronize the movement of information on the address and data bus.

CONTROL/MONITOR (INPUT/OUTPUT) DEVICES

CONTROL DEVICES are *outputs*, or *actuators*, that can affect the world around them when supplied with a voltage or current.

MONITORING DEVICES are *inputs*, or *sensors*, that are stimulated by temperature pressure, light, motion, etc. and convert this to voltage or current read by the computer Note: The interface circuitry converts the voltage or current to binary data, or vice versa.

1.4 TYPES OF MICROCONTROLLERS

Microcontrollers can be classified on the basis of internal bus width, architecture, memory and instruction set. Figure 1.4 shows the various types of microcontrollers.

1.4.1 THE 8,16 AND 32-BIT MICROCONTROLLERS

THE 8-BIT MICROCONTROLLER

When the ALU performs arithmetic and logical operations on a byte (8-bits) at an instruction, the microcontroller is an 8-bit microcontroller. The internal bus width o 8-bit microcontroller is of 8-bit. Examples of 8-bit microcontrollers are Intel 8051 famil and Motorola MC68HC11 family.

THE 16-BIT MICROCONTROLLER

When the ALU performs arithmetic and logical operations on a word (16-bits) at a instruction, the microcontroller is an 16-bit microcontroller. The internal bus width c 16-bit microcontroller is of 16-bit. Examples of 16-bit microcontrollers are Intel 809 family and Motorola MC68HC12 and MC68332 families. The performance an computing capability of 16 bit microcontrollers are enhanced with greater precision a compared to the 8-bit microcontrollers.

THE 32-BIT MICROCONTROLLER

When the ALU performs arithmetic and logical operations on a double word (32 bits) at an instruction, the microcontroller is an 32-bit microcontroller. The internal bu width of 32-bit microcontroller is of 32-bit. Examples of 32-bit microcontrollers are Int 80960 family and Motorola M683xx and Intel/Atmel 251 family. The performance an computing capability of 32 bit microcontrollers are enhanced with greater precision compared to the 16-bit microcontrollers.

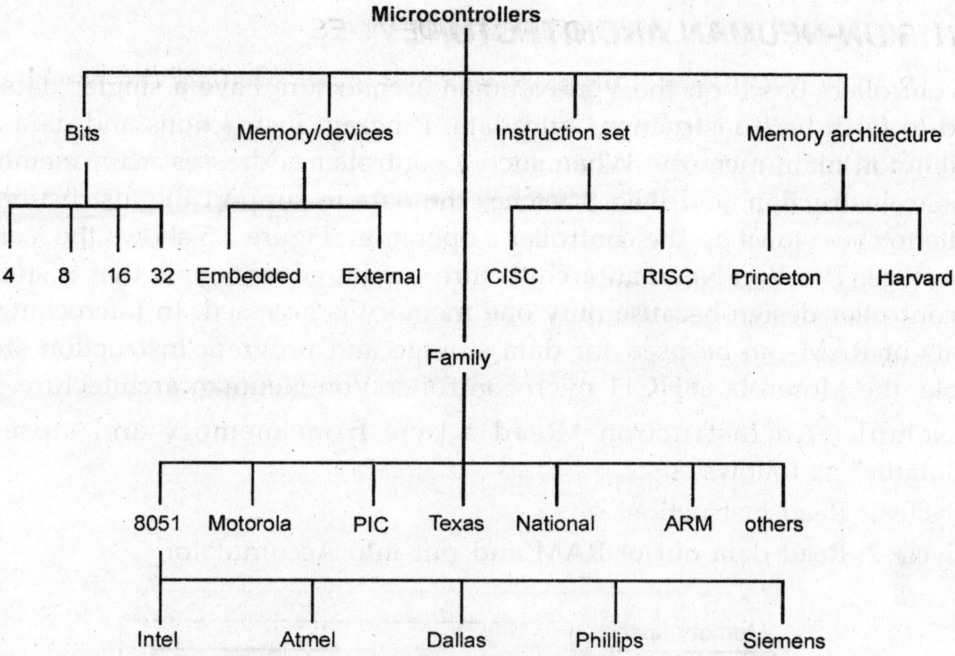

Figure 1.4 Types of microcontrollers

1.4.2 EMBEDDED AND EXTERNAL MEMORY MICROCONTROLLERS

EMBEDDED MICROCONTROLLERS

When an embedded system has an microcontroller unit that has all the functional blocks (including program as well as data memory) available on a chip is called an embedded microcontroller. For example, 8051 having Program & Data Memory, I/O Ports, Serial Communication, Counters and Timers and Interrupt Control logic on the chip is an embedded microcontroller.

EXTERNAL MEMORY MICROCONTROLLERS

When an embedded system has an microcontroller unit that has not all the functional blocks available on a chip is called an external memory microcontroller. In external memory microcontroller, all or part of the memory units are externally interfaced using an interfacing circuit called the glue circuit. For example, 8031 has no program memory on the chip is an external memory microcontroller.

1.4.3 MICROCONTROLLER ARCHITECTURAL FEATURES

There are mainly two categories of processors, namely, Von-Neuman (or Princeton) architecture and Harvard Architecture. These two architecture differ in the way data and programs are stored and accessed.

1.4.3.1 VON-NEUMAN ARCHITECTURE

Microcontrollers based on the Von-Neuman architecture have a single "data" bus that is used to fetch both instructions and data. Program instructions and data are stored in a common main memory. When such a controller addresses main memory, it first fetches an instruction, and then it fetches the data to support the instruction. The two separate fetches slows up the controller's operation. Figure 1.5 shows the Von-Neuman Architecture. The Von-Neuman architecture's main advantage is that it simplifies the microcontroller design because only one memory is accessed. In microcontrollers, the contents of RAM can be used for data storage and program instruction storage. For example, the Motorola 68HC11 microcontroller Von-Neuman architecture.

Example: An Instruction "Read a byte from memory and store it in the accumulator" as follows:

Cycle 1: Read instruction

Cycle 2: Read data out of RAM and put into Accumulator

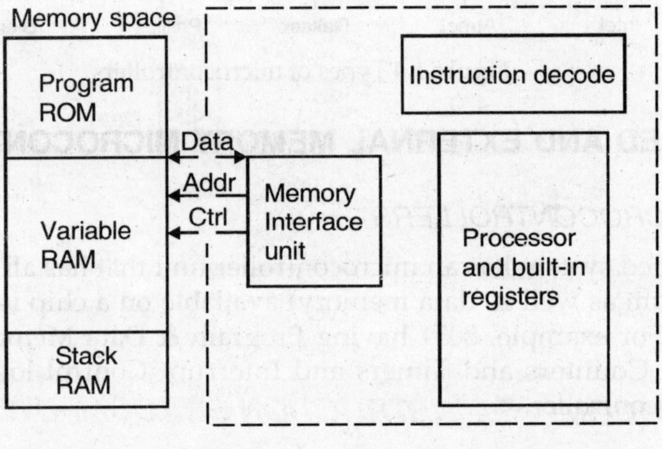

Figure 1.5 Von-Neuman architecture block diagram

1.4.3.2 HARVARD ARCHITECTURE

Microcontrollers based on the Harvard Architecture have separate data bus and an instruction bus. This allows execution to occur in parallel. As an instruction is being "pre-fetched", the current instruction is executing on the data bus. Once the current instruction is complete, the next instruction is ready to go. This pre-fetch theoretically allows for much faster execution than Von-Neuman architecture, on the expense of complexity. Figure 1.6 shows the Harvard Architecture.The Harvard Architecture executes instructions in fewer instruction cycles than the Von-Neuman architecture. For example,the intel Mcs-51 family of microcontrollers and PIC microcontrollers uses Harvard Architecture.

The same instruction (as shown under Von-Newman architecture) would be executed as follows:

Cycle 1: – Complete previous instruction
– Read the "Move Data to Accumulator" instruction

Cycle 2: – Execute "Move Data to Accumulator" instruction
– Read next instruction

Hence each instruction is effectively executed in one instruction cycle.

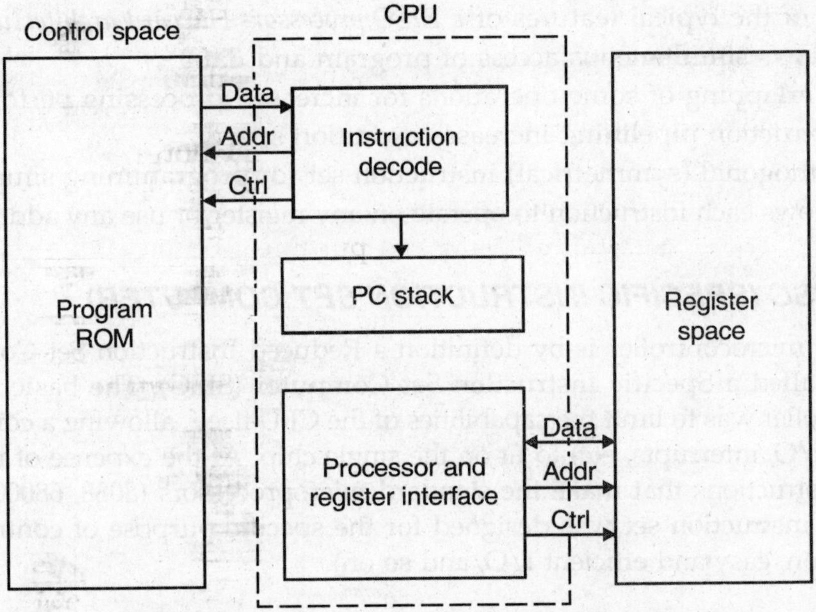

Figure 1.6 Harvard architecture block diagram

1.4.3.3 CISC (COMPLEX INSTRUCTION SET COMPUTER) ARCHITECTURE MICROCONTROLLERS

Almost all of today's microcontrollers are based on the CISC (Complex Instruction Set Computer) concept. When an microcontroller has an instruction set that supports many addressing modes for the arithmetic and logical instructions, data transfer and memory accesses instructions, the microcontroller is said to be of CISC architecture.

The typical CISC microcontroller has well over 80 instructions, many of them very powerful and very specialized for specific control tasks. It is quite common for the instructions to all behave quite differently. Some might only operate on certain address spaces or registers, and others might only recognize certain addressing modes.

The advantages of the CISC architecture are that many of the instructions are macro-like, allowing the programmer to use one instruction in place of many simpler instructions. An example of CISC architecture microcontroller is Intel 8096 family.

1.4.3.4 RISC (REDUCED INSTRUCTION SET COMPUTER) ARCHITECTURE MICROCONTROLLERS

The industry trend for microprocessor design is for Reduced Instruction Set Computers (RISC) designs. When a microcontroller has an instruction set that supports fewer addressing modes for the arithmetic and logical instructions and for data transfer instructions, the microcontroller is said to be of RISC architecture.

The benefits of RISC design simplicity are a smaller chip, smaller pin count, and very low power consumption.

Some of the typical features of a *RISC processor- Harvard architecture* are

1. Allows simultaneous access of program and data.
2. Overlapping of some operations for increased processing performance.
3. Instruction pipelining increases execution speed.
4. Orthogonal (symmetrical) instruction set for programming simplicity.
5. Allows each instruction to operate on any register or use any addressing mode.

1.4.3.5 SISC (SPECIFIC INSTRUCTION SET COMPUTER)

Actually, a microcontroller is by definition a Reduced Instruction Set Computer. It could really be called a Specific Instruction Set Computer (SISC). The basic idea behind the microcontroller was to limit the capabilities of the CPU itself, allowing a complete computer (memory, I/O, interrupts, etc) to fit on the single chip. At the expense of the more general purpose instructions that make the standard microprocessors (8088, 68000, 32032) so easy to use, the instruction set was designed for the specific purpose of control (powerful bit manipulation, easy and efficient I/O, and so on).

1.5 MICROCONTROLLER APPLICATIONS

In addition to control applications such as the home monitoring system, microcontrollers are frequently found in embedded applications. Among the many uses that you can find one or more microcontrollers: automotive applications, appliances (microwave oven, refrigerators, television and VCRs, stereos), automobiles (engine control, diagnostics, climate control), environmental control (greenhouse, factory, home), instrumentation, aerospace, and thousands of other uses.

Microcontrollers are used extensively in robotics. In this application, many specific tasks might be distributed among a large number of microcontrollers in one system. Communications between each microcontroller and a central, more powerful microcontroller (or microcomputer, or even large computer) would enable information to be processed by the central computer, or to be passed around to other microcontrollers in the system.

A special application that microcontrollers are well suited for is data logging. By stick one of these chips out in the middle of a corn field or up in a balloon, one can monitor and record environmental parameters (temperature, humidity, rain, etc). Small size, low power consumption, and flexibility make these devices ideal for unattended data monitoring and recording.

1.6 COMMERCIAL MICROCONTROLLER DEVICES

Microcontrollers come in many varieties. Depending on the power and features that are needed, one might choose a 4 bit, 8 bit, 16 bit, or 32 bit microcontroller. In addition, some specialized versions are available which include features specific for communications, keyboard handling, signal processing, video processing, and other tasks. The examples of different types of commercial microcontroller devices are given in the following tables.

Table 1.1 *4 Bit Microcontrollers*

Model (Manufacturer)	I/O	Pins	RAM (bytes)	ROM (bytes)	Counters	Extra Features
COP400 Family (National)	23	28	64	1K	1	Serial bit I/O
HMCS40 (Hitachi)	10	28	32	512	-	10-bit ROM
TMS 1000 (Texas Instruments)	23	28	64	1K	-	LED display

Table 1.2 *8 Bit Microcontrollers*

Model (Manufacturer)	I/O	Pins	RAM (bytes)	ROM (bytes)	Counters	Extra Features
8048 (Intel)	27	40	64	1K	1	8k External memory
8051 (Intel)	32	40	128	4K	2	128k External memory, Boolean processing, serial port
COP800 Family (National)	24	28	64	1K	1	Serial bit I/O, 8- channel A/D converter
6805 (Motorola)	20	28	64	1K	1	PLL frequency synthesizer,
68hc11(Motorola)	40	52	256	8K	2	A/D, PWM generator, pulse accumulator
TMS370 (Texas)	55	68	256	4K	2	watchdog timer, Instruments) Serial ports, A/D (8 bit, 8 channel)
PIC (Micro Chip)	12	18	25	1K	0	small pin count, very low power consumption

Table 1.3. *16 Bit Microcontrollers*

Model (Manufacturer)	I/O	Pins	RAM (bytes)	ROM (bytes)	Counters	Extra Features
80c196 (Intel)	40	68	232 8K	2		PWM generator, watchdog timer
HPC Family (National)	52	68	512 16K	4		PWM generator, watchdog timer, 8-channel A/D, serial port

1.7 PROBLEMS

1. Write major differences between a microprocessor and a microcontroller.
2. Discuss the evolution of microcontrollers.
3. What are the applications of microcontrollers?
4. Discuss the advantages and disadvantages of Harvard and Princeton architectures.
5. Discuss the advantages of microcontrollers over microprocessors in control operations.
6. What are the different ways of classifying the types of microcontrollers?
7. How does a microcontroller differ from a microprocessor?
8. What are the RISC and CISC microcontrollers?
9. Discuss microcomputer system. Is microcomputer as same as microcontroller?
10. What is the difference between an embedded and external memory microcontroller?

Chapter 2

8051 Microcontroller

2.1 INTRODUCTION

The 8051 is an 8-bit microcontroller originally designed in the 1980's by Intel. Its standard form includes several standard on-chip peripherals, including timers, counters, and UART, plus 4K bytes of on-chip program memory and 128 bytes of data memory, making single-chip implementations possible.

The 8051 have modified Harvard architecture with separate address spaces for program memory and data memory. The program memory can be increase to 64K. Up to 4K bytes of program instructions can be stored in the internal memory of the 8051. The 8051 can address up to 64K of external data memory, and is accessed only by indirect addressing. The 8051 memory architecture includes 128 bytes of data memory that are accessible directly by its instructions. A 32-byte segment of this 128-byte memory block is bit addressable by a subset of the 8051 instructions, namely the bit-instructions. The majority of the 8051's instructions are executed within 12 clock cycles.

The 8051 instruction set is optimized for the one-bit operations so often desired in real-time control applications. The 8051 features the so-called "boolean processor". The boolean processor provides direct support for bit manipulation. This refers to the way instructions can single out bits just about anywhere (RAM, accumulators, I/O registers, etc.), perform complex bit tests and comparisons, and then execute relative jumps based on the results. This leads to more efficient programs that need to deal with binary input and output conditions inherent in digital-control problems.

2.2 INTERNAL ARCHITECTURE OF 8051

The 8051 architecture consists of:

- Eight-bit CPU and data path with registers A and B
- 5 interrupts: 2 external and 3 internal with 2 priority levels
- 2 16-bit timer/counters: T 0 and T 1
- Programmable full-duplex serial port (baud rate provided by one of the timers)
- 32 I/O lines (four 8-bit ports P0-P3)
- 0K (8031), ROM 4K (8051), EPROM 4K (8751) –RAM 128 bytes (8XY1), 256 bytes (8XY2) (where X= 0 or 7 &Y=3 or 5)

- 16-bit PC and data pointer (DPTR)
- 8-bit PSW
- 8-bit SP
- Oscillator and clock circuits
- Variety of addressing modes

OSCILLATOR AND CLOCK CIRCUITS

The 8051 operates based on an external crystal oscillator. This is an electrical device which, when energy is applied, emits pulses at a fixed frequency. Most often a quartz crystal oscillator is connected to inputs XTAL1 (pin 19) and XTAL2 (pin 18). XTAL1 is input to the inverting oscillator amplifier and input to the internal clock generating circuits and XTAL2 is output from the inverting oscillator amplifier.

The quartz crystal oscillator connected to XTAL1 and XTAL2 also needs two capacitors of 30-pf values. One side of each capacitor is connected to the grounds as shown in Fig. 2.1.

When the 8051 is connected to a crystal oscillator and is powered up, we can observe the frequency on the XTAL2 pin using the oscilloscope.

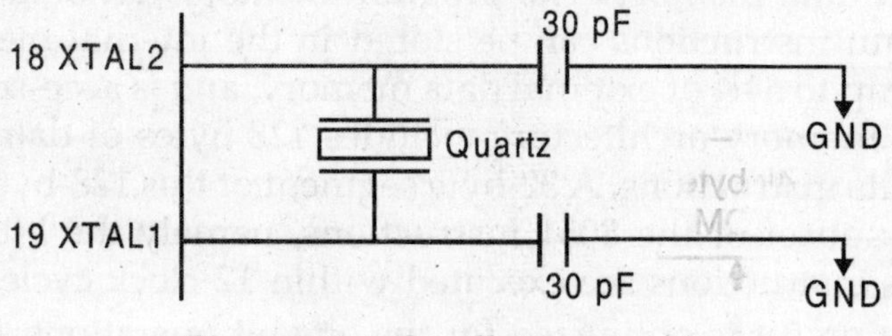

Figure 2.1 Oscillator circuit

When using an 8051, the most common crystal frequencies are 12 megahertz and 11.059 megahertz, with 11.059 being much more common.

The 8051 uses the crystal to synchronize it's operation. Effectively, the 8051 operates using what are called "machine cycles." A single machine cycle is the minimum amount of time in which a single 8051 instruction can be executed, although many instructions take multiple cycles.

In 8051, one machine cycle consists of twelve (12) clock cycles as shown in figure 2.1B. Machine cycle is sometimes called as instruction cycle by some authors. In 8051, each instruction cycle has six states (S_1 – S_6) and each state has two pulses (P1 and P2).

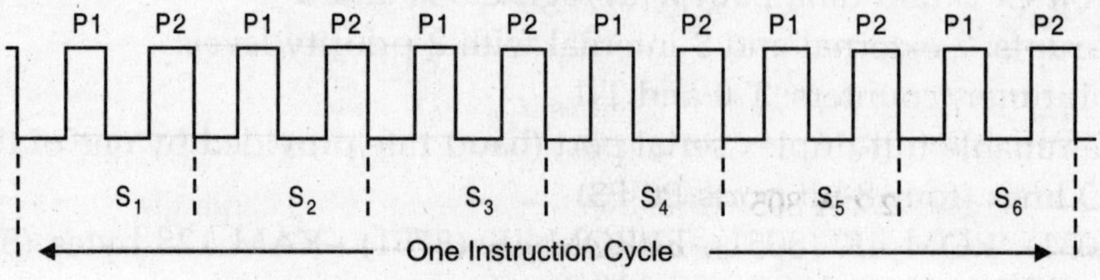

Figure 2.1B Instruction cycle of 8051

One 8051 machine cycle consists of twelve oscillator periods. The time (T) required for any 8051 instruction can be computed by dividing the clock frequency by 12, inverting that result and multiplying it by the number of machine cycles required by the instruction in question.

$$T = \frac{No\ of\ m/c\ cycles \times 12}{Crystal\ frequency}$$

Therefore, if a system which is using an 11.059 MHz clock, the number of instructions per second can be computed by dividing this value by 12.

11,059,000/12 = 921,583

This means that the 8051 can execute 921,583 single-cycle instructions per second. Inverting this will provide the amount of time taken by each instruction cycle (1.085 microseconds).

Figure 2.2A shows the simplified block diagram of 8051. While Intel® 8051 block diagram is shown in Fig. 2.2B.

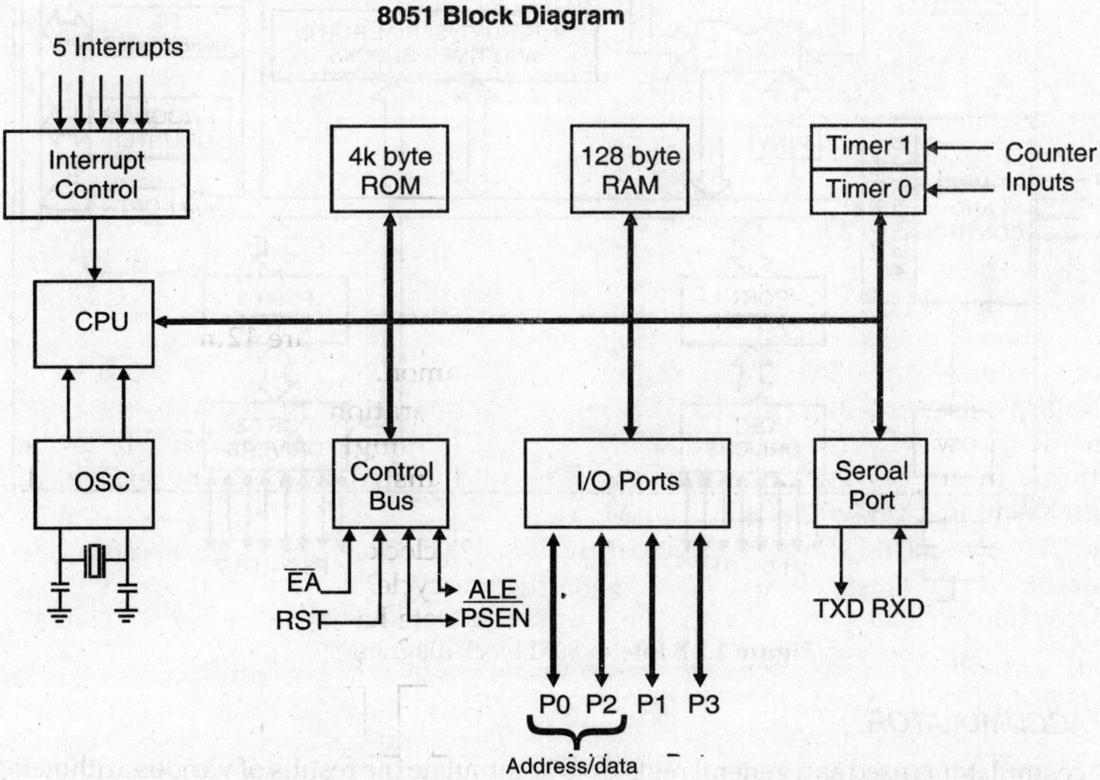

Figure 2.2 A 8051 core architecture→ 8051 block diaram

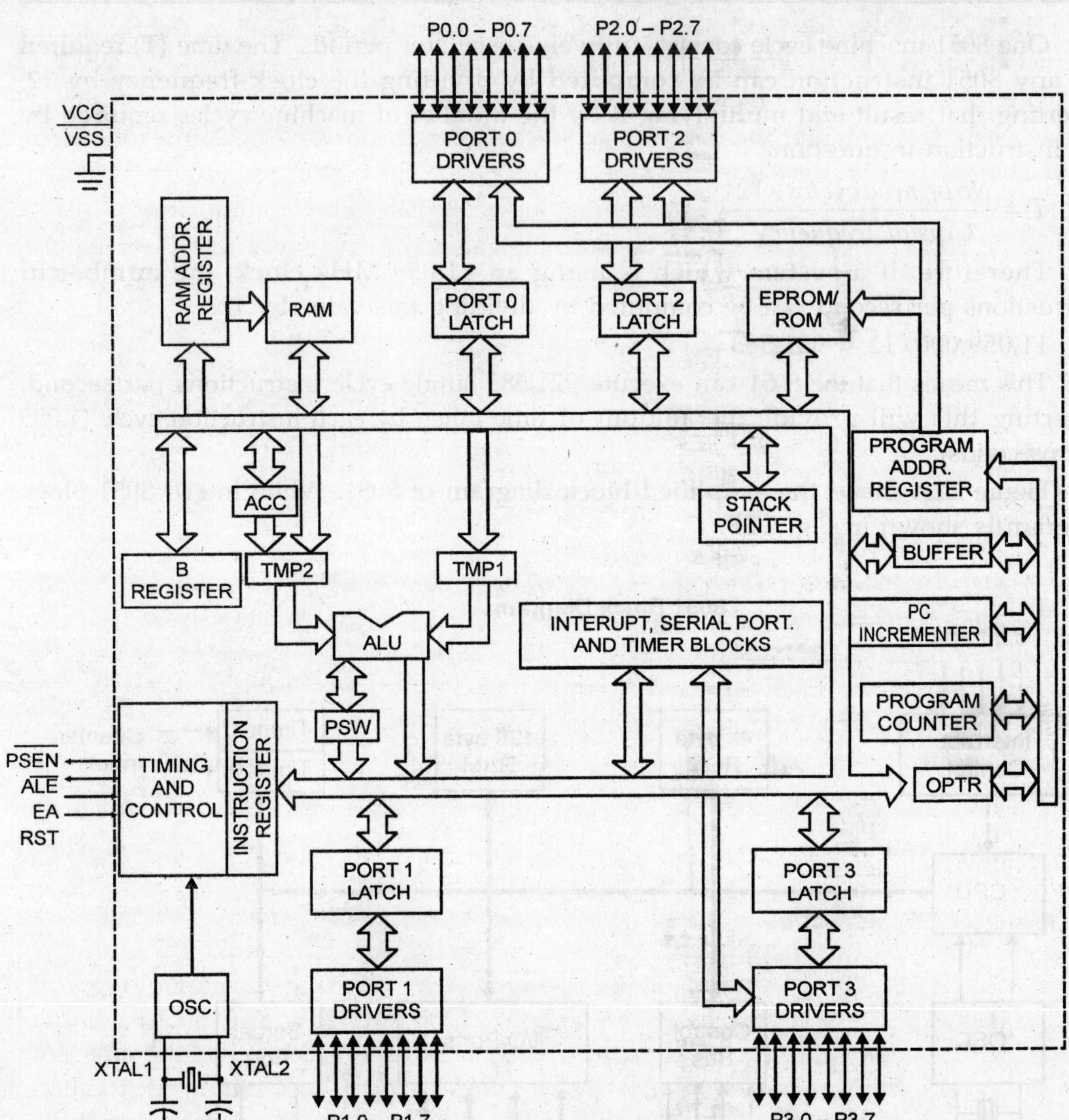

Figure 2.2 B Intel→ 8051 block diagram

THE ACCUMULATOR

The Accumulator is used as a general register to accumulate the results of various arithmetic and logic operations. It can hold an 8-bit (1-byte) value and is the most versatile register the 8051 has due to the shear number of instructions that make use of the accumulator.

The accumulator, referred to as ACC or A, is usually accessed explicitly using instructions such as:

```
INC A          ; Increment the accumulator
```

However, the accumulator is defined as an SFR register at address E0h. So the following two instructions have the same effect:

```
MOV A, #52h     ; Move immediate the value 52h to the accumulator
MOV E0h, #52h   ; Move immediate the value 52h to Internal RAM location
                ; E0h, which is, in fact, the accumulator SFR register.
```

B REGISTER

The B register is an SFR register at addresses F0h which is bit-addressable. The B register is used in two instructions only: *i.e.*, MUL (multiply) and DIV (divide). The B register can also be used as a general-purpose register.

THE "R" REGISTERS

The "R" registers are a set of eight registers that are named R0, R1, R2, R3, R4, R5, R6 and R7. These registers are used as auxiliary registers in many operations.

For example, if we add the number 10 and 20, the original number 10 may be stored in the Accumulator whereas the value 20 may be stored in, say, register R4.

To process the addition the command required will be

```
ADD A, R4    ; After executing this instruction the Accumulator will contain the
             value 30
```

PROGRAM COUNTER

The PC (Program Counter) is a 2 byte (16 bit) register which always contains the memory address of the next instruction to be executed. When the 8051 is reset the PC is always initialised to 0000h. If a 2 byte instruction is executed the PC is incremented by 2 and if a 3 byte instruction is executed the PC is incremented by three so as to correctly point to the next instruction to be executed. A jump instruction (*e.g.* LJMP) has the effect of causing the program to branch to a newly specified location, so the jump instruction causes the PC contents to change to the new address value. Jump instructions cause the program to flow in a non-sequential fashion.

SFRs

The 8051 is a flexible microcontroller with a relatively large number of modes of operations. Program may inspect and/or change the operating mode of the 8051 by manipulating the values of the 8051's Special Function Registers (SFRs).

SFRs are accessed as if they were normal Internal RAM. The only difference is that Internal RAM is from address 00h through 7Fh whereas SFR registers exist in the address range of 80h through FFh. Each SFR has an address (80h through FFh) and a name. We can categorized the SFR registers as follows:

1. CPU registers:

- ACC : Accumulator.
- B : B register.
- PSW : Program Status Word.
- SP : Stack Pointer.
- DPTR : Data Pointer (DPH, DPL).

2. Interrupt control:

- IE : Interrupt Enable.
- IP : Interrupt Priority.

3. I/O Ports:

- P0 : Port 0.
- P1 : Port 1.
- P2 : Port 2.
- P3 : Port 3.

4. TIMERS:

- TMOD : Timer mode.
- TCON : Timer control.
- TH0 : Timer 0 high byte.
- TL0 : Timer 0 low byte.
- TH1 : Timer 1 high byte.
- TL1 : Timer 1 low byte.

5. SERIAL I/O:

- SCON : Serial port control.
- SBUF : Serial data registers.

6. OTHER:

- PCON : Power control.

SFRs are covered in details in memory organization section.

2.3 SIGNALS AND PIN DESCRIPTION

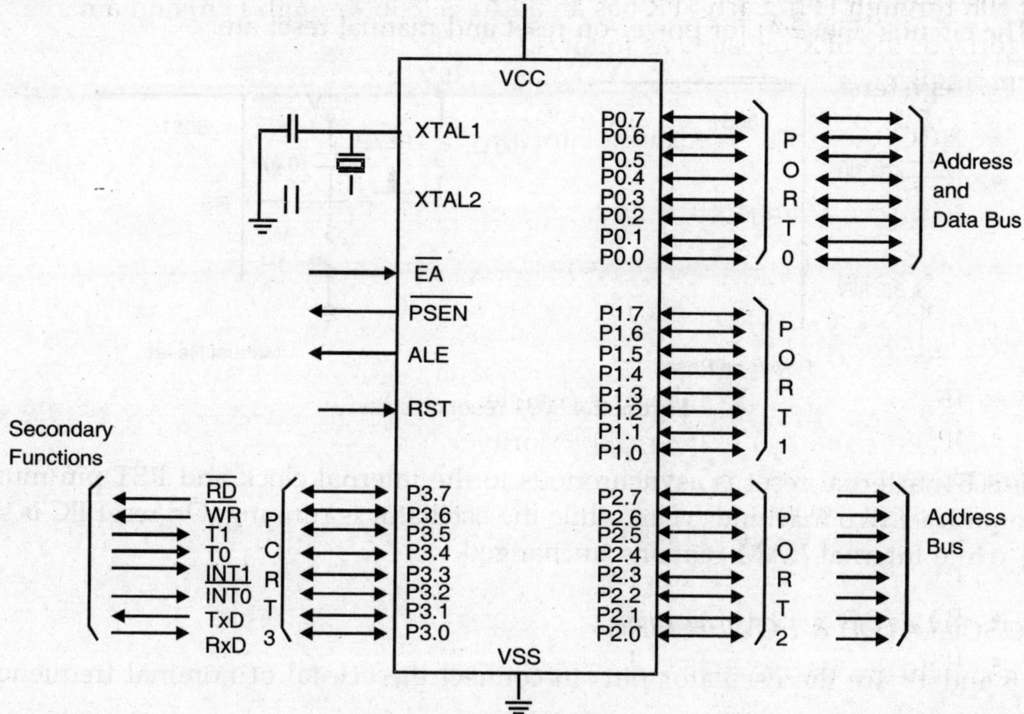

Figure 2.3 8051 Pin descriptions

Intel 8051 has 40 pins that are dedicated for various functions such as I/O, RD, WR, address, data and interrupts. A total of 32 pins are set aside for the four ports P0, P1, P2 and P3 where each port takes 8 pins. The rest of the pins are designed as V_{CC}, GND, XTAL1, XTAL2, RST, EA, and PSEN.

THE 8051 BUS CONTROL SIGNALS

The 8051 has 4 bus control signals:

- $\overline{PSEN}$ (pin 29): (Program Store Enable) enables external program (code) memory. Usually connected to EPROM's output enable ($\overline{OE}$). It pulses low during fetch stage of an instruction. It remains high while executing a program from internal ROM.
- ALE (pin 30): (Address Latch Enable) used for demultiplexing the address and data bus when port 0 is used as the data bus and low-byte of address bus.
- $\overline{EA}$ (pin 31): (External Access) high to execute programs from internal ROM and low to execute from external memory only.
- RST (pin 9): (RESET) master reset of 8051.

8051 RESET

In 8051 there are two ways by which reset could be used, *i.e.*, power-on reset and manual reset. The circuits (Fig. 2.4) for power-on reset and manual reset are:

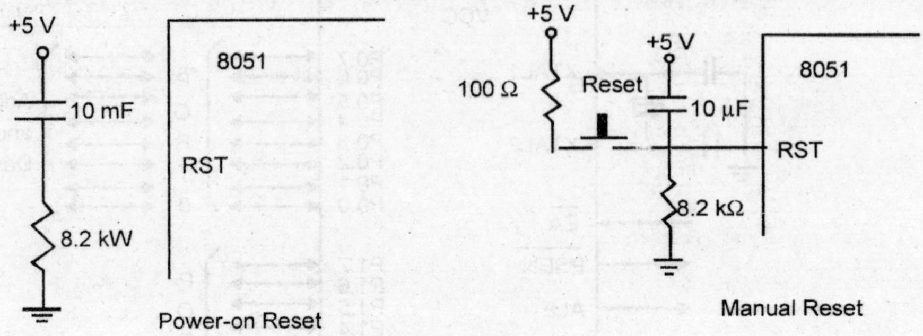

Figure 2.4 8051 reset circuits

In 8051, external reset is asynchronous to the internal clock and RST pin must be high for at least two machine cycles while the oscillator is running. On reset PC is set to 0000H while Internal RAM remains unchanged.

8051 OSCILLATOR & POWER PINS

Pins 18 and 19 are the oscillator pins to connect the crystal of nominal frequency 12 MHz.

Pin 40 is for +5 V and pin 20 is for GND.

I/O PORTS

The 8051 have four 8-bit bi-directional I/O ports. All the ports upon RESET are configured as output, ready to use as output ports. To use any of these ports as an input port, it must be programmed.

PORT 0 (PIN 32-39)

Port 0 occupies a total of 8 pins (pins 32-39). It can be used for input or output. To use the pins of port 0 as both input and output ports, each pin must be connected externally to a 10 K ohm pull up resistor. With external pull-up resistor connected upon reset, port 0 is configured as an output port.

Port 0 is also designated as AD0–AD7, allowing it to be used for both address and data. When connecting an 8051/31 to an external memory, port 0 provides both address and data. The 8051 multiplexes address and data through port 0 to save pins. ALE indicates if P0 has address or data. When ALE = 0, it provides data D0–D7, but when ALE = 1 it has address A0–A7.

PORT 1 (PIN 1-8)

Port1 occupies a total of 8 pins (pins 1 through 8). It can be used as I/O port. As an I/O port it is a standard bi-directional general purpose I/O port .In contrast to port 0, this port does not need any pull up resistor since it already has pull up resistor internally.

PORT 2 (PIN 21-28)

Port 2 occupies a total of 8 pins (pins 21 through 28). It is a dual purpose I/O port. As an I/O port it is a standard bi-directional general purpose I/O port. Just like port1, port 2 does not need any pull up resistors since it already has pull-up resistors internally.

The alternate functions of p2 is: High byte of address bus for external program and data memory accesses.

PORT 3 (PIN 10-17)

Port 3 occupies a total of 8-pins 10 through 17. It is a dual purpose I/O port. As an I/O port it is a standard bi-directional general purpose I/O port . P3 does not need any pull up resistor. The alternate functions of P3 are:

Serial I/O	-TXD, RXD
Timer clocks	-T0, T1
Interrupts	-INT0, INT1
Data memory	-RD, WR

2.4 I/O CONFIGURATIONS

The four ports P0, P1, P2, and P3,each use 8 pins, making them 8-bit ports. Each port has a D-type output latch for each pin. Each port SFR is made up of these eight latches, which can be addressed at the SFR address for that port. The data on the port latches does not have to be same as that on the port pins. All the ports upon RESET are configured as output, ready to use as output ports. To use any of these ports as an input port, it must be programmed.

PORT 0

Port 0 occupies a total of 8 pins (pins 32-39). It can be used for input or output. To use the pins of port 0 as both input and output ports, each pin must be connected externally to a 10K ohm pull up resistor. With external pull-up resistor connected upon reset, port 0 is configured as an output port. Port 0 receives the code bytes during EPROM programming, and outputs the code bytes during program verification. External pull ups are required during program verification. Port 0 is also the multiplexed low-order address and data bus during accesses to external memory. Figure 2.5 shows the 8051 port 0 structure.

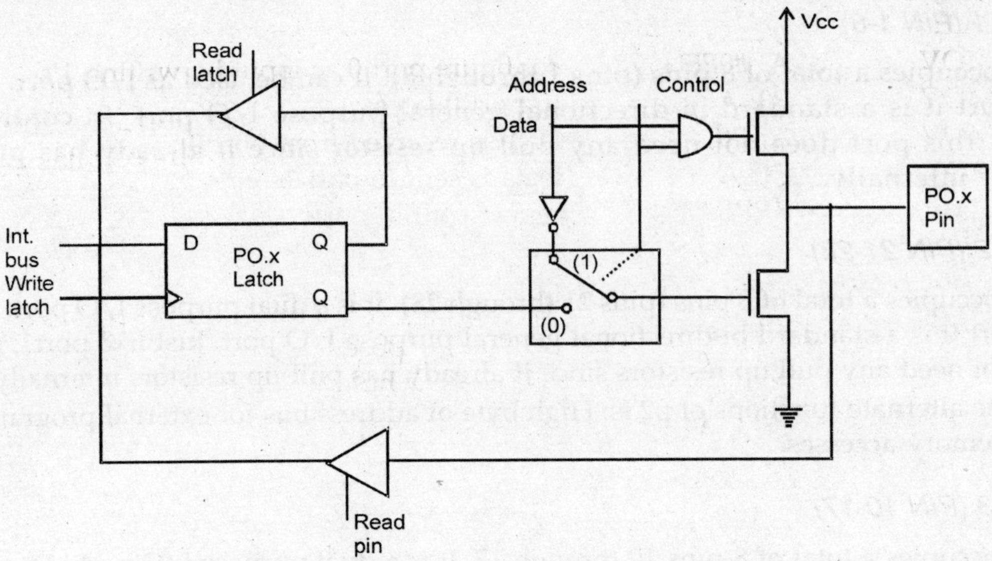

Figure 2.5 8051 Port 0 structure (open-drain)

Port-0 can be configured as a normal bidirectional I/O port or it can be used for address/data interfacing for accessing external memory. When control is '1', the port is used for address/data interfacing. When the control is '0', the port can be used as a normal bidirectional I/O port.

Let us assume that control is '0'. When the port is used as an input port, '1', written to the latch. In this situation both the output MOSFETs are 'off'. Hence the output pin floats. This high impedance pin can be pulled up or low by an external source. When the port is used as an output port, a '1' written to the latch again turns 'off' both the output MOSFETs and causes the output pin to float. An external pull-up is required to output a '1'. But when '0' is written to the latch, the pin is pulled down by the lower MOSFETs. Hence the output becomes zero.

When the control is '1', address/data bus controls the output driver MOSFETs. If the address/data bus (internal) is '0', the upper MOSFETs is 'off' and the lower MOSFET is 'on'. The output becomes '0'. If the address/data bus is '1', the upper transistor is 'on' and the lower transistor is 'off'. Hence the output is '1'. Hence for normal address/data interfacing (for external memory access) no pull-up resistors are required.

Port-0 latch is written to with 1's when used for external memory access.

PORT 0 AS INPUT

With resistors connected to port 0, in order to make it an input, the port must be programmed by writing 1 to all the bits.

For example, in the following code, port 0 is configured first as an input port by writing 1's to it, and then data is received from that port 0 and sent to P1.

```
REPEAT:
    MOV     A, #0FFH    ; configure port 0 as input by writing 1's
    MOV     P0, A       ; to port 0 latch
    MOV     A, P0       ; Data is received from port 0
    MOV     P1, A       ; Data is sent to port 1
    SJMP    REPEAT      ; repeat continuously
```

DUAL ROLE OF PORT 0

Port 0 is also designated as AD0 – AD7, allowing it to be used for both address and data. When connecting an 8051/31 to an external memory, port 0 provides both address and data. The 8051 multiplexes address and data through port 0 to save pins. ALE indicates if P0 has address or data. When ALE = 0, it provides data D0 – D7, but when ALE = 1 it has address A0 –A7.

PORT 1

Port 1 occupies a total of 8 pins (pins 1 through 8). It can be used as input or output. In contrast to port 0, this port does not need any pull up resistor since it already has pull up resistor internally. Upon reset, port 1 is configured as an output port. Port 1 also receives the low-order address bytes during EPROM programming and program verification. Figure 2.6 shows the 8051 port 1 structure.

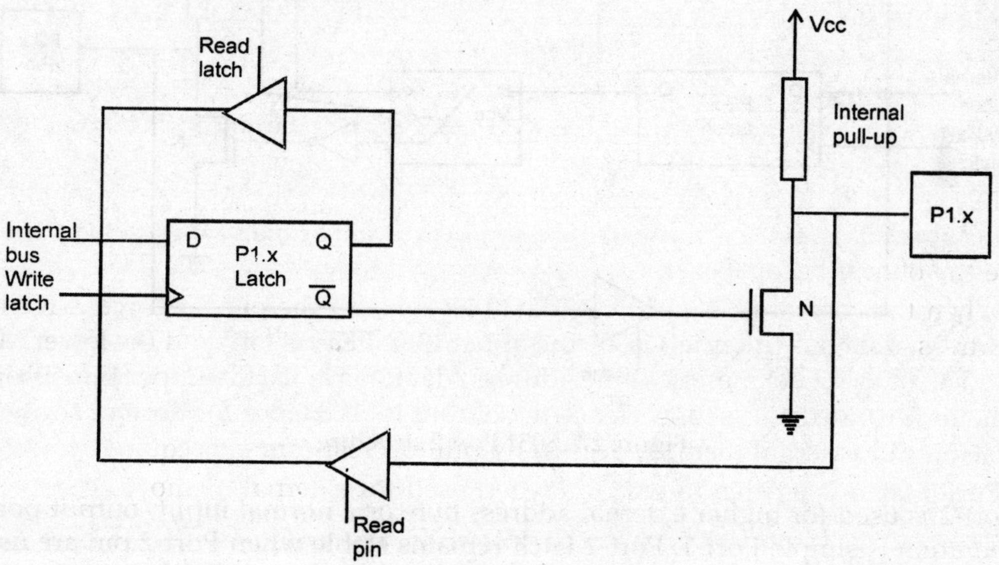

Figure 2.6 8051 Port1 structure

Port-1 does not have any alternate function i.e. it is dedicated solely for I/O interfacing. When used as output port, the pin is pulled up or down through internal pull-up. To use port-1 as input port, '1' has to be written to the latch. In this input mode when '1' is written to the pin by the external device then it read fine. But when '0' is written to the pin by the external device then the external source must sink current due to internal pull-up. If the external device is not able to sink the current the pin voltage may rise, leading to a possible wrong reading.

PORT 1 AS INPUT

To make port 1 as input port, it must programmed as such by writing 1 to all its bits.

PORT 2

Port 2 occupies a total of 8 pins (pins 21 through 28). It can be used as input or output. Just like P1, port 2 does not need any pull up resistors since it already has pull-up resistors internally. Upon reset, port 2 is configured as an output port.

Port 2 emits the high-order address byte during fetches from external program memory and during accesses to external data memory that use 16-bit address (MOVX @DPTR). Port 2 also receives some control signals and the high-order address bits during EPROM programming and program verification. Fig. 2.7 shows the 8051 port 2 structure.

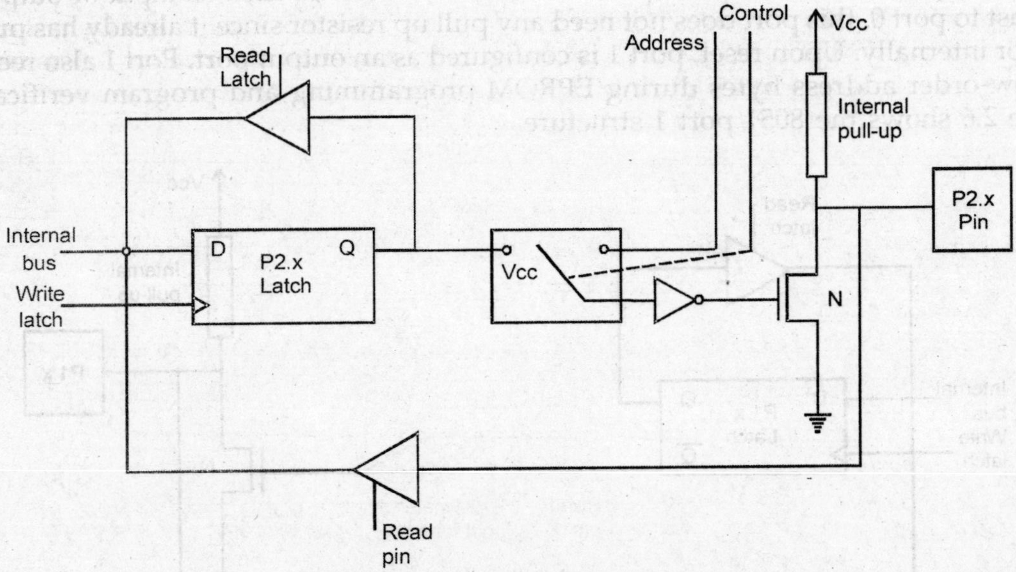

Figure 2.7 8051 Port 2 structure

Port-2 is used for higher external address byte or a normal input/output port. The I/O operation is simple Port-1. Port-2 latch remains stable when Port-2 pin are used for external memory access. Here again the internal pull-up there is limited current driving capability.

PORT 2 AS INPUT

To make pin 2 as it must be programmed as such by writing 1 to all its bits.

PORT 3

Port 3 occupies a total of 8-pins 10 through17. It can be used as input or output. The structure of a port-3 pin is shown in fig. 2.8. Port 3 receives some control signals for EPROM programming and program verification.

Port 3 also serves the functions of various special features of the 8051 microcontroller family, as follows:

Pin	Name	Alternate Function
P3.0	RXD	Serial Input Line
P3.1	TXD	Serial Output Line
P3.2	INT0	External Interrupt 0
P3.3	INT1	External Interrupt 1
P3.4	T0	Timer 0 External Input
P3.5	T1	Timer 1 External Input
P3.6	WR	External Data Memory Write Strobe
P3.7	RD	External Data Memory Read Strobe

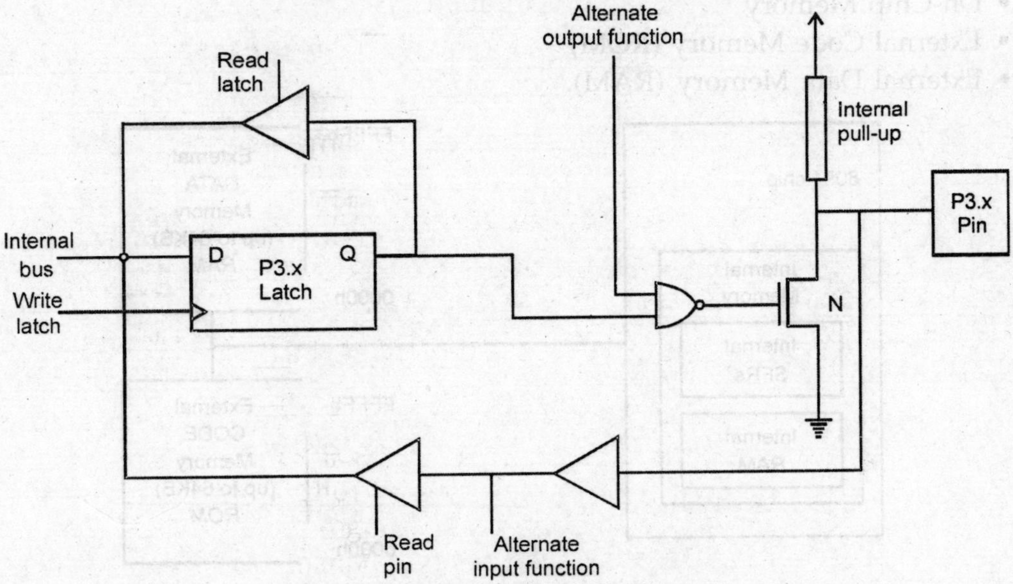

Figure 2.8 8051 Port 3 structure

Note:

1. Port 1, 2, 3 each can drive 4 LS TTL inputs.
2. Port-0 can drive 8 LS TTL inputs in address/data mode. For digital output port, it needs external pull-up resistors.
3. Port-1, 2 and 3 pins can also be driven by open-collector or open-drain outputs.
4. Each Port 3 bit can be configured either as a normal I/O or as a special function bit.

READING A PORT (PORT-PINS) VERSUS READING A LATCH

There is subtle difference between reading a latch and reading the output port pin.

The status of the output port pin is sometimes dependant on the connected load. For instance if a port is configured as an output port and a '1' is written to the latch, the output pin should also show '1'. If the output is used to drive the base of a transistor, the transistor turns 'on'.

If the port pin is read, the value will be '0' which is corresponding to the base-emitter voltage of the transistor.

Reading a latch: Usually the instructions that read the latch, read a value, possibly change it, and then rewrite it to the latch. These are called "read-modify-write" instructions.

2.5 MEMORY AND REGISTER ORGANISATION

The 8051 has three types of memory. As shown in Fig. 2.9 they are

- On-Chip Memory
- External Code Memory (ROM)
- External Data Memory (RAM).

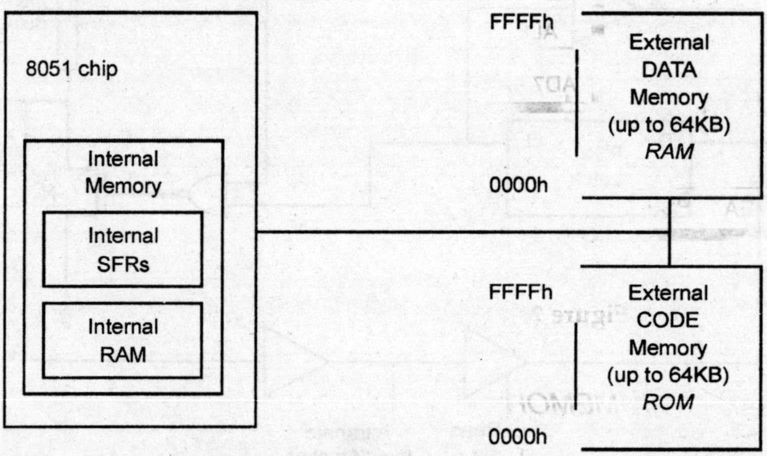

Figure 2.9 Memory types

EXTERNAL CODE MEMORY

The executable program code is stored in this code memory. The code memory size is limited to 64KBytes (in a standard 8051). The code memory is *read-only* in normal operation and is programmed under special conditions e.g. it is a PROM or a Flash type of memory However, code memory is most commonly implemented as off-chip EPROM, especially in low-cost development systems. The access of external program (code) memory is shown in Fig. 2.10, which is enabled by PSEN signal.

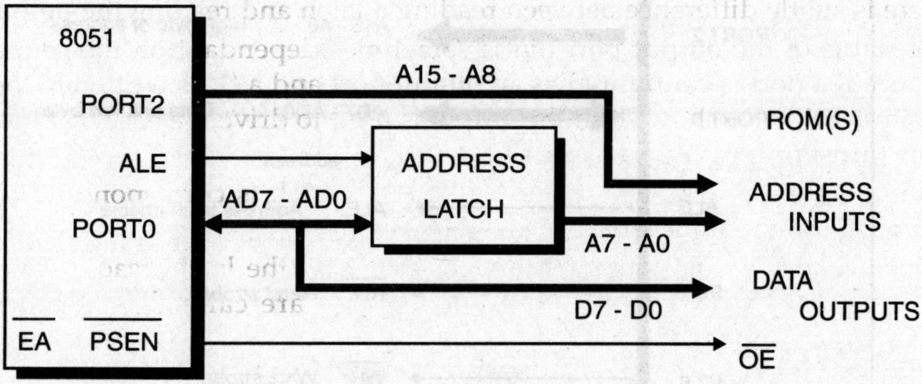

Figure 2.8 **External program memory access**

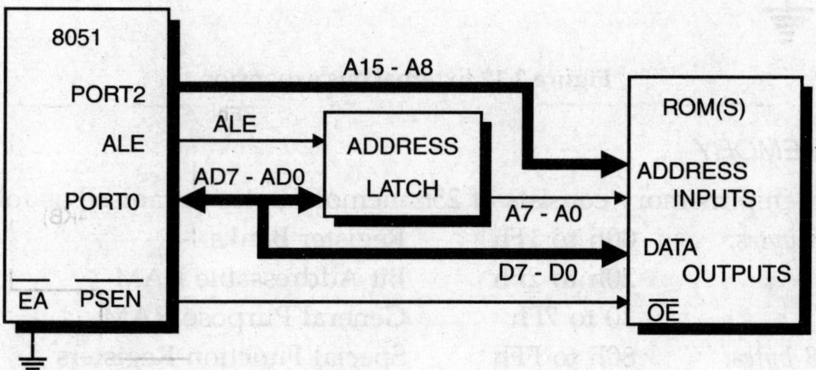

Figure 2.9 External program memory access

EXTERNAL RAM DATA MEMORY

This *is read-write* memory and is available for storage of data. Up to 64KBytes of external RAM data memory is supported (in a standard 8051).

While internal RAM is limited to 128 bytes, the 8051 supports external RAM up to 64K. Figure 2.9 shows how to use the External Data Memory.

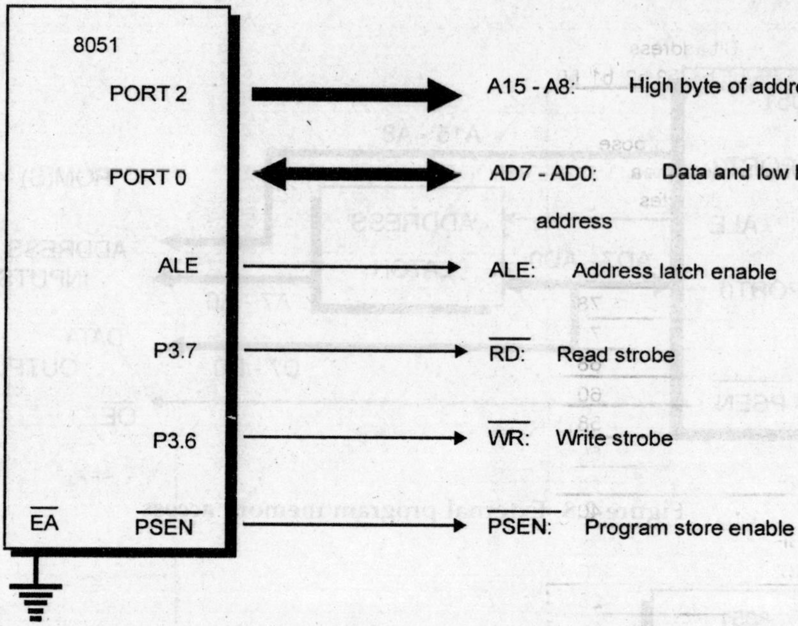

Figure 2.12 External bus expansion

INTERNAL MEMORY

The 8051's on-chip memory consists of 256 memory bytes organised as follows:

First 128 bytes:	00h to 1Fh	Register Banks
	20h to 2Fh	Bit Addressable RAM
	30 to 7Fh	General Purpose RAM
Next 128 bytes:	80h to FFh	Special Function Registers

The first 128 bytes of internal memory is organised as shown in Fig. 2.13, and is referred to as Internal RAM, or IRAM.

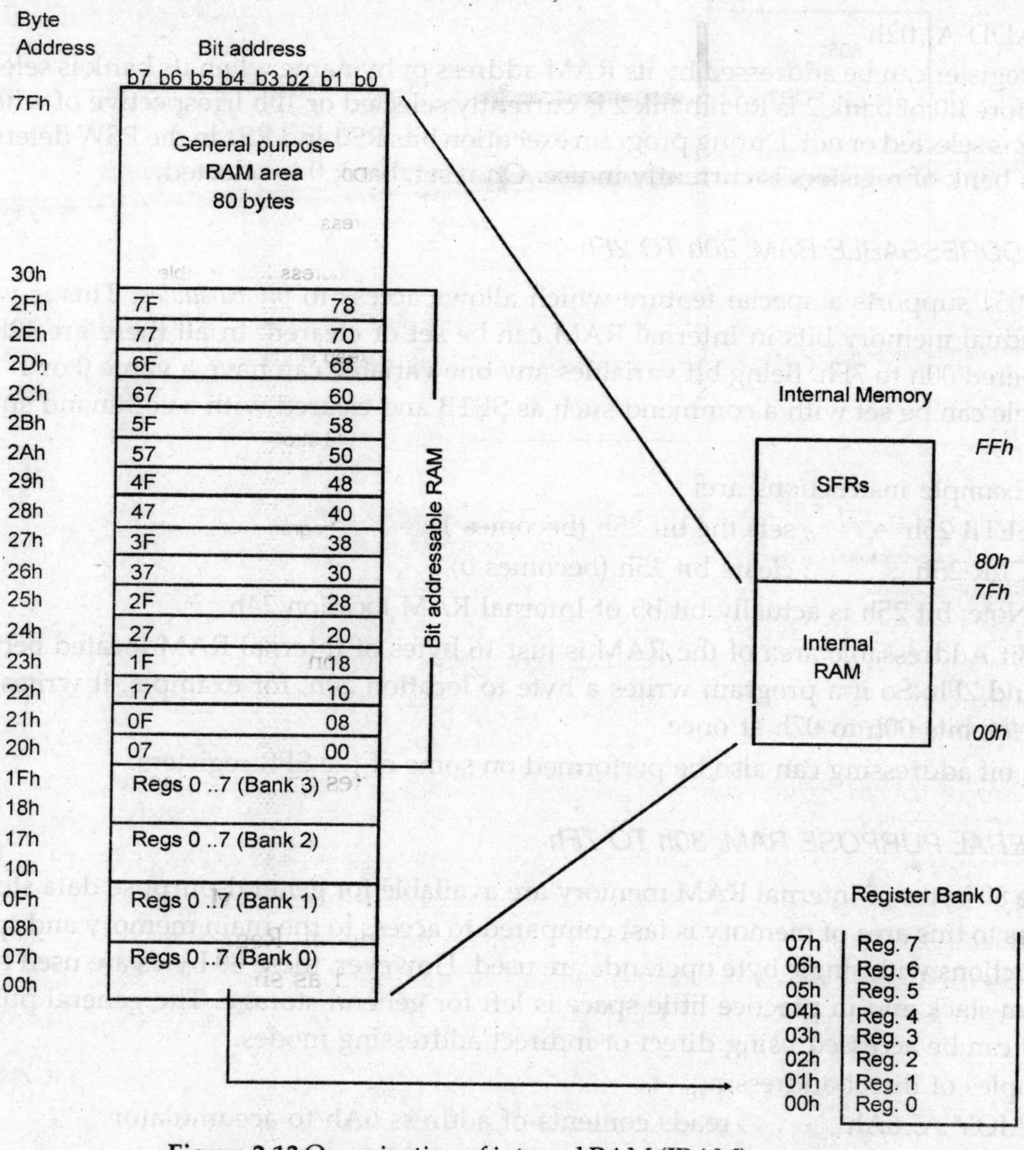

Figure 2.13 Organization of internal RAM (IRAM) memory

REGISTER BANKS: 00h TO 1Fh

The 8051 uses 8 general-purpose registers R0 through R7 (R0, R1, R2, R3, R4, R5, R6, and R7). These registers are used in instructions such as:

```
ADD A, R2        ; adds the value contained in R2 to the accumulator
```

Note: since R2 happens to be memory location 02h in the Internal RAM the following instruction has the same effect as the above instruction.

ADD A, 02h

Each register can be addressed by its RAM address or by name when its bank is selected. Therefore R0 of bank 2 is R0 if bank 2 is currently selected or 10h irrespective of whether bank 2 is selected or not. During program execution bits RS0 and RS1 in the PSW determine which bank of registers is currently in use. On reset, bank 0 is selected.

BIT ADDRESSABLE RAM: 20h TO 2Fh

The 8051 supports a special feature which allows access to *bit variables*. This is where individual memory bits in Internal RAM can be set or cleared. In all there are 128 bits numbered 00h to 7Fh. Being bit variables any one variable can have a value 0 or 1. A bit variable can be set with a command such as SETB and cleared with a command such as CLR.

Example instructions are:

```
SETB 25h        ; sets the bit 25h (becomes 1)
CLR 25h         ; clears bit 25h (becomes 0)
```

Note, bit 25h is actually bit b5 of Internal RAM location 24h.

The Bit Addressable area of the RAM is just 16 bytes of Internal RAM located between 20h and 2Fh. So if a program writes a byte to location 20h, for example, it writes 8 *bit variables*, bits 00h to 07h at once.

Note: bit addressing can also be performed on some of the SFR registers.

GENERAL PURPOSE RAM: 30h TO 7Fh

These 80 bytes of Internal RAM memory are available for general-purpose data storage. Access to this area of memory is fast compared to access to the main memory and special instructions with single byte operands are used. However, these 80 bytes are used by the system stack and in practice little space is left for general storage. The general purpose RAM can be accessed using direct or indirect addressing modes.

Examples of direct addressing:

```
MOV A, 6Ah      ; reads contents of address 6Ah to accumulator
```

Examples for indirect addressing (use registers R0 or R1):

```
MOV R1, #6Ah    ; move immediate 6Ah to R1
MOV A, @R1      ; move indirect: R1 contains address of Internal RAM
                ; which contains data that is moved to A.
```

These two instructions have the same effect as the direct instruction above.

SFR REGISTERS

The SFR registers are located within the Internal Memory in the address range 80h to FFh, as shown in Fig. 2.14. Not all locations within this range are defined. Each SFR has a very specific function. Each SFR has an address (within the range 80h to FFh) and a name which reflects the purpose of the SFR. Although 128 bytes of the SFR address space is defined only 21 SFR registers are defined in the standard 8051.

Undefined SFR addresses should not be accessed as this might lead to some unpredictable results.

Note some of the SFR registers are *bit addressable*. SFRs are accessed just like normal Internal RAM locations.

Special Function Register Map

Bit Addressable ↓ (column A)

BYTE ADDRESS	A (0)	B (1)	C (2)	D (3)	E (4)	F (5)	G (6)	H (7)
F8								
F0	B							
E8								
E0	ACC							
D8								
D0	PSW							
C8								
C0								
B8	IP							
B0	P3							
A8	IE							
A0	P2							
98	SCON	SBUF						
90	P1							
88	TCON	TMOD	TL0	TL1	TH0	TH1		
80	P0	SP	DPL	DPH				PCON

Figure 2.14 SFRs register layout

We can categorized the SFRs register as follows:

1. CPU REGISTERS:
   - ACC : Accumulator.
   - B : B register.
   - PSW : Program Status Word.
   - SP : Stack Pointer.
   - DPTR : Data Pointer (DPH, DPL).
2. INTERRUPT CONTROL:
   - IE : Interrupt Enable.
   - IP : Interrupt Priority.

3. I/O PORTS:
- P0 : Port 0.
- P1 : Port 1.
- P2 : Port 2.
- P3 : Port 3.

4. TIMERS:
- TMOD : Timer mode.
- TCON : Timer control.
- TH0 : Timer 0 high byte.
- TL0 : Timer 0 low byte.
- TH1 : Timer 1 high byte.
- TL1 : Timer 1 low byte.

5. SERIAL I/O:
- SCON : Serial port control.
- SBUF : Serial data registers.

6. OTHER:
- PCON : Power control

CPU REGISTERS:

THE ACCUMULATOR

The Accumulator is used as a general register to accumulate the results of various arithmetic and logic operations. It can hold an 8-bit (1-byte) value and is the most versatile register the 8051 has due to the shear number of instructions that make use of the accumulator.

The accumulator, referred to as ACC or A, is usually accessed explicitly using instructions such as:

INC A ; Increment the accumulator

However, the accumulator is defined as an SFR register at address E0h. So the following two instructions have the same effect:

MOV A, #52h ; Move immediate the value 52h to the accumulator

MOV E0h, #52h ; Move immediate the value 52h to Internal RAM location; E0h, which is, in fact, the accumulator SFR register.

B REGISTER

The B register is an SFR register at addresses F0h which is bit-addressable. The B register is used in two instructions only: *i.e.* MUL (multiply) and DIV (divide). The B register can also be used as a general-purpose register.

PSW (PROGRAM STATUS WORD, ADDRESSES D0H, BIT-ADDRESSABLE)

The Program Status Word is used to store a number of important bits that are set and cleared by 8051 instructions. The PSW SFR contains the carry flag, the auxiliary carry flag, the overflow flag, and the parity flag. Additionally, the PSW register contains the register bank select flags that are used to select which of the "R" register banks are currently selected. The Fig. 2.15 shows the PSW register.

PSW : Program Status World

CY	AC	F0	RS1	RS0	OV	----	P

Symbol Bit	Address	Description
C (or CY)	PSW .7 D7h	Carry flag
AC	PSW .6 D6h	Auxilary carry flag
F0	PSW .5 D5h	Flag 0
RS1	PSW .4 D4h	Register bank select 1
RS0	PSW .3 D3h	Register bank select 0
0V	PSW .2 D2h	Overflog flag
	PSW .1 D1h	Reserved
P	PSW .0Dh	Even Parity flag

Figure 2.15 Program status word

CARRY FLAG. CY

This is a conventional carry, or borrow, flag used in arithmetic operations. The carry flag is also used as the 'Boolean accumulator' for Boolean instruction operating at the bit level.

For example,

(1) As traditional CY for arithmetic operations

If A contains FFh then the instruction

ADD A, #1 ;leaves A equal to 00H and sets the CY in PSW. (A=00h & ;CY=1)

(2) As Boolean accumulator

If ANL C, 25H ; ANDs bit 25H with the carry flag and places the results ; back in the CY.

AUXILIARY CARRY FLAG. AC

This is a conventional auxiliary carry (half carry) used in addition of BCD numbers, is set if a carry was generated out of bit 3 into bit 4. If the values are added are BCD, then the add instruction must be followed by DAA (decimal adjust accumulator) to bring results greater than 9 back into range.

FLAG 0. F0

This is a general-purpose flag bit available for user applications.

REGISTER BANK SELECT 0 AND REGISTER BANK SELECT 1.

RS1 & RS0 are used to select different register banks.

RS1	RSO	Register Bank	Address
0	0	0	00h - 07h
0	1	1	08h - 0Fh
1	0	2	10h - 17h
1	1	3	18h - 1Fh

These bits define the active register bank (bank 0 is the default register bank).

OVERFLOW FLAG. OV

This is a conventional overflow bit for signed arithmetic to determine if the result of a signed arithmetic operation is out of range. OV is set after an addition or subtraction operation if there was an arithmetic overflow. Results greater than +127 or less than –128 will set OV bit

EVEN PARITY FLAG. P

The parity flag is the accumulator parity flag, set to a value, 1 or 0, such that the number of '1' bits in the accumulator plus the parity bit add up to an even number.
Note: If one writes an interrupt handler routine, it is advisable to save the PSW SFR on the stack and restore it when the interrupt is complete. Many 8051 instructions modify the bits of PSW. If interrupt routine does not guarantee that PSW is the same upon exit as it was upon entry, program is bound to behave rather erratically and unpredictably, and it will be tricky to debug since the behavior will tend not to make any sense.

SP (STACK POINTER, ADDRESS 81H)

The Stack Pointer, SP, is an 8-bit SFR register at address 81h. The small address field (8 bits) and the limited space available in the Internal RAM confines the stack size . The SP contains the address of the data byte currently on the top of the stack. The SP pointer in initialised to a defined address. A new data item is 'pushed' on to the stack using a PUSH instruction which will cause the data item to be written to address SP + 1.

Typical instructions, which cause modification to the stack are: PUSH, POP, LCALL, RET, RETI etc. The SP SFR, on start-up, is initialised to 07h so this means the stack will start at 08h and expand upwards in Internal RAM. If register banks 1 to 3 are to be used the SP SFR should be initialised to start higher up in Internal RAM.

The following instruction is often used to initialise the stack:

```
MOV SP, #2Fh
```

Note: The SP SFR, on startup, is initialized to 07h. This means the stack will start at 08h and start expanding upward in internal RAM. Since alternate register banks 1, 2, and 3 as well as the user bit variables occupy internal RAM from addresses 08h through 2Fh, it is necessary to initialize SP in program to some other value if someone will be using the alternate register banks and/or bit memory.

DATA POINTER (DPL/DPH, ADDRESSES 82h/83h)

The Data Pointer, DPTR, is a special 16-bit register used to address the external code or external data memory. The SFRs DPL and DPH work together to represent a 16-bit value called the Data Pointer. Since the SFR registers are just 8-bits wide the DPTR is stored in two SFR registers, where DPL (82h) holds the low byte of the DPTR and DPH (83h) holds the high byte of the DPTR.

For example, to write the value 46h to external data memory location 2500h, one might use the following instructions:

```
MOV A, #46h          ; Move immediate 8 bit data 46h to A (accumulator)
MOV DPTR, #2504h     ; Move immediate 16 bit address value 2504h to A.
                     ; Now DPL holds 04h and DPH holds 25h.
MOVX @DPTR, A        ; Move the value in A to external RAM location 2500h.
                     ; uses indirect addressing.
```

Note: DPTR is really DPH and DPL taken together as a 16-bit value. To push DPTR onto the stack one must first PUSH DPL and then DPH. One can't simply PUSH DPTR onto the stack. Additionally, there is an instruction to "increment DPTR." When one execute this instruction, the two bytes are operated upon as a 16-bit value. However, there is no instruction that decrements DPTR. To decrement the value of DPTR, one must write their own code to do so.

INTERRUPT CONTROL

INTERRUPT ENABLE (IE, ADDRESSES A8h)

The Interrupt Enable SFR is used to enable and disable specific interrupts. The low 7 bits of the SFR are used to enable/disable the specific interrupts, where as the highest bit is used to enable or disable ALL interrupts. Thus, if the high bit of IE is 0 all interrupts are disabled regardless of whether an individual interrupt is enabled by setting a lower bit.

INTERRUPT PRIORITY (IP, ADDRESSES B8h, BIT-ADDRESSABLE)

The Interrupt Priority SFR is used to specify the relative priority of each interrupt. On the 8051, an interrupt may either be of low (0) priority or high (1) priority. An interrupt may only interrupt, interrupts of lower priority. For example, if we configure the 8051 so that all interrupts are of low priority except the serial interrupt, the serial interrupt will always be able to interrupt the system, even if another interrupt is currently executing. However, if a serial interrupt is executing no other interrupt will be able to interrupt the serial interrupt routine since the serial interrupt routine has the highest priority.

I/O PORT

The standard 8051 has four 8 bit I/O ports: P0, P1, P2 and P3.

PORT 0 (P0, ADDRESS 80h, BIT-ADDRESSABLE)

Port 0 is a physical 8 bit I/O port on the 8051. Read (input) and write (output) access to this port is done in software by accessing the SFR P0 register which is located at address 80h. SFR P0 is also bit addressable. Each bit corresponds to a physical I/O pin on the 8051.

Example access to port 0:

```
SETB P0.7        ; sets the MSB bit of Port 0
CLR P0.7         ; clears the MSB bit of Port 0
```

The operand P0.7 uses the dot operator and refers to bit 7 of SFR P0. The same bit could be addressed by accessing bit location 87h.

Thus the following two instructions have the same meaning:

```
CLR P0.7
CLR 87h
```

PORT 1 (P1, ADDRESS 90h, BIT-ADDRESSABLE)

This is input/output port 1. Each bit of this SFR corresponds to one of the pins on the microcontroller.

PORT2 (P2, ADDRESS A0h, BIT-ADDRESSABLE)

This is input/output port 2. Each bit of this SFR corresponds to one of the pins on the microcontroller.

P3 (PORT 3, ADDRESS B0h, BIT-ADDRESABLE)

This is input/output port 3. Each bit of this SFR corresponds to one of the pins on the microcontroller.

Note: While the 8051 has four I/O port (P0, P1, P2, and P3) but if hardware uses external RAM or external code memory (i.e. program is stored in an external ROM or EPROM chip or if using external RAM chips) one may not use P0 or P2. This is because the 8051 uses ports P0 and P2 to address the external memory. Thus if one is using external RAM or code memory he may only use ports P1 and P3.

TIMERS

The set up and operation of the on-chip hardware timers will be described later, but the associated registers are:

TIMER CONTROL (TCON, ADDRESSES 88h, BIT-ADDRESSABLE)

TCON, the Timer Control register is an SFR at address 88h, which is bit-addressable. TCON is used to configure and monitor the 8051 timers. The TCON SFR also contains some interrupt control bits.

TIMER MODE (TMOD, ADDRESSES 89h)

TMOD, the Timer Mode register is an SFR at address 89h and is used to define the operational modes for the timers.

TIMER 0 LOW/HIGH (TL0/TH0, ADDRESSES 8Ah/8Ch)

These two SFRs, taken together, represent timer 0. Their exact behavior depends on how the timer is configured in the TMOD SFR; however, these timers always count up. What is configurable is how and when they increment in value.

TIMER 1 LOW/HIGH (TL1/TH1, ADDRESSES 8Bh/8Dh)

These two SFRs, taken together, represent timer 1. Their exact behavior depends on how the timer is configured in the TMOD SFR; however, these timers always count up. What is configurable is how and when they increment in value.

SERIAL I/O

Programming of the on-chip serial communications port will be described later but the associated SFR registers are, SBUF and SCON.

SERIAL CONTROL (SCON, ADDRESSES 98h, BIT-ADDRESSABLE)

The SCON (Serial Control) is an SFR register located at addresses 98h, and it is bit addressable. SCON configures the behavior of the on-chip serial port, setting up parameters such as the baud rate of the serial port, activating send and/or receive data, and setting up some specific control flags.

SERIAL BUFFER (SBUF, ADDRESSES 99h)

The Serial Buffer SFR is used to send and receive data via the on-board serial port. Any value written to SBUF will be sent out the serial port's TXD pin. Likewise, any value which the 8051 receives via the serial port's RXD pin will be delivered to the user program via SBUF. In other words, SBUF serves as the output port when written to and as an input port when read from.

OTHER

POWER CONTROL REGISTER (PCON, ADDRESSES 87h)

The Power Control SFR is used to control the 8051's power control modes. Certain operation modes of the 8051 allow the 8051 to go into a type of "sleep" mode which requires much less power. These modes of operation are controlled through PCON. Additionally, one of the bits in PCON is used to double the effective baud rate of the 8051's serial port.

Note: SFRs are used to control the way the 8051 functions. Each SFR has a specific purpose and format. Not all addresses above 80h are assigned to SFRs. However, this area may not be used as additional RAM memory even if a given address has not been assigned to an SFR.

2.6 POWER SAVING MODES OF OPERATION

The CHMOS versions of the 8051 feature two power saving modes that can be activated by software: idle mode and power down mode. These modes are accessed via the PCON (Power CONtrol) SFR which is shown in Fig. 2.14.

SM0D	-	-	-	GF1	GF0	PD	IDL

Bit	Name	Bit Address	Explanation of Function
7	SM0D	PCON.7	Serial baud rate modify bit. (Double Baud rate bit)
6	-	PCON.6	Not implemented
5	-	PCON.5	Not implemented
4	-	PCON.4	Not implemented
3	GF1	PCON.3	General purpose user flag bit 1.
2	GF0	PCON.2	General purpose user flag bit 0.
1	PD	PCON.1	Power down bit.
0	IDL	PCON.0	Idle mode bit.

Figure 2.16A PCON Register

The Idle mode freezes the CPU while allowing the RAM, timer/counters, serial port, and interrupt system to continue functioning. The Power Down mode saves the RAM contents but freezes the oscillator, causing all other chip functions to be inoperative.

The schematic diagram for 'Power down' mode and 'Idle' mode is given is as follows:

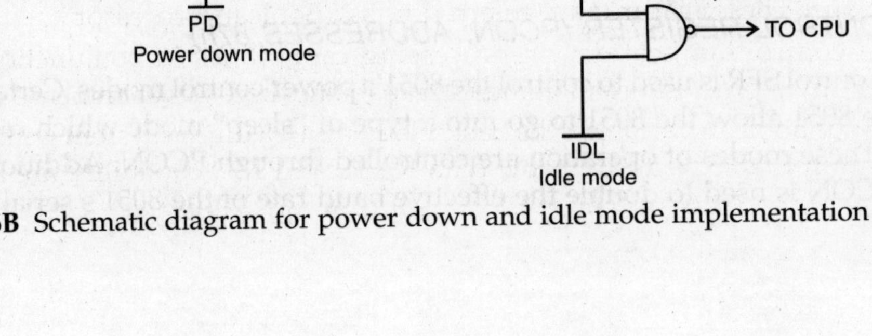

Figure 2.16B Schematic diagram for power down and idle mode implementation idle mode

IDLE MODE

The idle mode is activated by setting the IDL bit high. An instruction that sets PCON register bit 0 (PCON.0) bring microcontroller in Idle mode. The idle mode causes all program execution to stop. Internal RAM contents are preserved and the oscillator continues to run but is blocked from the CPU. The timers and the UART continue to function as normal.

Idle mode is terminated by the activation of any interrupt or by a hardware reset. Activation of any enabled interrupt terminates Idle mode by clearing PCON.0. Upon completion of the interrupt service routine, execution will continue from the instruction following the instruction which set the IDLE bit. On-chip hardware inhibits access to internal RAM in this event, but access to the port pins is not inhibited. To eliminate the possibility of an unexpected write to a port pin when Idle is terminated by reset, the instruction following the one that invokes Idle should not be one that writes to a port pin or to external memory.

POWER DOWN MODE

The power down mode is activated by setting the PDWN bit high. The instruction that sets PCON.1 invokes Power Down, is the last instruction executed. In the Power Down mode, the on-chip oscillator stopped. Thus, the timers and the UART as well as software execution are halted. The on-chip RAM and Special Function Registers retain their values until the Power Down mode is terminated. As long as a minimum of 2 volts are applied to the chip (assuming a five volt part) the contents of the internal RAM will be preserved.

The only way to force the processor out of power down mode is by applying a power on reset. Reset redefines the SFRs but does not change the on-chip RAM. The reset should not be activated before V_{CC} is restored to its normal operating level and must be held active long enough to allow the oscillator to restart and stabilize.

Before entering the Power Down mode, the contents of the Carry Bit and B.7 must be equal and at power on, the voltage on V_{CC} and RST must come up at the same time for a proper start-up.

2.7 BOOLEAN PROCESSOR

The 8051 includes a number of special features which support the direct manipulation and testing of individual bits and allow the use of single-bit variables in performing logical operations. These features are referred to as "Boolean Processor".

In digital control application, bit-processing capabilities in conjunction with the microcomputer's byte-processing and numerical capabilities becomes of immense significance.

In relation of Boolean variables, the basic elements of a digital system with associated registers, program memory, addressable data RAM, and I/O capability are as follows.

CPU

The 8051 CPU incorporates special logic devoted to executing several bit-wide operations. There are 17 such bit level instructions.

PROGRAM MEMORY

Bit-processing instructions are fetched from the same program memory as other arithmetic and logical operations. In addition to the 17 bit level instructions, several sophisticated program control features like multiple addressing modes, subroutine nesting, and a two-level interrupt structure are useful in structuring Boolean Processor based programs.

Boolean instructions are one, two, or three bytes long, depending on what function they perform, shown in Fig. 2.17. Those involving only the carry flag have either a single-byte opcode or an opcode followed by a conditional-branch destination byte. The more general instructions add a "direct address" byte after the opcode to specify the bit affected, yielding two or three byte encoding. Though this format allows potentially 256 directly addressable bit locations, not all of them are implemented in the 8051 family.

DATA MEMORY

The instructions in Fig. 2.17 can operate directly upon 144 general purpose bits forming the Boolean processor "RAM." These bits can be used as software flags or to store program variables. Two operand instructions use the CPU's carry flag ("C") as a special one-bit register: in a sense, the carry is a "Boolean accumulator" for logical operations and data transfers.

INPUT/OUTPUT

All 32 I/O pins can be addressed as individual inputs, outputs, or both, in any combination. Any pin can be a control strobe output, status (Test) input, or serial I/O link implemented via software. An additional 33 individually addressable bits reconfigure, control, and monitor the status of the CPU and all on chip peripheral functions (timer counters, serial port modes, interrupt logic etc).

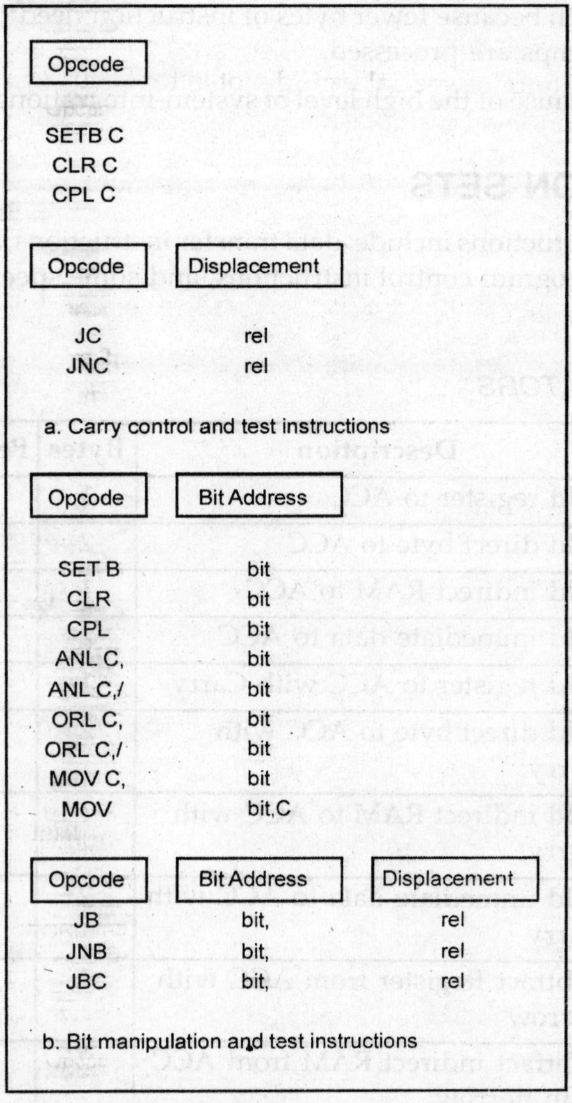

Figure 2.17 Bit addressing instruction formats

ADVANTAGE OF BOOLEAN PROCESSOR

- Applications are simple to write since the architecture correlates more closely with the problems being solved.
- Easier to debug because more individual instructions have no unexpected or undesirable side effects.
- More byte efficient due to direct bit addressing and program counter relative branching.

- Faster execution because fewer bytes of instruction need to be fetched and fewer conditional jumps are processed.
- Lower cost because of the high level of system-integration within one component.

2.8 INSTRUCTION SETS

The assembly level instructions include: data transfer instructions, arithmetic instructions, logical instructions, program control instructions, and some special instructions such as the rotate instructions.

ARITHMETIC OPERATORS

Instruction	Description	Bytes	Periods	C	OV	AC
ADD A, Rn	Add register to ACC	1	12	x	x	x
ADD A, direct	Add direct byte to ACC	2	12	x	x	x
ADD A, @Ri	Add indirect RAM to ACC	1	12	x	x	x
ADD A, #data	Add immediate data to ACC	2	12	x	x	x
ADDC A, Rn	Add register to ACC with Carry	1	12	x	x	x
ADDC A, direct	Add direct byte to ACC with Carry	2	12	x	x	x
ADDC A, @Ri	Add indirect RAM to ACC with Carry	1	12	x	x	x
ADDC A, #data	Add immediate data to ACC with Carry	2	12	x	x	x
SUBB A, Rn	Subtract Register from ACC with borrow	1	12	x	x	x
SUBB A, direct	Subtract indirect RAM from ACC with borrow	2	12	x	x	x
SUBB A, @Ri	Subtract indirect RAM from ACC with borrow	1	12	x	x	x
SUBB A, #data	Subtract immediate data from ACC with borrow	2	12	x	x	x
INC A	Increment ACC	1	12			
INC Rn	Increment register	1	12			
INC direct	Increment direct byte	2	12			
INC @Ri	Increment direct RAM	1	12			

DEC A	Decrement ACC	1	12			
DEC Rn	Decrement Register	1	12			
DEC direct	Decrement direct byte	2	12			
DEC @Ri	Decrement indirect RAM	1	12			
INC DPTR	Increment Data Pointer	1	24			
MUL AB	Multiply A & B	1	48	0	x	
DIV AB	Divide A by B	1	48	0	x	
DA A	Decimal Adjust ACC	1	12	x		

LOGICAL OPERATIONS

Instruction	Description	Bytes	Periods	C	OV	AC
ANL A, Rn	AND register to ACC	1	12			
ANL A, direct	AND direct byte to ACC	2	12			
ANL A, @Ri	AND indirect RAM to ACC	1	12			
ANL A, #data	AND immediate data to ACC	2	12			
ANL direct, A	AND ACC to direct byte	2	12			
ANL direct, #data	AND immediate data to direct byte	3	24			
ORL A, Rn	OR register to ACC	1	12			
ORL A, direct	OR direct byte to ACC	2	12			
ORL A, @Ri	OR indirect RAM to ACC	1	12			
ORL A, #data	OR immediate data to ACC	2	12			
ORL direct, A	OR ACC to direct byte	2	12			
ORL direct, #data	OR immediate data to direct byte	3	24			
XRL A, Rn	XOR register to ACC	1	12			
XRL A, direct	XOR direct byte to ACC	2	12			
XRL A, @Ri	XOR indirect RAM to ACC	1	12			
XRL A, #data	XOR immediate data to ACC	2	12			
XRL direct, A	XOR ACC to direct byte	2	12			
XRL direct, #data	XOR immediate data to direct byte	3	24			
CLR A	Clear the ACC	1	12			
CPL A	Complement the ACC	1	12			
RL A	Rotate the ACC left	1	12			
RLC A	Rotate the ACC left through Carry	1	12	x		
RR A	Rotate the ACC right	1	12			
RRC A	Rotate the ACC right through Carry	1	12	x		
SWAP A	Swap nibbles in the ACC	1	12			

DATA TRANSFER

Instruction	Description	Bytes	Periods	C	OV	AC
MOV A, Rn	Move Register to ACC	1	12			
MOV A, direct	Move Direct byte to ACC	2	12			
MOV A,@Ri	Move Indirect byte to ACC	1	12			
MOV A,#data	Move Immediate data to ACC	2	12			
MOV Rn,A	Mov ACC to Register	1	12			
MOV Rn,direct	Move Direct byte to Register	2	24			
MOV Rn,#data	Move Immediate data to Register	2	12			
MOV direct,A	Move ACC to Direct byte	2	12			
MOV direct,Rn	Move Register to Direct byte	2	24			
MOV direct,direct	Move Direct byte to Direct byte	3	24			
MOV direct,@Ri	Mov Indirect RAM to Direct byte	3	24			
MOV direct,#data	Move Immediate data to Direct byte	3	24			
MOV @Ri,A	Move ACC to Indirect RAM	1	12			
MOV @Ri,direct	Move direct byte to indirect RAM	2	24			
MOV @Ri,#data	Move Immediate data to Indirect RAM	2	12			
MOV DPTR, #data16	Load data pointer with 16 bit constant	3	24			
MOVC A, @A +DPTR	Move code byte at ACC+DPTR to ACC	1	24			
MOVC A,@A+PC	Move code byte at ACC+PC to ACC	1	24			
MOVX A,@Ri	Move external RAM to ACC	1	24			
MOVX @Ri,A	Move ACC to external RAM	1	24			
MOVX A,@DPTR	Move external RAM to ACC	1	24			
MOVX @DPTR,A	Move ACC to external RAM	1	24			
PUSH direct	Push direct byte to stack	2	24			
POP direct	Pop direct byte from stack	2	24			
XCH A,Rn	Exchange register with ACC	1	12			
XCH A, direct	Exchange direct byte with ACC	2	12			

Instruction	Description	Bytes	Periods	C	OV	AC
XCH A,@Ri	Exchange indirect RAM with ACC	1	12			
XCHD A,@Ri	Exchange low order digit indirect RAM with ACC	1	12			

BOOLEAN MANIPULATION

Instruction	Description	Bytes	Periods	C	OV	AC
CLR C	Clear carry flag	1	12	0		
CLR bit	Clear direct bit	2	12			
SETB C	Set carry flag	1	12	1		
SETB bit	Set direct bit	2	12			
CPL C	Complement carry flag	1	12	x		
CPL bit	Complement direct bit	2	12			
ANL C,bit	AND direct bit to carry	2	24	x		
ANL C,/bit	AND complement of direct bit to	2	24	x		
ORL C,bit	OR direct bit to carry	2	24	x		
ORL C,/bit	OR complement of direct bit to carry	2	24	x		
MOV C,bit	Move direct bit to carry	2	12	x		
MOV bit,C	Move carry to direct bit	2	24			
JC rel	Jump if carry is set	2	24			
JNC rel	Jump if carry is NOT set	2	24			
JB bit,rel	Jump if direct bit is set	3	24			
JNB bit,rel	Jump if direct bit is NOT set	3	24			
JBC bit,rel	Jump if direct bit is set and clear that bit	3	24			

2.9 SOLVED EXAMPLES

1Q: Can the ports P0 and P2 be used for I/O when using external memory? Explain.

Ans: No. The output drivers of Ports 0 and 2, and the input buffers of port 0, are used to access external memory. Port 0 outputs the low byte of the external memory address, time-multiplexed with the byte being read/written. Port 2 outputs the high byte of the external memory address when the address is 16 bits wide. Otherwise, the P2 SFR contents available at the port 2 pins. Therefore, when external memory is being used, ports 0 and 2 are unavailable for their primary use as general I/O lines.

2Q: Is there anything one can do to use these ports for I/O when using external memory?

Ans: Normally ports P0, P1, P2, P3 can not be used for I/O, But in some cases it can be used. For example, one can use port 2 for output, when PSEN, RD and WR are all inactive. The chip will emit the contents of the P2 SFR at that time. Because the contents of the SFR latch for port 2 are not modified during the execution of a Data Memory fetch cycle on the Expanded Bus. If an instruction requiring a cycle on the Expanded Bus is not followed by another instruction requiring a cycle on the Expanded Bus, then the original contents of the port 2 SFR latch will appear during the next machine cycle.

3Q: Port 0 has open drain outputs. Ports 1, 2, and 3 have internal pullups. What does this mean?

Ans: When used as outputs, all port pins will drive the state to which the associated SFR latch bit has been set. Except for port 0,which will only drive low (not high). When a 0 is written to a bit in port 0, the pin is pulled low (0). But, when a 1 is written to a bit in port 0, the pin goes into a high impedance state - or in other words, "disconnected", no value.

To be able to get a 1 as output, an external pull up resistor are needed to pull up the port (to +5V, or 1) when the port is in its high impedence state. Typical values for pullups might be 470 ohm to drive a LED, and 4.7K or higher to drive logic circuits. (Any port pin may be used as a general purpose input simply by writing a 1 into the associated SFR latch bit. Since ports 1, 2, and 3 have internal pull-up devices they will pull high and will source current when pulled low. When a port 0 bit is programmed for input (set to 1) it will go to a high impedance state.)

4Q: Why is such an "odd" crystal frequency of 11.0592 MHz used so often for 8051 designs.

Ans: When Timer 1 is used as the baud rate generator, the baud rates in Modes 1 and 3 are determined by the Timer 1 overflow rate and the value of SMOD (PCON.7 - double speed baud rates) as follows:

$$Baud\,rate = \frac{2^{smod}}{32} \times (Timer\,1\,overflow\,rate)$$

Most typically, the timer is configured in the auto-reload mode (mode 2, high nibble of TMOD = 0100B). In this case, the baud rate is given as:

$$Baud\,rate = \frac{2^{smod}}{32} \times \frac{Oscillator\ frequency}{12 \times (256 - Thl)}$$

Some typical baud rates for an 11.0592 crystal:

Baud rate	SMOD	TH1
19200	1	0FDH
9600	0	0FDH
4800	0	0FAH
2400	0	0F4H
1200	0	0E8H
300	0	0A0H

5Q: The Intel MCS-51 assembly language defines alternate symbols AR0... AR7 for registers R0 ... R7. What is meaning of this?

Ans: Some 8051 instructions do not support all possible addressing modes. For example, the PUSH and POP instructions are only available with direct addressing. Since the registers R0 ... R7 are mapped into the internal memory, they must also have a DATA (= direct) address. The special assembler symbols AR0 ... AR7 are simply the absolute DATA addresses of registers R0 ... R7.

Although there is no instruction PUSH R5 with true register addressing, one can do it with PUSH AR5 (= direct addressing).

2.10 PROBLEMS

1. Name three features of the 8051.
2. What is the major difference between the 8051 and 8052 microcontrollers?
3. Give the size of RAM in 8051, 8052 and 8031.
4. Give the size of the on chip ROM in 8051, 8052 and 8031.
5. What are the different power-saving modes of 8051?Differentiate them.
6. Which port has no alternate functions?
7. What component are normally put together with the microcontroller into a single chip?
8. Name registers that can do division.
9. Why a low-address byte latch for external memory is needed?
10. What is a SFR?Can you identify the bit addressable SFRs from their addresses?
11. If a microcontroller architecture has both 8-bit and 16-bit versions, which of the following statement is true.
    (a) The 8-bit software will run on the 16-bit system.
    (b) The 16-bit software will run on the 8-bit system.
12. List the different addressing modes used in 8051 with one example for each.
13. With a diagram, show the memory mapping of 8051.
14. True or False
    I. A general – purpose microprocessor has on-chip ROM.
    II. A microcontroller has on-chip ROM.

III. A microcontroller has on-chip I/O ports.

IV. A microcontroller has a fixed amount of RAM on the chip.

15. Fill in the blanks.

I. The 8051 is a _______ -bit microprocessor.

II. The 8751 has ________ bytes of on-chip ROM.

III. The 8051 has _______ on-chip timers.

IV. The 8052 has _______ bytes of on-chip RAM.

V. The ROMless version of the 8051 uses ____________ as the part number.

VI. The 8051 family has ____________ pins for I/O.

VII. The 8051 family has circuitry to support ___________ serial ports.

VIII. The 8751 on-chip ROM is of type__________.

Chapter 3

Assembly Language Programming with 8051 Microcontroller

3.1 INTRODUCTION

The instructions executed by the CPU are defined by a binary code called *machine code*. The instructions and corresponding codes are microprocessor dependent. Each instruction is represented by a unique binary string that causes the microprocessor to perform a low-level function (e.g., add a number to a register or move a register's value to a memory location).

Microprocessors can be programmed using assembly language, which has a mnemonic command corresponding to each instruction (*e.g.*, ADD to add a number to a register and MOV to move a register's value to a memory location). However, assembly language must be converted to machine code, using software called an *assembler*, before it can be executed on the microprocessor/microcontroller. These are the reasons to write computer instructions in assembly language.

- To speed computer operation
- To reduce the size of the program
- To write programs for special situations
- To better understand how computer operates

3.2 MICROCONTROLLER PROGRAMMING LANGUAGES

3.2.1 MACHINE/ASSEMBLY LANGUAGE

Machine language is the program representation as the microcontroller understands it. A program that consists of 0s and 1s is called *machine language*. It is not simple for one to understand machine language. Therefore, Assembly languages were developed which provided mnemonics for the machine code instructions. Assembly language is a human-readable form of machine language which makes it much easier. Each assembly language statement corresponds to one machine language statement. Assembly language is referred to as a *low-level language* because it deals directly with the internal architecture of machine (CPU).

An assembly/machine language program is fast and small. This is because programmer are in complete charge of what goes into the program. Assembly language (assembler) can't correct wrongly written programs.

If beginners are starting out learning about microcontrollers, it would be worth first learning assembler. By programming in assembler, beginners master the underlying architecture of the chip, which is important if beginners intend to do anything significant with microcontroller.

3.2.2 INTERPRETERS

An interpreter is a high level language translator that is closer to natural language. The interpreter itself is a program that sits resident in the microcontroller. It executes a program by reading each language statement one at a time and then doing what the statement says to do. The two most popular interpreters for microcontrollers are BASIC and FORTH. As low level language is translated into machine code by assembler, high level languages by *interpreter/compiler*.

BASIC's popularity is due to its simplicity and readability. Only disadvantage of [interpreted] BASIC is that it is slow. But, often using a different technique for performing the desired task can solve this.

FORTH interpreter is important due to its speed (approaching that of assembler language) and its incremental approach to building a system from reusable parts. Many FORTH systems come with a host system which turns desktop computer into a development system. FORTH can be quite difficult to write in (if one have no experience with it) and is probably even harder to read. However, it is a very useful and productive language for control systems and robotics, and can be mastered in time. The nicest thing about developing a system with an interpreter is that one can build program interactively. One can first write a small piece of code and then try it out immediately to see how it works. When the results are satisfactory, one can then add additional components until the final result is achieved.

3.2.3 COMPILERS

A compiler is a high level language translator that combines the programming ease of an interpreter with greater speed. This is accomplished by translating the program (on a host machine such as a desktop PC) directly into machine language. The machine language program is then burned onto an EPROM or downloaded directly to the microcontroller. The microcontroller then executes the translated program directly, without having to interpret first.

The most popular microcontroller compilers are C and BASIC. PL/M, from Intel, also has some popular support due to that company's extensive use of that language.

Due to both its popularity and its slow speed, it was only logical that BASIC would appear as a compiled language. A few companies supply a BASIC compiler for several of the more popular microcontrollers. Execution speed is drastically increased over interpreted BASIC since the microcontroller is freed from the task of interpreting the statements as the program runs.

There are several very good and cheap C compilers available for the popular microcontrollers.

While interpreted forth approaches the speed of many compilers, compiled forth screams along. Today there are many high performance optimizing native code Forth compilers. Of course it still has compactness and more elegant factoring of functionality than in most languages.

3.2.4 FUZZY LOGIC AND NEURAL NETWORKS

Fuzzy Logic and neural networks are two design methods that are coming into favor in embedded systems. The two methods are very different from each other, from conception to implementation. However, the advantages and disadvantages of the two can complement each other.

The advantage of neural networks is that it is possible to design them without completely understanding the underlying logical rules by which they operate. The neural network designer applies a set of inputs to the network and "trains" it to produce the required output. The inputs must represent the behavior of the system that is being programmed, and the outputs should match the desired result within some margin of error. If the network's output does not agree with the desired result, the structure of the neural network is altered until it does. After training it is assumed that the network will also produce the desired output, or something close to it, when it is presented with new and unknown data.

In contrast, a fuzzy-logic system can be precisely described. Before a fuzzy control system is designed, its desired logical operation must be analyzed and translated into fuzzy-logic rules. This is the step where neural networks technology can be helpful to the fuzzy-logic designer. The designer can first train a software neural network to produce the desired output from a given set of inputs and outputs and then use a software tool to extract the underlying rules from the neural network. The extracted rules are translated into fuzzy-logic rules.

Fuzzy logic is not a complete design solution. It supplements rather than replaces traditional event control and PID (proportional, integral, and derivate) control techniques. Fuzzy logic relies on grade of membership and artificial intelligence techniques. It works best when it is applied to non-linear systems with many inputs that cannot be easily expressed in either mathematical equations used for PID control or IF-THEN statements used for event control.

3.3 DEVELOPMENT TOOLS

Having a programming language is usually not enough to develop a program for a microcontroller. Some way of debugging the program is needed.

3.3.1 SIMULATORS

A simulator runs microcontroller program on a host machine (such as PC). One can step through the code to see exactly what is happening as the program runs. Contents of registers or variables can be altered to change the way the program runs. One can work out ideas or learn about microcontrollers by experimenting with small code fragments and watching on the screen what happens. A simulator can't support real interrupts or devices, and usually runs much slower than the real device the program is intended for.

3.3.2 RESIDENT DEBUGGERS

A resident debugger runs program on the microcontroller itself, while showing the progress on host machine (such as a PC). Has many of the same advantages as simulator, with the additional benefit of seeing how the program runs on the real target machine. A resident debugger needs to "steal" some resources from the target machine, including: a communications port to communicate with the host, an interrupt to handle single stepping, and a certain amount of memory for the resident part (on the target) of the debugger.

3.3.3 EMULATORS

An emulator is a sophisticated device that pretends that it is the microprocessor itself, while at the same time capturing information. It provides full and total control over the target, while at the same time not requiring any resources from the target. The emulator can either be a stand alone device with its own display, or it can be interface to a PC.

3.4 ASSEMBLY LANGUAGE PROGRAMMING

Assembly language programs are written as a sequence of text lines. Each line of text is an instruction to the CPU, a directive to the assembler, or a combination of the two. The Complete syntax of a line of program code (an assembly language instruction line) is label: instruction; comment(s)

3.4.1 LABELS IN ASSEMBLY LANGUAGE

By choosing label names that are meaningful, a programmer can make a program readable and easier to maintain. There are several rules that names must follow.

- First, each label name must be unique. The names used for labels in Assembly language programming consist of alphabetic letters in both upper and lower case, the digits 0 to 9, and the special characters question mark (?), period (.), at (@), underline (_), and dollar sign ($).
- The first character of the label must be an alphabetic character. In other words it cannot be a number.
- Every assembler has some reserved words which must not be used as labels in the program. Foremost among the reserved words are the mnemonics for the

instructions. For example, "MOV" and "ADD" are reserved since they are instruction mnemonics. Aside from the mnemonics there are some other reserved words. Programmer should check assembler for the list of reserved words.

INSTRUCTIONS

Each 8051 instructions is generally made up of three distinct parts, as shown

1 (mnemonic)	2 destination,	3 source (operands)

COMMENTS

Comments begin with a semicolon (;) to indicate that they are not one of the operands. Anything typed after semicolon is a comment.

3.4.2 8051 DATA TYPES AND DIRECTIVES

Assembler program at concerns deal with such things as setting the PC contents, assigning names to numbers, and defining fixed numbers. The title given to an assembler program language instruction is a directive.

The 8051 microcontroller has only one data type. It is 8 bits, and the size of each register is also 8 bits. It is the job of the programmer to break down data larger than 8 bits (00 to FFH, or 0 to 255 in decimal) to be processed by the CPU.

DB (DEFINE BYTE)

The DB directive is the most widely used data directive in the assembler. It is used to define the 8-bit data. When DB is used to define data, the numbers can be in decimal, binary, hex, or ASCII formats. For decimal, the "D" after the decimal number is optional, but using "B" (binary) and "H" (hexadecimal) for the others is requisite. Regardless of which is used, the assembler will convert the numbers into hex. To indicate ASCII, simply place it in quotation marks (' '). The assembler will assign the ASCII code for the numbers or characters automatically. The DB directive is the only directive that can be used to define ASCII strings larger than two characters; therefore, it should be used for all ASCII data definitions.

NOTE: Either single or double quotes can be used around ASCII strings. This can be useful for strings, which contain a single quote such as "A'Singh". DB is also used to allocate memory in byte-sized chunks.

ASSEMBLER DIRECTIVES

Most frequently used directives of the 8051 are as follows.

ORG (ORIGIN)/.ORG

The ORG/.ORG directive is used to indicate the beginning of the address. The number that comes after ORG can be either in hex or in decimal. If the number is not followed by H, it is decimal and the assembler will convert it to hex.

EQU (EQUATE)

This is used to define a constant without occupying a memory location. The EQU directive does not set aside storage for a data item but associates a constant value with a data label so that when the label appears in the program, its constant value will be substituted for the label. The following uses EQU for the counter constant and then the constant is used to load the R3 register.

```
COUNT      EQU      100
...                 ...
MOV                 R3, #COUNT
```

When executing the instruction "MOV R3, #COUNT", the register R3 will be loaded with the value 100 (notice the # sign). What is the advantage of using EQU? Assume that there is a constant (a fixed value) used in many different places in the program, and the programmer wants to change its value throughout. By the use of EQU, one can change it once and the assembler will change all of its occurrences, rather than search the entire program trying to find every occurrence.

It is good practice to use EQU directive in professional programming.

END/.END

Another important pseudo code is the END/.END directive. This indicates to the assembler the end of the source (asm) file. The END directive is the last line of an 8051 program, meaning that in the source code anything after the END directive is ignored by the assembler.

NOTE: Programmer should refer assembler before using assembler directives.

3.5 8051 PROGRAMMING TECHNIQUES

3.5.1 SAVING CPU STATUS DURING INTERRUPTS

When the 8051 hardware recognizes an interrupt request, program control branches automatically to the corresponding service routine, by forcing the CPU to process a long CALL (LCALL) instruction to the appropriate address. The return address is stored on the top of the stack. After completing the service routine, an RETI instruction returns the processor to the background program at the point from which it was interrupted.

3.5.2 PASSING PARAMETERS ON THE STACK

The stack area of the internal RAM is used to automatically store the address, called the return address, of the instruction found immediately after the call. The Stack Pointer register holds the address of the last space used on the stack. It stores the return address above this space, adjusting itself upward the return address is stored.

The stack may also pass parameters to and from subroutines. The stack parameter passing can be easily understood with the help of the Fig. 3.1.The Fig. 3.1 depicts the following sequence of events.

- A call opcode occurs in the program software, or an interrupt is generated in hardware in hardware circuitry.
- The return address of the next instruction after the call instruction or interrupt is found in the program counter.
- The return address bytes are pushed on the stack, low byte first.
- The stack pointer is incremented for each push on the stack.
- The subroutine address is placed in the program counter.
- The subroutine is executed.
- A RET (return) opcode is encountered at the end of the subroutine.
- Two pop operations restore the return address to the PC from the stack area in internal RAM.
- The stack pointer is decremented for each address byte pop.

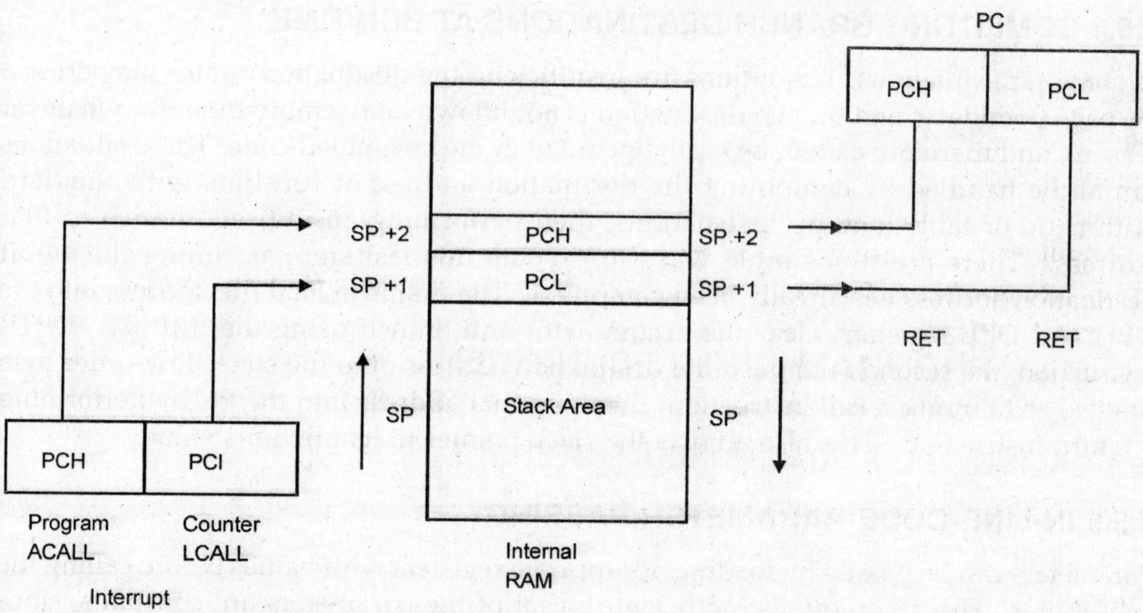

Fig. 3.1 Stack parameter passing

For example, to intialize of stack with RAM address 25h one may use

```
MOV 81,#25h    ;sets the stack pointer to 25h in RAM
```

3.5.3 N-WAY BRANCHING

There are several different means for branching to sections of code determined or selected at run time. (The single destination address incorporated into conditional and unconditional jumps are, of course, fixed at assembly time). Each has advantages for different applications.

In a typical N-way branch situation, the potential destinations are generally known at assembly time. One of a number of small routines is selected according to the value of an index variable determined while the program is running. The most efficient way to solve this problem is with the MOVC and an indirect jump instruction, using a short table of offset values in ROM to indicate the relative starting addresses of the several routines.

JMP@A+DTPR is an instruction which performs an indirect jump to an address determined during program execution. The instruction adds the eight-bit unsigned accumulator contents with the contents of the sixteen-bit data pointer, just like MOVC, A,@A+DPTR. The resulting sum is loaded in to the program counter and is used as the address for subsequent instruction fetches. Again, a sixteen-bit addition is performed; a carry-out from the low-order eight-bits may propagate through the higher-order bits. In this case, neither the accumulator contents nor the data pointer is altered.

3.5.4 COMPUTING BRANCH DESTINATIONS AT RUN TIME

In some rare situations, 128 options are insufficient, the destination routes may cross a 2K page boundary, or a branch destination is not known at assembly time (for whatever reason), and therefore cannot be easily included in the assembled code. These situations can all be handled by computing the destination address at run-time with standard arithmetic or table look-up instructions, then performing an indirect branch to that address. There are two simple ways to execute this last step, assuming the 16-bit destination address has already been computed. The first is to load the address into the DPH and DPL registers, clear the accumulator and branch using the JMP @A+DPTR instruction; the second is to push the destination address onto the stack, low-order byte first (so as to mimic a call instruction) then pop that address into the PC by performing a return instruction. This also adjusts the stack pointer to its previous value.

3.5.5 IN-LINE-CODE PARAMETER PASSING

Parameters can be passed by loading appropriate registers with values before calling the subroutine. This technique is inefficient if a lot of the parameters are constants, since each would require a separate register to carry it and a separate instruction to load the register each time the routine is called.

If the routine is called frequently, a more code-efficient way to transfer constants is "in-line-code" parameter-passing. The constants are actually part of the program code, immediately following the call instruction. The subroutine determines where to find them from the return address on the stack, and then reads the parameters it needs from program memory.

3.5.6 LOOKUP TABLES

A lookup table is a way of organising a set of data object in memory such that each object is consecutively placed from the base and can be looked directly by using the an offset or index value with respect to table origin address. The two instructions that are available for reading lookup tables in Program Memory are MOVC A, @A+DPTR (Read Program memory at A+DPTR) and MOVC A, @A+PC (Read Program Memory at A+PC). Since these instructions access only Program Memory, the lookup tables can only be read, not updated. The mnemonic is MOVC for "move constant".

3.6 ADDRESSING MODES

An instruction is divided in to groups of bits, or fields, with one field, called the operation code (opcode), indicating what the computer is to do and other fields called the operands, indicating the information needed by the instruction in carrying out its task.

The way in which an operand is specified is called its addressing mode. In simple words, an "addressing mode" refers to how one is addressing a given memory location. In summary, the addressing modes are as follows, with an example of each:

Immediate Addressing
Direct Addressing
Register Addressing
Indirect Addressing
Relative Addressing
Absolute addressing
Long Addressing
Indexed Addressing

Each of these addressing modes provides important flexibility.

IMMEDIATE ADDRESSING

Immediate addressing is so-named because the value to be stored in memory immediately follows the operation code (opcode) in memory. That is to say, the instruction itself dictates what value will be stored in memory. The mnemonic for immediate data is the pound sign (#).

Example:

```
MOV Rn, #data      ;copy the immediate data byte 'data' to register Rn
MOV A, #data       ;copy the immediate data byte 'data' to A register
```

For example, the instruction:

MOV A, #99d

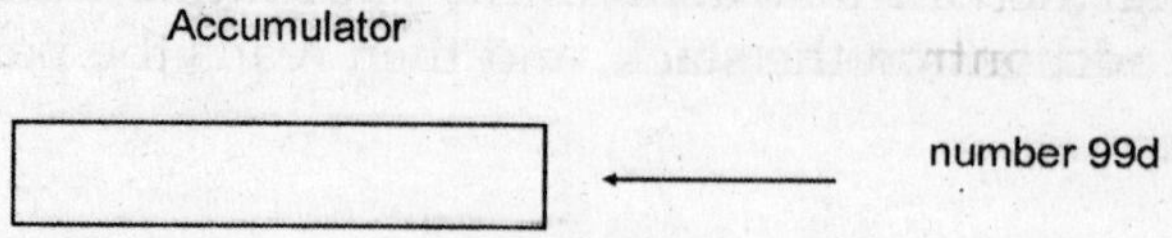

This instruction uses Immediate Addressing because the Accumulator will be loaded with the value that immediately follows; in this case 99 (decimal).

Immediate addressing is very fast since the value to be loaded is included in the instruction. However, since the value to be loaded is fixed at compile-time it is not very flexible.

DIRECT ADDRESSING

Direct addressing is so-named because the value to be stored in memory is obtained by directly retrieving it from another memory location. The SFRs and all 128 bytes of internal RAM may be addressed directly using the single-byte address.

Example:

```
MOV A, direct        ;copy data from direct address 'direct' to register A
MOV Rn, direct       ;copy data from direct address 'direct' to register Rn
```

For example:

MOV A, 47h

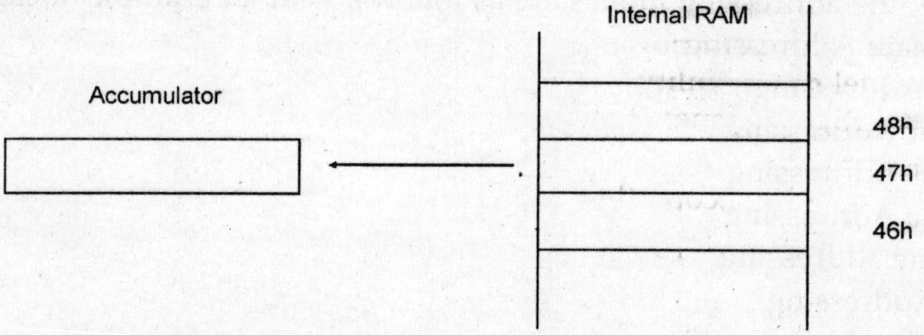

This instruction will read the data out of Internal RAM address 47 (hexadecimal) and store it in the Accumulator.

It is for programmer to use a name for an SFR or absolute address for the SFR.

For example:

```
MOV 80h, #0b3h
MOV p0, #0b3h      ;both moves a constant number into port 0.
```

Direct addressing is generally fast since, although the value to be loaded isn't included in the instruction, it is quickly accessible since it is stored in the 8051's Internal RAM. It is also much more flexible than Immediate Addressing since the value to be loaded is whatever is found at the given address, which may be variable.

Also, it is important to note that when using direct addressing any instruction which refers to an address between 00h and 7Fh is referring to Internal Memory. Any instruction which refers to an address between 80h and FFh is referring to the SFR control registers that control the 8051 microcontroller itself.

REGISTER ADDRESSING

Some register names may be used as part of the mnemonic as sources or destinations of data. Register A, R0 to R7 and DPTR may be named as the part of the mnemonic.

Example:

```
MOV Rn, A      ;copy data from register A to register Rn
MOV A, Rn      ;copy data from register Rn to register A
```

For example:

```
MOV A, R5
```

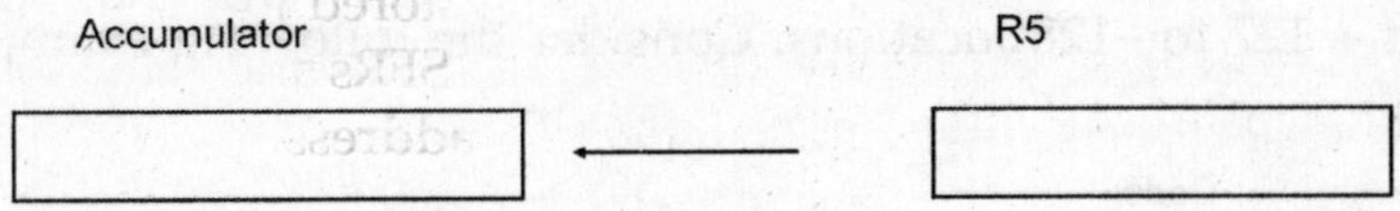

This instruction will read the data out of register R5 and store it in the Accumulator.

In the register addressing mode, register-to-register moves occur between registers A and R0 to R7.

INDIRECT ADDRESSING

Indirect addressing is a very powerful addressing mode which in many cases provides an exceptional level of flexibility. It uses a register to hold the final address, known as pointing register (Ri). The mnemonic for indirect addressing is the "at" sign (@). Indirect addressing appears as follows:

```
MOV A, @Ri          ;copy the contents of the address in Ri to A register
MOV @ RI, #data     ;copy the immediate byte 'data' to the address in Ri.
```

For example:

```
MOV A, @ R0
```

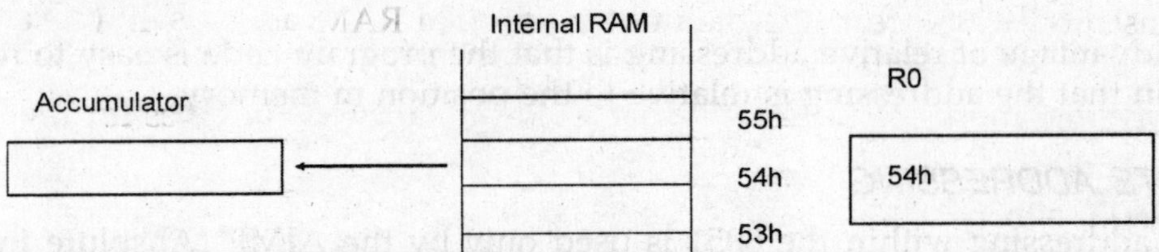

This instruction causes the 8051 to analyze the value of the R0 register. The 8051 will then load the accumulator with the value from Internal RAM which is found at the address indicated by R0.

For example, let's say R0 holds the value 54h and Internal RAM address 54h holds the value 67h. When the above instruction is executed the 8051 will check the value of R0. Since R0 holds 54h the 8051 will get the value out of Internal RAM address 54h (which holds 67h) and store it in the Accumulator. Thus, the Accumulator ends up holding 67h. Indirect addressing refers to Internal RAM only and cannot be used to refer to SFR registers.

Note: Only R0 or R1 can be used as register data pointers for indirect addressing when using MOV instructions.

The 8052 (as opposed to the 8051) has an additional 128 bytes of internal RAM. These 128 bytes of RAM can be accessed only using indirect addressing.

RELATIVE ADDRESSING

This is a special addressing mode used with certain jump instructions. The relative address, often referred to as an offset, is an 8-bit signed number, which is automatically added to the PC to make the address of the next instruction. The 8-bit signed offset value gives an address range of + 127 to –128 locations. Consider the following example:

SJMP LABEL_X

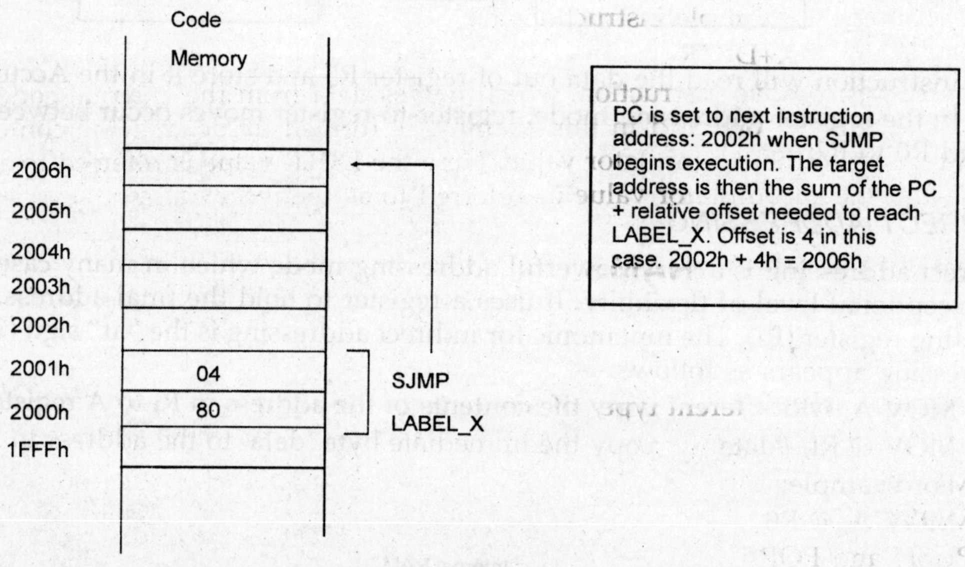

An advantage of relative addressing is that the program code is easy to relocate in memory in that the addressing is relative to the position in memory.

ABSOLUTE ADDRESSING

Absolute addressing within the 8051 is used only by the AJMP (Absolute Jump) and ACALL (Absolute Call) instructions.

LONG ADDRESSING

The long addressing mode within the 8051 is used with the instructions LJMP and LCALL. The address specifies a full 16 bit destination address so that a jump or a call can be made to a location within a 64K Byte code memory space (216 = 64K). An example instruction is:

```
LJMP 5000h        ;full 16 bit address is specified in operand
```

INDEXED ADDRESSING

With indexed addressing a separate register, either the program counter, PC, or the data pointer DTPR, is used as a base address and the accumulator is used as an offset address. The effective address is formed by adding the value from the base address to the value from the offset address. Indexed addressing in the 8051 is used with the JMP or MOVC instructions. Look up tables are easy to implemented with the help of index addressing.

Only Program Memory can be accessed with indexed addressing, and it can only be read. This addressing mode is intended for reading look-up tables in Program Memory. A 16-bit base register (either DPTR or the Program Counter) points to the base of the table, and the Accumulator is set up with the table entry number. The address of the table entry in Program Memory is formed by adding the Accumulator data to the base pointer.

Consider the example instruction:

```
MOVC A, @A+DPTR
```

MOVC is a move instruction, which moves data from the external code memory space. The address operand in this example is formed by adding the content of the DPTR register to the accumulator value. Here the DPTR value is referred to as the *base address* and the accumulator value us referred to as the *index address*.

3.7 SIMPLE PROGRAMS

DATA TRANSFER

The 8051 uses five different types of instruction to move data:

MOV
MOVX
MOVC
PUSH and POP
XCH

MOV

In the 8051 the MOV instruction is concerned with moving data internally, i.e. between Internal RAM, SFR registers, general registers etc. MOVX and MOVC are used in accessing external memory data.

The MOV instruction has the following format:

MOV *destination* <- *source*

The instruction copies *(copy* is a more accurate word than *move)* data from a defined source location to a destination location.

Example MOV instructions are:

```
MOV R2, #80h        ; Move immediate data value 80h to register R2
MOV R4, A           ; Copy data from accumulator to register R4
MOV DPTR, #0F22Ch   ; Move immediate value F22Ch to the DPTR register
MOV R2, 80h         ; Copy data from 80h (Port 0 SFR) to R2
MOV 52h, #52h       ; Copy immediate data value 52h to RAM location 52h
MOV 52h, 53h        ; Copy data from RAM location 53h to RAM 52h
MOV A, @R0          ; Copy contents of location addressed in R0 to A
                      (indirect addressing)
```

MOVX

The 8051 the external memory can be addressed using *indirect* addressing only. The DPTR register is used to hold the address of the external data (since DPTR is a 16-bit register it can address 64KByte locations: $2^{16} = 64K$). The 8 bit registers R0 or R1 can also be used for indirect addressing of external memory but the address range is limited to the lower 256 bytes of memory ($2^8 = 256$ bytes).

The MOVX instruction is used to access the external memory (X indicates external memory access). All external moves must work through the A register (accumulator).

Examples of MOVX instructions are:

```
MOVX @DPTR, A    ; Copy data from A to the address specified in DPTR
MOVX A, @DPTR    ; Copy data from address specified in DPTR to A
```

MOVC

MOVX instructions operate on RAM, which is (normally) a volatile memory. Program tables often need to be stored in ROM since ROM is non volatile memory. The MOVC instruction is used to read data from the external code memory (ROM).

Like the MOVX instruction the DPTR register is used as the indirect address register.

The indirect addressing is enhanced to realize an indexed addressing mode where register A can be used to provide an offset in the address specification. Like the MOVX instruction all moves must be done through register A.

An example of MOVC instruction:

```
MOV DPTR, # 2000h   ; Copy the data value 2000h to the DPTR register
MOV A, #80h         ; Copy the data value 80h to register A
MOVC A, @A+DPTR     ; Copy the contents of the address 2080h (2000h + 80h)
                    ; to register A
```

Note, for the MOVC the program counter, PC, can also be used to form the address.

PUSH AND POP

PUSH and POP instructions are used with the stack only. The SFR register SP contains the current stack address. Direct addressing is used as shown in the following examples:

PUSH 4Ch ; Contents of RAM location 4Ch is saved to the stack. SP is incremented.

PUSH 00h ; The content of R0 (which is at 00h in RAM) is saved to the stack and; SP is incremented.

POP 80h ; The data from current SP address is copied to 80h and SP is; decremented.

XCH

The above move instructions copy data from a source location to a destination location, leaving the source data unaffected. A special XCH (eXCHange) instruction will actually swap the data between source and destination, effectively changing the source data. Immediate addressing may not be used with XCH. XCH instructions must use register A. XCHD is a special case of the exchange instruction where just the lower nibbles are exchanged.

Examples using the XCH instruction are:

XCH A, R3 ; Exchange bytes between A and R3

XCH A, @R0 ; Exchange bytes between A and RAM location whose address is in R0

XCH A, A0h ; Exchange bytes between A and RAM location A0h (SFR port 2)

ARITHMETIC

Some key flags within the PSW, i.e. C, AC, OV, P, are utilized in many of the arithmetic instructions. The arithmetic instructions can be grouped as follows:

Addition
Subtraction
Increment/decrement
Multiply/divide
Decimal adjust

ADDITION

Register A (the accumulator) is used to hold the result of any addition operation.

Some simple addition examples are:

ADD A, #25h ; Adds the number 25h to A, putting sum in A

ADD A, R3 ; Adds the register R3 value to A, putting sum in A

The flags in the PSW register are affected by the various addition operations, as follows:

The C (carry) flag is set to 1 if the addition resulted in a carry out of the accumulator's MSB bit, otherwise it is cleared.

The AC (auxiliary) flag is set to 1 if there is a carry out of bit position 3 of the accumulator, otherwise it is cleared.

For signed numbers the OV flag is set to 1 if there is an arithmetic overflow.

Simple addition is done within the 8051 based on 8 bit numbers, but it is often required to add 16 bit numbers, or 24 bit numbers etc. This leads to the use of multiple byte (multi-precision) arithmetic. The least significant bytes are first added, and if a carry results, this carry is carried over in the addition of the next significant byte etc. This addition process is done at 8-bit precision steps to achieve multiprecision arithmetic. The ADDC instruction is used to include the carry bit in the addition process.

Example instructions using ADDC are:

```
ADDC A, #55h  ; Add contents of A, the number 55h, the carry bit; and put the;
                sum in A
ADDC A, R4    ; Add the contents of A, the register R4, the carry bit; and put; the
                sum in A.
```

SUBTRACTION

Computer subtraction can be achieved using 2's complement arithmetic. Most computers also provide instructions to directly subtract signed or unsigned numbers.

The accumulator, register A, will contain the result (difference) of the subtraction operation. The C (carry) flag is treated as a borrow flag, which is always subtracted from the minuend during a subtraction operation.

Some examples of subtraction instructions are:

```
SUBB A, #55d  ; Subtract the number 55 (decimal) and the C flag from A
              ; and put the result in A.
SUBB A, R6    ; Subtract R6 the C flag from A; and put the result in A.
SUBB A, 58h   ; Subtract the number in RAM location 58h and the C flag from A
              ; and put the result in A.
```

INCREMENT/DECREMENT

The increment (INC) instruction has the effect of simply adding a binary 1 to a number while a decrement (DEC) instruction has the effect of subtracting a binary 1from a number. The increment and decrement instructions can use the addressing modes: direct, indirect and register. The flags C, AC, and OV are not affected by the increment or decrement instructions. If a value of FFh is increment it overflows to 00h. If a value of 00h is decrement it underflows to FFh. The DPTR can overflow from FFFFh to 0000h. The DPTR register cannot be decremented using a DEC instruction.

Some example INC and DEC instructions are as follows:

```
INC R7    ; Increment register R7
INC A     ; Increment A
```

```
INC @R1     ; Increment the number which is the content of the address in R1
DEC A       ; Decrement register A
DEC 43h     ; Decrement the number in RAM address 43h
INC DPTR    ; Increment the DPTR register
```

MULTIPLY/DIVIDE

The 8051 supports 8-bit multiplication and division. This is low precision (8 bit) arithmetic but is useful for many simple control applications. The arithmetic is relatively fast since multiplication and division are implemented as single instructions. If better precision, or indeed, if floating point arithmetic is required then special software routines need to be written. For the MUL or DIV instructions the A and B registers must be used and only unsigned numbers are supported.

MULTIPLICATION

The MUL instruction is used as follows (note absence of a comma between the A and B operands):

```
MUL AB                ; Multiply A by B.
```

The resulting product resides in registers A and B, the low-order byte is in A and the high order byte is in B.

DIVISION

The DIV instruction is used as follows:

```
DIV AB                ; A is divided by B.
```

The remainder is put in register B and the integer part of the quotient is put in register A.

DECIMAL ADJUST (SPECIAL)

The 8051 performs all arithmetic in binary numbers (i.e. it does not support BCD arithmetic). If two BCD numbers are added then the result can be adjusted by using the DA, decimal adjust, instruction:

```
DA A    ; Decimal adjust A following the addition of two BCD numbers.
```

LOGICAL

BOOLEAN OPERATIONS

Most control applications implement control logic using Boolean operators to act on the data. Most microcomputers provide a set of Boolean instructions that act on byte level data. However, the 8051 (somewhat uniquely) additionally provides Boolean instruction which can operate on bit level data.

The following Boolean operations can operate on byte level or bit level data:

ANL Logical AND
ORL Logical OR
CPL Complement (logical NOT)
XRL Logical XOR (exclusive OR)

LOGICAL OPERATIONS AT THE BYTE LEVEL

The destination address of the operation can be the accumulator (register A), a general register, or a direct address. Status flags are not affected by these logical operations (unless PSW is directly manipulated).

Example instructions are:

```
ANL A, #55h      ; AND each bit in A with corresponding bit in number 55h,
                 leaving
                 ; the result in A.
ANL 42h, R4      ; AND each bit in RAM location 42h with corresponding bit in
                 R4,
                 ; leaving the result in RAM location 42h.
ORL A, @R1       ; OR each bit in A with corresponding bit in the number whose
                 ; address is contained in R1 leaving the result in A.
XRL R4, 80h      ; XOR each bit in R4 with corresponding bit in RAM location
                 80h
                 ; (port 0), leaving result in A.
CPL R0           ; Complement each bit in R0
```

LOGICAL OPERATIONS AT THE BIT LEVEL

The C (carry) flag is the destination of most bit level logical operations. The carry flag can easily be tested using a branch (jump) instruction to quickly establish program flow control decisions following a bit level logical operation.

The following SFR registers only are addressable in bit level operations:

PSW, IE, IP, TCON, SCON

Examples of bit level logical operations are as follows:

```
SETB 2Fh     ; Bit 7 of Internal RAM location 25h is set
CLR C        ; Clear the carry flag (flag = 0)
CPL 20h      ; Complement bit 0 of Internal RAM location 24h
MOV C, 87h   ; Move to carry flag the bit 7of Port 0 (SFR at 80h)
ANL C, 90h   ; AND C with the bit 0 of Port 1 (SFR at 90)
ORL C, 91h   ; OR C with the bit 1 of Port 1 (SFR at 90)
```

ROTATE INSTRUCTIONS

The ability to rotate the A register (accumulator) data is useful to allow examination of individual bits. The options for such rotation are as follows:

RL A ; Rotate A one bit to the left. Bit 7 rotates to the bit 0 position

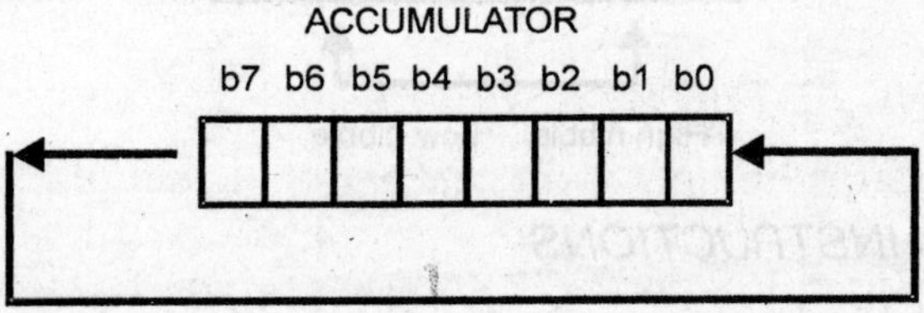

RLC A ; The Carry flag is used as a ninth bit in the rotation loop

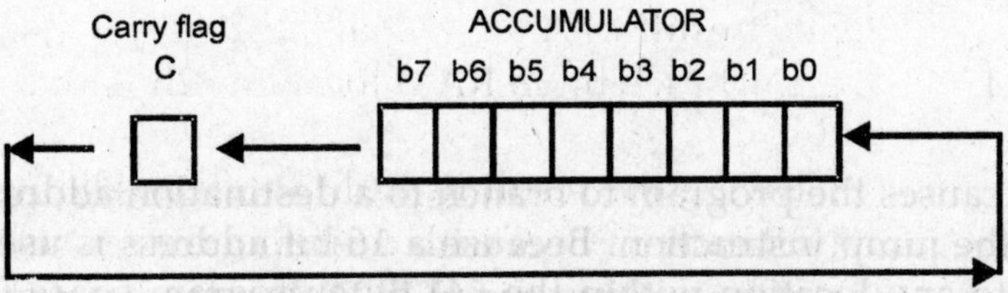

RR A ; Rotates A to the right (clockwise)

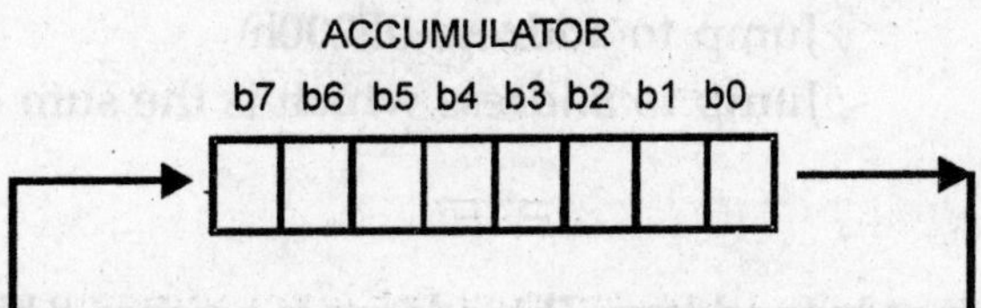

RRC A ; Rotates to the right and includes the carry bit as the 9th bit.

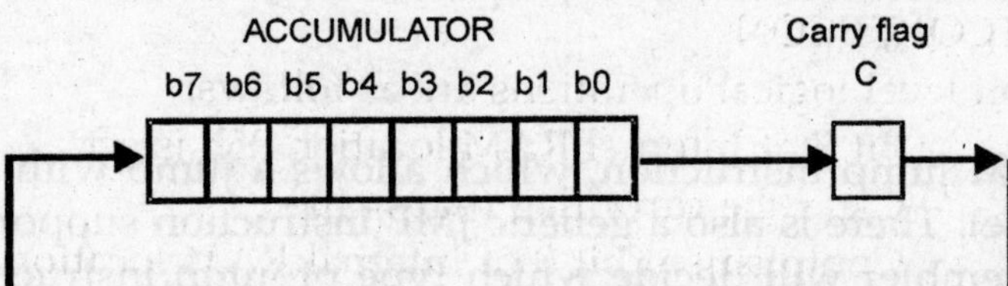

SWAP

The Swap instruction swaps the accumulator's high order nibble with the low-order nibble using the instruction:

SWAP A

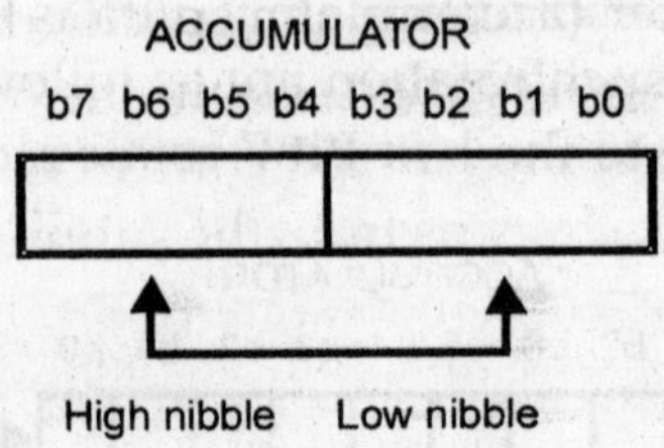

PROGRAM CONTROL INSTRUCTIONS

The 8051 supports three kinds of jump instructions:

LJMP
SJMP
AJMP

LJMP

LJMP (long jump) causes the program to branch to a destination address defined by the 16-bit operand in the jump instruction. Because a 16-bit address is used the instruction can cause a jump to any location within the 64KByte program space (216 = 64K).

Example instructions are:

```
LJMP LABEL_X        ; Jump to the specified label
LJMP 0F200h         ; Jump to address 0F200h
LJMP @A+DPTR        ; Jump to address which is the sum of DPTR and Reg. A
```

SJMP

SJMP (short jump) uses a singe byte address. This address is a signed 8-bit number and allows the program to branch to a distance –128 bytes back from the current PC address or +127 bytes forward from the current PC address. The address mode used with this form of jumping (or branching) is referred to as *relative addressing,* introduced earlier, as the jump is calculated relative to the current PC address.

AJMP

This is a special 8051 jump instruction, which allows a jump with a 2KByte address boundary (a 2K page). There is also a generic JMP instruction supported by many 8051 assemblers. The assembler will decide which type of jump instruction to use, LJMP, SJMP or AJMP, so as to choose the most efficient instruction.

SUBROUTINES AND PROGRAM FLOW CONTROL

A subroutine is called using the LCALL or the ACALL instruction.

LCALL

This instruction is used to call a subroutine at a specified address. The address is 16 bits long so the call can be made to any location within the 64KByte memory space. When a LCALL instruction is executed the current PC content is automatically pushed onto the stack of the PC. When the program returns from the subroutine the PC contents is returned from the stack so that the program can resume operation from the point where the LCALL was made. The return from subroutine is achieved using the RET instruction, which simply pops the PC back from the stack.

ACALL

The ACALL instruction is logically similar to the LCALL but has a limited address range similar to the AJMP instruction.

CALL is a generic call instruction supported by many 8051 assemblers. The assembler will decide which type of call instruction, LCALL or ACALL, to use so as to choose the most efficient instruction.

PROGRAM CONTROL USING CONDITIONAL JUMPS

Most 8051 jump instructions use an 8-bit destination address, based on relative addressing, i.e. addressing within the range –128 to +127 bytes.

When using a conditional jump instruction the programmer can simply specify a program label or a full 16-bit address for the conditional jump instruction's destination. The assembler will position the code and work out the correct 8-bit relative address for the instruction.

Examples of conditional jump instructions are:

```
JZ LABEL_1              ; Jump to LABEL_1 if accumulator is equal to zero
JNZ LABEL_X             ; Jump to LABEL_X if accumulator is not equal to
                        ; zero
JNC LABEL_Y             ; Jump to LABEL_Y if the carry flag is not set
DJNZ R2, LABEL          ; Decrement R2 and jump to LABEL if the resulting
                        ; value of R2 is not zero.
CJNE R1, #55h , LABEL_2 ; Compare the magnitude of R1 and the number 55h
                        ; and
                        ; jump to LABEL_2 if the magnitudes are not equal.
```

Note, jump instructions such as DJNZ and CJNE are very powerful as they carry out a particular operation (e.g.: decrement, compare) and then make a decision based on the result of this operation. Some example code later will help to explain the context in which such instructions might be used.

3.8 SOLVED PROBLEMS

ADDRESSING MODES

1Q: Write program to send 44h to ports P1 and P2, using (a) their addresses (b) their names.

Solution:

```
(a)  MOV A, #44h      ; load data 44h to accumulator
     MOV P1, A        ; transfer acc data to port1 using register addressing
     MOV P2, A        ; transfer acc data to port2
(b)  MOV A, #44h
     MOV 90,A         ; transfer acc data to port1 using direct addressing
     MOV 0A0h,A       ; transfer acc data to port2 using direct addersing
```

Note: Moving data to a port changes the port latch; moving data from a port gets data from the port pins.

2Q: Write program to copy a block of 8 bytes of data to RAM locations starting at 50H from RAM locations 30h.

Solution:

```
         MOV    R0, #30h     ; source pointer
         MOV    R1, #50h     ; destination pointer
         MOV    R3, #8       ; destination pointer
                             ; counter
RETURN:  MOV A, @R0          ; get a byte from source
         MOV @R1, A          ; copy it to destination
         INC R0              ; increment source pointer
         INC R1              ; increment destination pointer
         DJNZ R3, RETURN     ; keep doing it for all eight bytes
```

3Q: Write program to transfer the bytes into RAfM locations starting at 50H, assuming that ROM space starting at 240H contains "INDIA"

Solution: (a) By using a counter

```
        ORG    0000
        MOV    DPTR,#MY_DATA   ;load rom pointer
        MOV    R0,#50h         ;load ram pointer
        MOV    R2,#5           ;load counter
REPEAT: CLR A                  ;A=0
        MOVC A,@A+DPTR         ;move data from program
                               ;memory
        MOV  @R0,A             ;save it in ram
        INC  DPTR              ;increment rom pointer
```

```
                INC  R0                 ;increment ram pointer
                DJNZ R2,REPEAT          ;loop until counter = 0
HERE:       SJMP HERE
; ON-CHIP CODE SPACE USED FOR STORING DATA
   ORG  240h
MY_DATA: DB   "INDIA"
   END
```

(b) By using null char for end of string

```
ORG         0000
MOV         DPTR, #MY_DATA      ;load rom pointer
MOV         R0, #50h            ;load ram pointer
REPEAT:     CLR A               ;A=0
            MOVC A,@A+DPTR      ;move data from ;code space
            JZ  HERE            ;exit if null char
            MOV  @R0,A          ;save it in ram
            INC  DPTR           ;increment rom pointer
            R0                  ;increment ram pointer
            SJMP REPEAT         ;loop
HERE:   SJMP HERE
; ON-CHIP CODE SPACE USED FOR STORING DATA
   ORG  240h
  MYDATA: DB "INDIA",0    ; null char for end of string
   END
```

4Q: Write program to get the x value from P1 and send x^2 to P2, continuously.

Solution:

```
        ORG         0
        MOV         DPTR,#300h          ; load look-up table address
        MOV         A,#0FFh             ; a=ff
        MOV         P1,A                ; configure p1 as input port
REPEAT:             MOV A,P1            ; get x
                    MOVC A, @A+DPTR     ; get x sqaure from table
                    MOV P2,A            ; issue it to p2
                    SJMP REPEAT         ; keep doing it
                    ORG 300h
XSQR_TABLE:
   DB    0,1,4,9,16,25,36,49,64,81
   END
```

Note: This program uses look-up table instead of calculating.

ARITHMETIC/LOGIC OPERATIONS

1Q: Assume that RAM locations 50-55 have the following values. Write a program to find the sum of the values. At the end of the program, register A should contain the low byte and R7 the high byte. All values are in hex.

50=(2E)
51=(5B)
52=(A2)
53=(30)
54=(C5)
55=(EB)

Solution:

```
         MOV  R0,#50h        ;load pointer
         MOV  R2,#6          ;load counter
         CLR  A              ;A=0
         MOV  R7, A          ;clear R7
REPEAT:  ADD  A,@R0          ;add the byte pointer to by R0
         JNC  NEXT           ;if CY=0 don't accumulate carry
         INC  R7             ;keep track of carries
NEXT:    INC  R0             ;increment pointer
         DJNZ R2,REPEAT      ;repeat until R2 is zero
```

2Q: Write program to add two 16-bit numbers. The numbers are 2E5Fh and A3B4h.Store the sum in R7 and R6;R6 should have the lower byte.

Solution:

```
CLR C           ;make CY=0
MOV  A,#05Fh    ;load the low byte now A=5Fh
ADD A,#B4h      ;add the low byte now
MOV  R6,A       ;save the low byte of the sum in R6
MOV  A,#2Eh     ;load the high byte
ADDC A,#A3h     ;add with the carry
MOV  R7,A       ;save the high byte of the sum
```

3Q: Assume that RAM locations 50-55 have the following 6 BCD data. Write a program to find the sum of the values. The result must be in BCD.

50=(43)
51=(54)
52=(65)
53=(27)
54=(78)
55=(91)

Solution:

```
         MOV  R0,#40h        ;load pointer
         MOV  R2,#5          ;load counter
         CLR A               ;A=0
         MOV  R7,A           ;clear R7
REPEAT:  ADD  A,@R0          ;add the byte pointer to by R0
         DA   A              ;adjust for BCD
         JNC NEXT            ;if CY=0 don't accumulate carry
         INC  R7             ;keep track of carries
NEXT:    INC  R0             ;increment pointer
         DJNZ R2,REPEAT      ;repeat until R2 is zero
```

4Q: Write a program to get hex data in the range of 00-FFh from the port 0 and convert it to decimal. Save the digits in R7,R6 and R5,where the least significant digit is in R7.

Solution:

```
         MOV  A,#0FFh
         MOV  P0,A           ;make P0 an input port
         MOV  A,P0           ;read data from P0
         MOV  B,#10          ;B=0A hex (10 dec)
         DIV  AB             ;divide by 10
         MOV  R7,B           ;save lower digit
         MOV  B,#10
         DIV  AB             ;divide by 10 once more
         MOV  R6,B           ;save the next digit
         MOV  R5,A           ;save the last digit
```

5Q: Write a program to convert packed BCD to two ASCII numbers and place them in R2 and R6.it to decimal. Assuming A has packed BCD.

Solution:

```
         MOV  A,#29h         ;A=29h, packed BCD
         MOV  R2,A           ;keep a copy of BCD data in R2
         ANL  A,#0Fh         ;mask the upper nibble(A=09)
         ORL  A,#30h         ;make it an ASCII, A=39h ('9')
         MOV  R6,A           ;save it (R6=39h ASCII char)
         MOV  A,R2           ;A=29h;get the original data
         ANL  A,#0F0h        ;mask the lower nibble(A=20)
         RR   A              ;rotate right
         RR   A              ;rotate right
         RR   A              ;rotate right
```

```
        RR   A          ;rotate right,(A=02)
        ORL  A,#30h     ;A=32h,ASCII char.'2'
        MOV  R2,A       ;save ASCII char in R2
```

3.9 PROBLEMS

1. Write code to send 55h to ports P1 and P2, using (a) their names (b) their address.
2. Show the code to push R5, R6 and A onto the stack and then pop them back into R2, R3 and B, where register B = register A, R2 = R6, and R3 = R5.
3. Write a program to copy the value 55h into RAM memory location 40h to 45h using
   (a) direct addressing mode
   (b) register indirect addressing mode without a loop, and
   (c) with a loop.
4. Write a program to add all the digits of your ID number and save the result in R3. The result must be in BCD.
5. Write a program to add the following numbers and save the result in R2,R3.

   ```
   ORG      250h
   MYDATA:      DB    53,94,56,92,74,65,43,23,83
   ```
6. Modify the above program to make result in BCD.
7. Write a program to (a) write the values 55h to RAM locations 40h – 4Fh, and
   (b) add all these RAM location contents together, and save result in RAM locations 60h and 61h.
8. State the step that the SUBB instruction will go through and for each of the following.
   (a) 23h – 12h (b) 43h – 53h (c) 99 – 99
9. For above problem , write a program to perform each operation.
10. Write a program to add 897F9Ah to 34BC48h, and save the result in RAM memory location starting at 40h.
11. Write a program to subtract 197795h to 344548h and save the BCD result in RAM memory location starting at 40h.
12. Show how to perform 77 * 34 in the 8051.
13. Show how to perform 77/3 in the 8051.
14. Write a program with three subroutines to (a) transfer the following data from on-chip ROM to RAM locations starting at 30h (b) add them and save the result in

70h(c) find the average of data and store it in R7. Notice that the data is stored in a code space of on-chip ROM.

```
ORG        250h
MYDATA:    DB    3,9,6,9,7,6,4,2,8
```

15. Show how the following are represented by assembler.
    (a) −23 (b) +12 (c) -28 (d) +6Fh (e) -128 (f) +127
16. The memory address in computers are __________ (signed, unsigned) numbers.
17. Write a program for each of the following and indicate the status of the OV flag for each.
    (a) (+15) + (−12) (b) (−123) + (−127)
    (c) (+25H) + (+34H) (d) (-127)(+127)
18. Explain the difference between the CY and OV flags and where each one is used.
19. Explain when OV flag is raised.
20. Which register holds the OV flag?
21. How do you detect 'the OV flag in the 8051? How do you detect the CY flag?
22. Show the result of the following.

```
MOV    A,#35h    ;A = 35h
ANL    A,#0Fh    ;A = A AND 0Fh (now A = 05)
```

23. Show the result of the following .

```
MOV    A,#04     ;A = 04
ORL    A,#68     ;A = 6C
```

24. Show the results of the following.

```
MOV    A,#54h
XRL    A,#78h
```

25. Find 2's complement of the value 85h.
26. Examine the following code, then answer the following questions.
    (a) Will it jump to NEXT?
    (b) What is in A after the CJNE instruction is executed?

```
MOV    A,#55h
CJNE   A,#99h,NEXT
NEXT:  ...
```

27. Write a program to monitor P1 continuously for the value 63h. It should get out of the monitering only if P1 = 63h.

28. What values must R4 have in order for the following instruction not to jump?

```
CJNE    R4,#53,OVER
```

29. Find the contents of register A after execution of the following code.

```
CLR     A
ORL     A,#99h
CPL     A
```

30. What is the value of register A after each of the following instructions?

```
MOV     A,#25h
RR      A
RR      A
RR      A
RR      A
```

31. What is the value of register A after each of the following instructions?

```
MOV  A,#A2h
RL   A
RL   A
RL   A
RL   A
```

32. What is the value of register A after each of the following instructions?

```
CRL     A
SETB    C
RRC     A
SETB
RRC     A
```

33. Why does "RLC   R1" give an error in the 8051?

34. What is in register A after the execution of the following code?

```
MOV     A,#85h
SWAP    A
ANL     A,#0F0h
```

35. For the following decimal numbers, give the packed BCD and unpacked BCD representation.

(a) 15 (b) 99

36. Show the binary and hex formats for "76" and its BCD version.

37. Does the register A have BCD data after the following interaction is executed?

```
MOV     A,#54
```

38. 67h in BCD when converted to ASCII is __________ h and __________ h.

39. Does the following convert unpacked BCD in register A to ASCII?

```
MOV     A,#09
ADD     A,#30h
```

40. Assume that register A has packed BCD, write a program to convert packed BCD to two ASCII numbers and place them in R2 and R6.

41. Write a program to convert a series of packed BCD numbers to ASCII. Assume that the packed BCD is located in ROM locations starting at 300h. Place the ASCII codes in RAM locations starting at 40h.

```
        ORG         300h
        MYDATA:     DB          76h, 87h, 98h, 43h
```

42. Write a program to convert a series of ASCII numbers to packed BCD. Assume that the ASCII data located in ROM locations starting at 300h. Place the BCD data in RAM locations starting at 60h.

```
        ORG         300h
        MYDATA:     DB          "87675649"
```

43. Write a program to get an 8-bit binary number from P1, convert it to ASCII, and save the result in RAM locations 40h ,41h and 42h. What is the result if P1 has 1000 1101 binary as input?

44. Write the following programs.

    (a) Create a square wave of 50% duty cycle on bit 0 of port 1.

    (b) Create a square wave of 60% duty cycle on bit 3 of port 1.

45. Write a program to see if accumulator contains an even number. If so, divide it by 2. If not make it even and then divide it by 2.

46. Write a program to see if bits 0 and 5 of register B are 1. If they are not, make them so and save it in R0.

47. Write a program to save the accumulator in R7 of bank 2.

48. While there are instruction such as JNC and JC to check the carry flag bit (CY), there are no such instructions for the overflow flag bit (OV). How would you write code to check OV?

49. Write instructions to save the CY flag bit in bit location 4.

50. Write instructions to save the AC flag bit in bit location 16h.

51. Write instructions to save the P flag bit in bit location 12h.
52. Write instruction to see weather the D0 and D1 bits of register A are high. If so, divide register A by 4.

Chapter 4

Interrupts, Serial Communication and Timer/Counter Operation

4.1 THE 8051 TIMER/COUNTERS

The 8051 has two internal sixteen bit Timer/Counters. Each Timer/Counter, both of which may be controlled, set, read, and configured individually. The 8051 timers have three general functions:

- Keeping time and/or calculating the amount of time between events,
- Counting the events themselves,
- Generating baud rates for the serial port.

The 8052 has an additional (third) Timer/Counter.

Figure 4.1 shows a circuit for a simple 3-bit counter which counts from 0 to 7 and then overflows, setting the overflow flag. A 3-bit counter would not be very useful in a microcomputer so it is more typical to find 8-bit and 16-bit counter circuits.

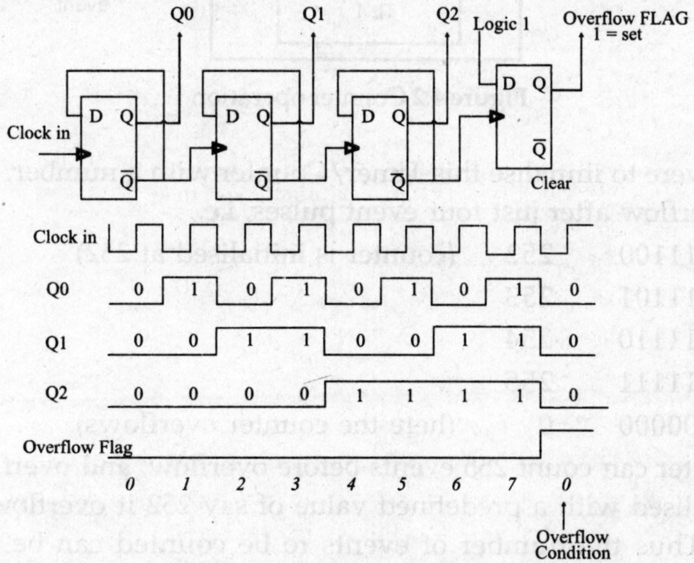

Figure 4.1 3-Bit counter circuits

4.1.1 8-BIT COUNTER OPERATION

First let us consider a simple 8-bit counter. Since this is a modulo-8 set up we are concerned with 256 numbers in the range 0 to 255 ($2^8 = 256$). The counter will count in a continuous sequence as follows:

Hex	Binary	Decimal	
00h	00000000	0	
01h	00000001	1	
02h	00000010	2	
...		.	
FEh	11111110	254	
FFh	11111111	255	
00h	00000000	0	here the counter **overflows** to zero 1
01h	00000001	1	
...			
...			

Timer/Counter 1 is used to explain the counter operation in example (Fig. 4.2) below.

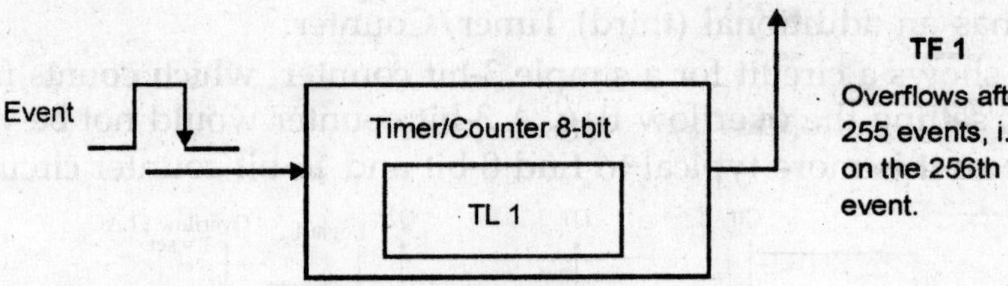

Figure 4.2 Counter operation

Suppose we were to initialise this Timer/Counter with a number, say 252, then the counter would overflow after just four event pulses, i.e.,

FCh	11111100	252	(counter is initialised at 252)
FDh	11111101	253	
FEh	11111110	254	
FFh	11111111	255	
00h	00000000	0	(here the counter overflows)

An 8-bit counter can count 255 events before overflow, and overflows on the 256th event. When initialised with a predefined value of say 252 it overflows after counting just four events. Thus the number of events to be counted can be programmed by preloading the counter with a given number value.

4.1.2 8-BIT TIMER OPERATION

The 8051 internally divides the processor clock by 12. If a 12 MHz. processor clock is used then a 1 MHz. instruction rate clock, or a pulse once every microsecond, is realised internally within the chip. If this 1 microsecond pulse is connected to a Timer/Counter input, in place of an *event* input, then the Timer/Counter becomes a timer which can delay by up to 255 microseconds. There is a clear difference between a timer and a counter. The counter will count events, up to 255 events before overflow, and the timer will count time pulses, thus creating delays up to 255 microseconds as given in fig. 4.3.

To be precise we would refer to the *counter* as an *event counter* and we would refer to the *timer* as an *interval timer*.

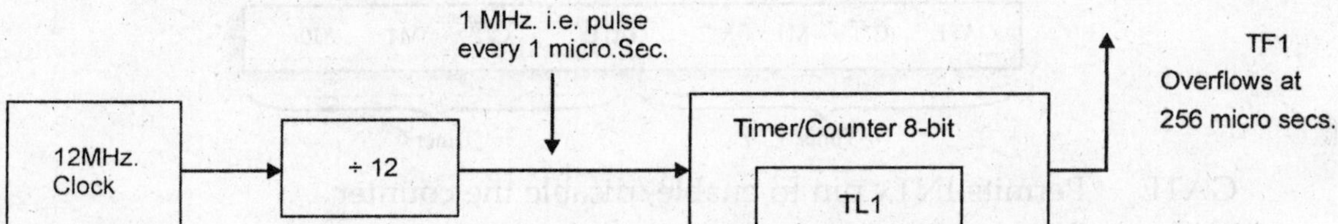

Figure 4.3 Timer operation

The hardware implementation of timer/counter function of 8051 is shown in figure 4.4. When used as a timer, the clock pulses are sourced from the oscillator through the divide-by-12 circuit. When used as a counter, pin T0 (P3.4) and pinT1 (P3.5) supplies pulses to counter 0 and counter1 respectively. The bit in TMOD must be set to1 to enable pulses from the TX pin to reach the control circuit as shown in figure 4.4.

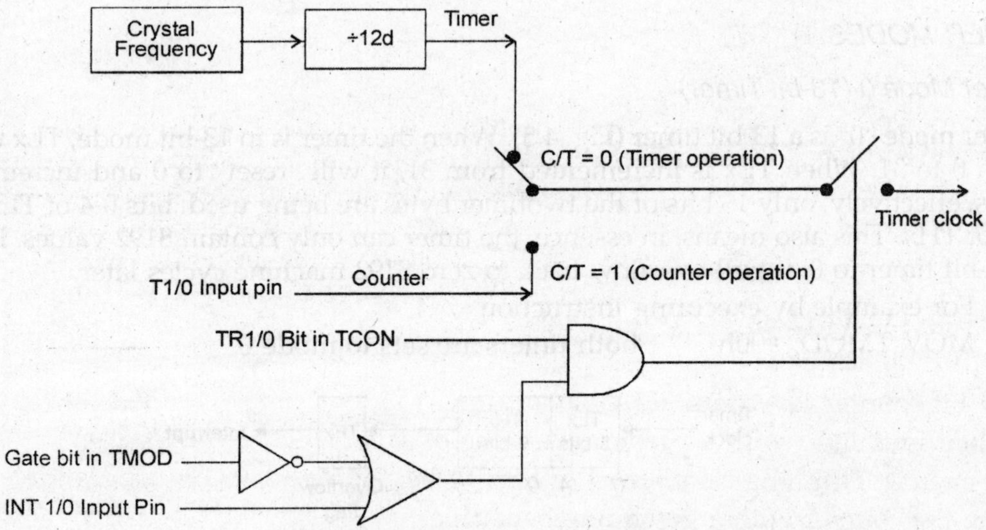

Figure 4.4 Timer/Counter operation

4.1.3 HOW DO WE PROGRAM THE TIMER/COUNTER?

Let's look at how to do the following:

- Configure the Timer/Counter as a TIMER or as a COUNTER.
- Program the Timer/Counter with a value between 0 and 255.
- Enable and disable the Timer/Counter.
- How to know when the timer has overflowed.

The TMOD register (Timer Mode Control) is an SFR register at location 89h in internal RAM and is used to define the Timer/Counter mode of operation. TMOD is not bit addressable. It is loaded, generally, by the software at the beginning of a program to initialize the timer mode.

TMOD : Counter/Timer MODE Register

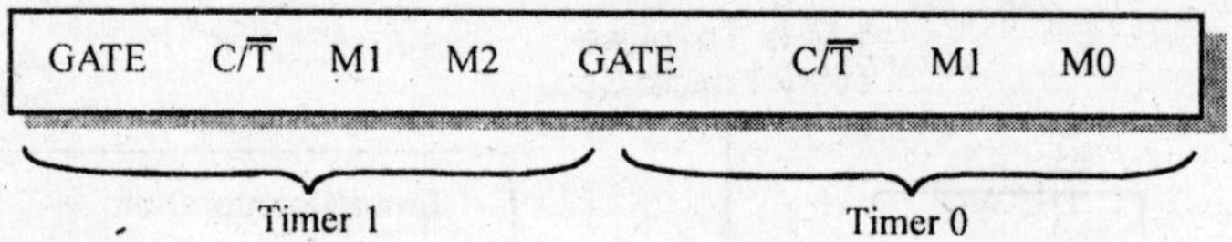

GATE	Permits INTx pin to enable/disable the counter	
$C/\overline{T}$	Set for counter operation, reset for timer operation	
M1,M0	To Select the Mode	
0 0	Mode 0	13-bit timer mode (Emulates 8048)
0 1	Mode 1	16-bit timer mode
1 0	Mode 2	8-bit auto-reload mode
1 1	Mode 3	Split timer mode (Timer 0 = two 8-bit timers).

For example to select timer 1 in TIMER mode using 8-bit operation, the TMOD register is initialised as follows:

```
MOV TMOD, #00100000b      ; assume timer 0 is not considered
```

TIMER MODES

Timer Mode 0 (13-bit Timer)

Timer mode "0" is a 13-bit timer (Fig. 4.5). When the timer is in 13-bit mode, TLx will count from 0 to 31. When TLx is incremented from 31, it will "reset" to 0 and increment THx. Thus, effectively, only 13 bits of the twotimer bytes are being used: bits 0-4 of TLx and bits 0-7 of THx. This also means, in essence, the timer can only contain 8192 values. If one sets a 13-bit timer to 0, it will overflow back to zero 8192 machine cycles later.

For example by executing instruction

```
MOV TMOD, #00h      ; both timers are sets to mode 0
```

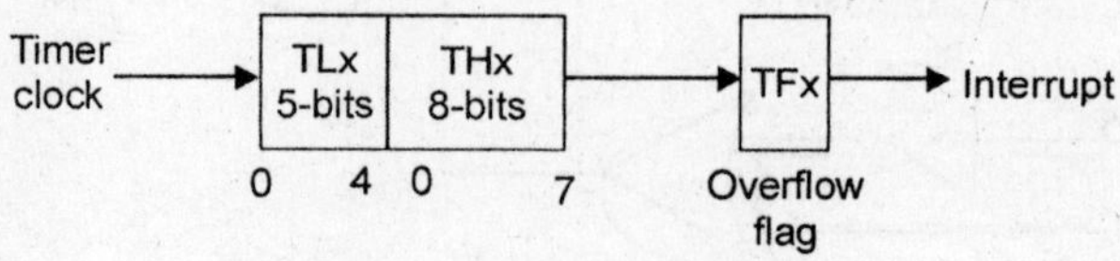

Figure 4.5 Timer mode 0

Timer Mode 1 (16-bit Timer)

Timer mode "1" is a 16-bit timer(Fig. 4.6). It functions just like 13-bit mode except that all 16 bits are used. Timer high-byte (THx) is cascaded the timer low-byte (TLx) to form a 16-bit timer, where x = 0 or 1.

TLx is incremented from 0 to 255. When TLx is incremented from 255, it resets to 0 and causes THx to be incremented by 1. Since this is a full 16-bit timer, the timer may contain up to 65536 distinct values. Overflow occurs on the FFFFh-to-0000h and sets the timer overflow flag. If programmer set a 16-bit timer to 0, it will overflow back to 0 after 65,536 machine cycles.

For Timer mode 1, a time delay can be created by loading TLx and THx with values derived from the formula:

$$\textit{Time Delay} = \frac{(12*(65,536 - \textit{Init Value}))}{\textit{Freq}}$$

where, InitValue = TLx + (256 * THx)

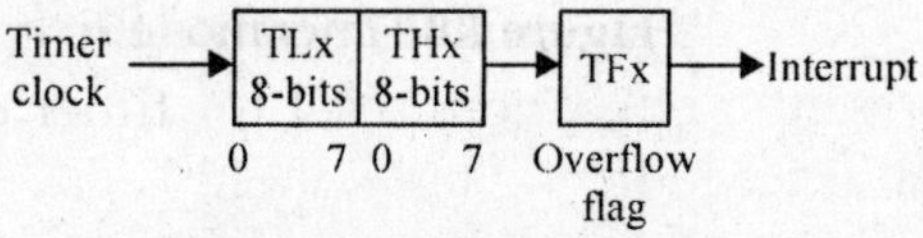

Figure 4.6 Timer mode 1

Figure 4.7 shows the timer 1 Operating in 16-bit (Mode 1)

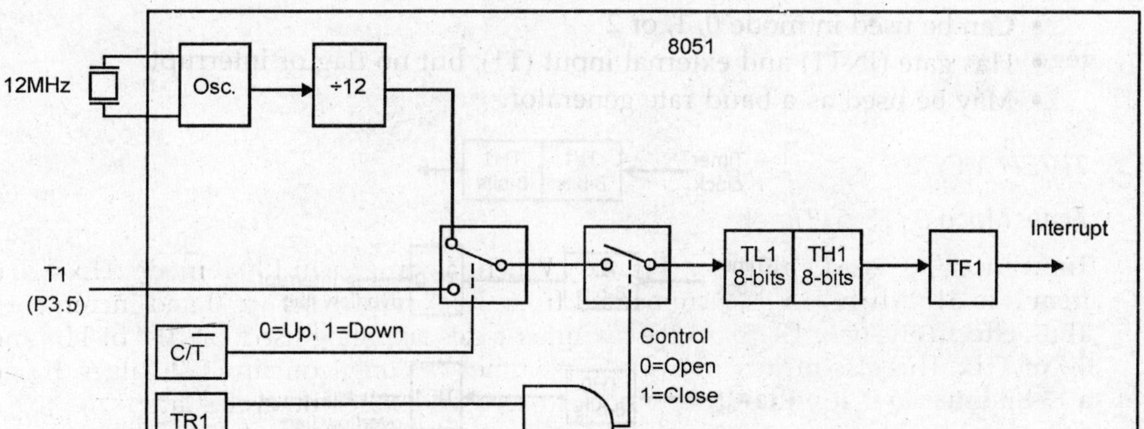

Figure 4.7 Timer 1 operating in 16-bit (Mode 1)

Timer Mode 2 (Auto-Reload)

Timer mode "2" is an 8-bit auto-reload mode (Fig. 4.8). When a timer is in mode 2, THx holds the "reload value" and TLx is the timer itself. Thus, TLx starts counting up. When TLx reaches 255 and is subsequently incremented, instead of resetting to 0 (as in the case of modes 0 and 1), it will be reset to the value stored in THx.

In Timer mode 2 ,when TLx overflows (goes from 0FFh to 0),it is reloaded with the value set in THx. The delays between overflows can be calculated from:

$$\text{Time delay} = \frac{[12 \cdot (256 - \text{THx})]}{\text{Frequency}}$$

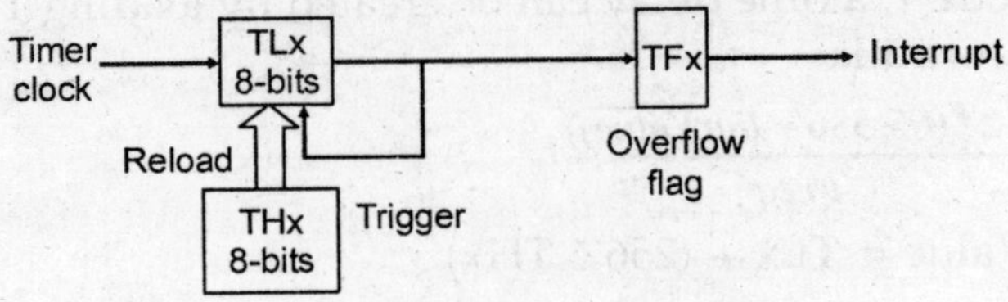

Figure 4.8 Timer mode 2

Timer Mode 3

In timer mode 3 the Timer 0 splits into two 8-bit counter/timers (Fig. 4.9). TL0 and TH0 act as two separate timers with overflows setting the TF0 and TF1 respectively. While Timer 1 (when timer 0 is in mode 3) worked as follows:

- Counter stopped if in mode 3
- Can be used in mode 0, 1, or 2
- Has gate (INT1) and external input (T1), but no flag or interrupt.
- May be used as a baud rate generator.

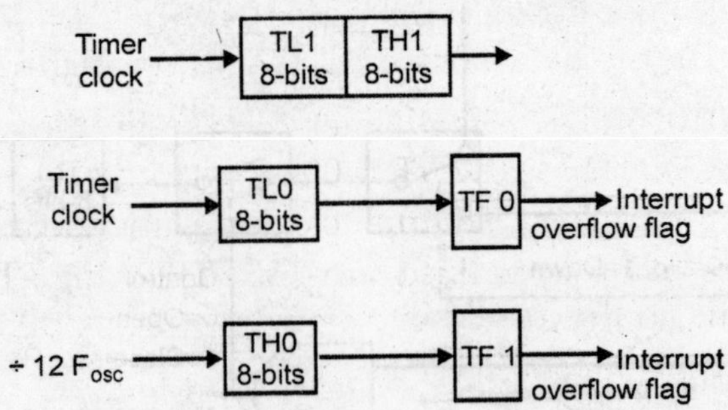

Figure 4.9 Timer mode 3

PROGRAM THE TIMER/COUNTER VALUE

The 8-bit Timer/Counter is pre-programmed with a value in the range 0...255. This is achieved by writing this value into the THx register for the Timer/Counter.

For example by executing instruction

```
MOV TH1, #129d        ; Timer/Counter 1 is programmed for 129 counts
```

START, STOP, AND CONTROL OF TIMERS

The TCON register (Timer Control) has some bits which represent Timer/Counter status flags as well as some bits which can be set or cleared to control the Timer/Counter operation.

TCON : Counter/Timer CONtrol Register

TF1	TR1	TF0	TR0	IE1	IT1	IE0	IT0
Timers				Interrupts			

TF1, TF0 : Overflow flags for Timer 1 and Timer 0.

TR1, TR0 : Run control bits for Timer 1 and Timer 0.(set to run, reset to hold)

IE1, IE0 : Edge flag for external interrupts 1 and 0. * (set by interrupt edge, cleared when interrupt is processed)

IT1, IT0 : Type bit for external interrupts. *(set for falling edge interrupts, reset for 0 level interrupts)

* not related to counter/timer operation but used to detect and initiate external interrupts.

Note: TRx bit in bit addressable register TCON is responsible for starting and stopping the counters (system reset clears TRx, so timers are disabled by default) i.e.,

TRx = 0 stops/disables the timers (e.g., CLR TR1)

TRx = 1 starts/enables the timers (e.g., SETB TR0)

INITIALIZING AND ACCESSING TIMER REGISTERS

Timers are usually initialized once at the beginning of the program to set the correct operating mode.Then, within the body of a program, the timers are started, stopped, flag bits are tested and cleared, timer registers read or updated, and so on, as required in the application. First register to be initialized is TMOD to set the mode of operation. e.g.,

```
MOV TMOD, #00010000B        ;sets Timer 1 in mode 1, leave C/T̄ = 0 and
                            GATE = 0 for
                            ;internal clocking, and clears the Timer 0 bits.
```

Secondly, registers to be initialized are TLx/THx. E.g., For 100μs interval, the following instruction will do the job

```
MOV     TL1, #9Ch     ; (–100)10 = FF9Ch
MOV     TH1, #FFh     ; load Timer 1 registers by FF9Ch
```

The timer is then started by setting the run control bit i.e.,

```
SETB    TR1
```

After starting, overflow flag is automatically set 100μs later. Following instruction will check that

```
WAIT:   JNB TF1, WAIT         ; wait until overflow flag is set.
```

When the timer overflows, it is necessary to stop the timer and clear the overflow flag in software by the following instructions:

```
        CLR  TR1            ;stop Timer 1
        CLR  TF1            ;clear overflow flag of Timer 1
```

Example 1: Write a program to generate a square wave of 2 KHz frequency on pin P1.5. Assuming crystal frequency 11.0592 MHz.

Solution:

```
        MOV  TMOD,#10h      ;timer 1, mode 1(16-bit)
REPEAT: MOV  TL1,#1Ah       ;TL1=1A,low byte of timer
        MOV  TH1,#0FFh      ;TH1=FF,high byte
        SETB  TR1           ;start the timer 1
RETURN: JNB  TF1,RETURN     ;stay until timer rolls over
        CLR  TR1            ;stop timer 1
        CPL  P1.5           ;comp. p1.5 to get high, low
        CLR  TF1            ;clear timer flag 1
        SJMP REPEAT         ;reload timer since mode 1 is not auto-reload
```

Example 2: Find the value of timer's registers to generate a time delay of 5 ms. Assuming crystal frequency 11.0592 MHz. Show the program for timer 0 to create a pulse width of 5 ms on p2.3.

Solution:

Since crystal freq=11.0592 MHz, the counter counts up every 1.085 microseconds. To get 5 ms we need (5 ms/1.085 μs)4608 clocks. To achieve that we need to load TH and TL the value 65536-4608 = 60928=EE00h i.e TH=EE and TL=00.

```
        CLR  P2.3           ;clear P2.3
        MOV  TMOD,#01       ;Timer 0,mode 1(16-bit mode)
START:  MOV  TL0,#0         ;TL0=0, the low byte
        MOV  TH0,#0EEh      ;TH0=EE(hex), the high byte
        SETB  P2.3          ;set high P2.3
        SETB  TR0           ;start timer 0
REPEAT: JNB  TF0,REPEAT     ;monitor timer Flag 0 until it rolls over
        CLR  TR0            ;stop timer 0
        CLR  TF0            ;clear timer 0 flag
```

Example 3: Write a program to generate a square wave of 50 Hz frequency on pin P1.5. Assuming crystal frequency 11.0592 MHz.

Solution:

```
        MOV  TMOD,#10h      ;timer 1, mode 1 (16-bit)
REPEAT: MOV  TL1,#00        ;TL1=00,low byte of timer
        MOV  TH1,#0DCh      ;TH1=DC,Hi byte
        SETB  TR1           ; start the timer 1
RETURN: JNB  TF1,RETURN     ; stay until timer rolls over
        CLR  TR1            ; stop timer 1
```

```
        CPL  P2.3               ; comp. p2.3 to get hi, lo
        CLR  TF1                ; clear timer flag 1
        SJMP REPEAT             ; reload timer since mode 1is not auto-reload
```

xample 4: Write a program to count 20,000 events and to generate an interrupt following the 20,000 events and then set bit P1.5. Assuming crystal frequency 11.0592 MHz.

olution:

To generate interrupt after 20,000 events, the timer 1 is loaded with a value (65,536-)000=45,536 or B1E0h).

```
  ORG 0000h                   ; entry address for 8051 RESET
  LJMP MAIN                   ; MAIN starts beyond interrupt vector space
  ORG 001Bh                   ; vector address for interrupt
  LJMP ISR_TIMER1             ; jump to start of ISR_TIMER1
  ORG 0100h                   ; entry address for main
IAIN:
  MOV TMOD, #01010000b        ; Timer 1 is set for mode 1, COUNTER operation
  MOV TH1, #0B1h              ; Timer 1 high byte is loaded
  MOV TL1, #0E0h              ; Timer 1 low byte is loaded
  MOV IE, #10001000b          ; enable Timer/counter 1 interrupt
  SETB TR1                    ; start Timer/counter 1
  LOOP: LJMP LOOP             ; just loop around doing nothing
R_TIMER1:
  CLR TR1                     ; stop Timer 1 to be safe
  SETB P1.5                   ; set high P1 bit 5
  RETI                        ; return from interrupt
  END
```

Note: This program have three different addresses using ORG directive, one is entry dress for 8051 RESET, second is vector address for interrupt and third is entry address r main program.

ample 5: Find time delays in seconds for following program. Exclude instructions in the loop.

```
          MOV  TMOD,#10H       ; Timer 1,mode 1(16-bit)
          MOV  R3,#500         ; counter for multiple delay
REPEAT:   MOV  TL1,#08         ; TL1=08,low byte of timer
          MOV  TH1,#01         ; TH1=01,Hi byte
          SETB TR1             ; start the timer 1
RETURN:   JNB  TF1,RETURN      ; stay until timer rolls over
          CLR  TR1             ; stop timer 1
          CLR  TF1             ; clear timer flag 1
          DJNZ R3,REPEAT       ; if R3 not zero then reload timer
```

Solution:

TH–TL = 0108h=264 in decimal and 65536–264 = 65272.

65272* 1.085 µs = 70.820 ms and for 500 we have 500* 70.820 ms = 35.41 seconds.

4.2 SERIAL COMMUNICATION (SERIAL PORT OPERATION)

4.2.1 BASICS OF SERIAL COMMUNICATION

The EIA RS-232 serial communication standard is a universal standard. The serial data is transmitted at a predefined rate, referred to as the baud rate. The term baud rate refers to the number of state changes per second which is the same as the bit rate for this particular communication scheme. Typical baud rates are: 9600bps; 19,200 bps; 56kbps etc.

In asynchronous Serial Communications, data is sent is a serial fashion, without any reference to a timing clock to help synchronize the receiver clock in terms of frequency and phase, the system is said to be non-synchronous, or asynchronous. Figure 4.10(a) shows three bytes transmitted by the microcontroller. Assume the bytes are *ASCII* coded to represent the characters A, B and C. The receiver needs to know exactly where each character starts and finishes. To achieve this the data character is framed with a start bit at the beginning of each character and a stop bit at the end of each character. Figure 4.10(b) shows the start bit as a low logic level and the stop bit as a high logic level. Thus the receiver can detect the start bit and it then clocks in the character bits. The receiver then expects to find the stop bit, existing as a logic high bit. Figure 4.10(c) shows the inclusion of an additional parity bit for error control purposes.

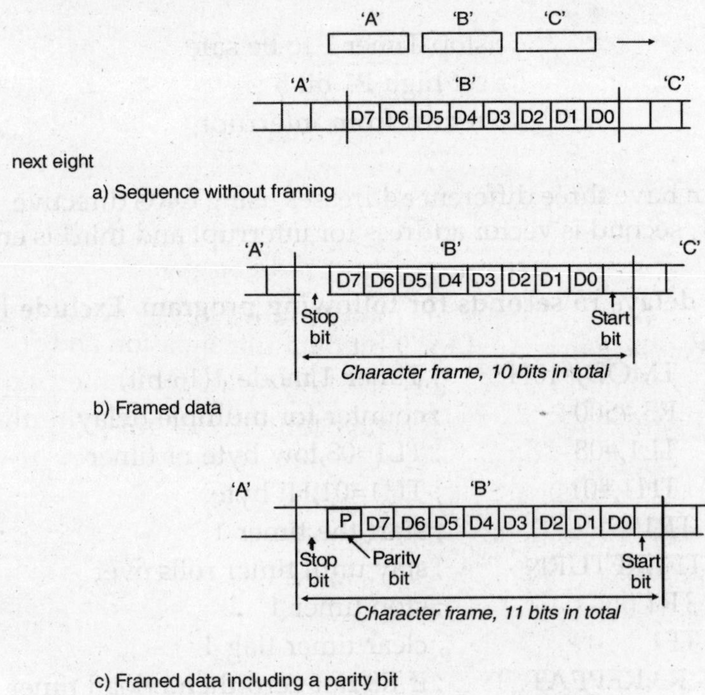

Figure 4.10 Asynchronous transmission

4.2.2 THE 8051 UART

The 8051 includes Full duplex UART (Universal Asynchronous Receiver/Transmitter), known as a serial port. (Full duplex UART is a device that receives and transmits serial data with each data character preceded by a start bit "0" and followed by a stop bit "1"). Essential function of serial port is to perform parallel-to-serial conversion for output data, and serial-to-parallel conversion for input data. The UART block diagram is shown in Fig. 4.11.

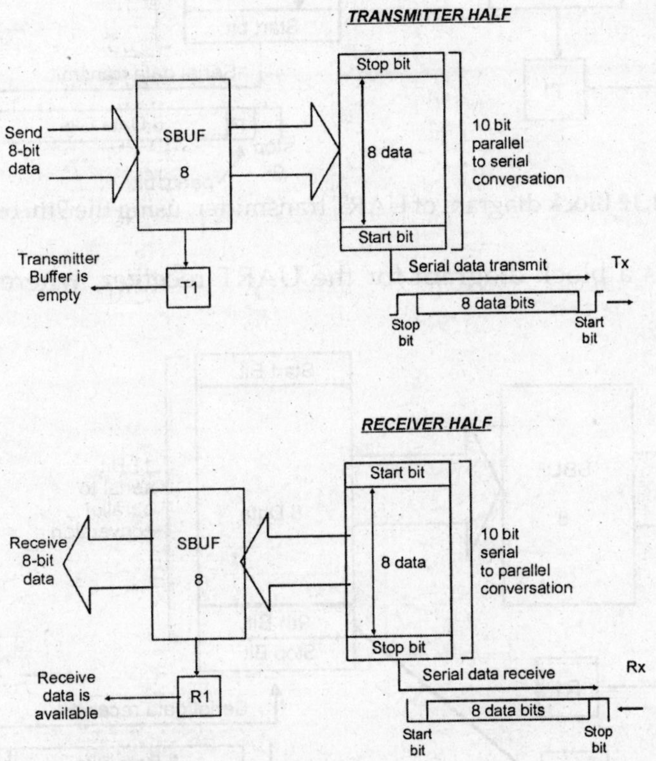

Figure 4.11 UART block diagram

The UART can be configured for 9-bit data transmission and reception. Here 8 bits represent the data byte (or character) and the ninth bit is the parity bit. Figure 4.12 shows a block diagram for the UART transmitter, where the ninth bit is used as the parity bit.

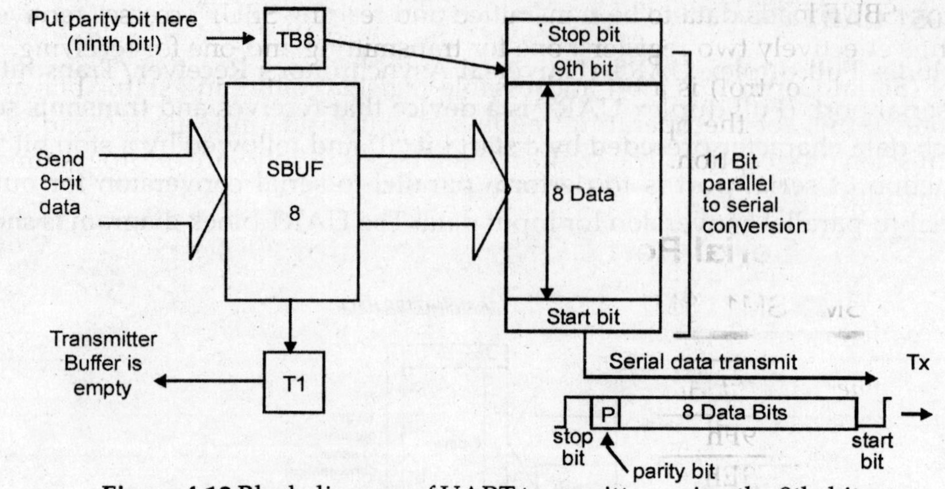

Figure 4.12 Block diagram of UART transmitter, using the 9th. bit

Figure 4.13 shows a block diagram for the UART receiver, where the ninth bit is used as the parity bit.

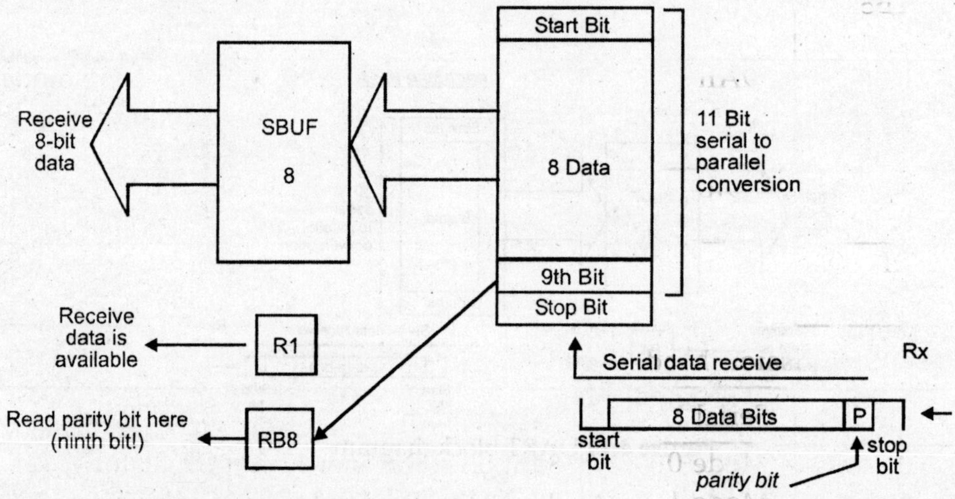

Figure 4.13 Block diagram of UART receiver, using the 9th. bit

Serial port can operate in four modes over a wide range of frequencies. Serial data transmission bit is **P3.1 on pin 11 (TXD)** and reception bit is **P3.0 on pin 10 (RXD).** Serial port frequency of operation (baud rate) can be fixed or variable. Fixed is derived from on-chip oscillator and variable is supplied by Timer 1 which must be programmed accordingly. There are two SFRs that controls and provide the software access to serial port in 8051 are SBUF & SCON.

SBUF is an SFR register which can be written to, so as to hold the next data byte to be transmitted. Also it can be read from to get the latest data byte received by the serial port.

That is, writing to SBUF loads data to be transmitted and reading SBUF accesses received data. SBUF is thus effectively two registers: one for transmitting and one for receiving.

The SCON (Serial Control) is a bit addressable register containing status bits and control bits. Control bits set the operating mode and status bits indicate the end of a character transmission or reception. The status bits are tested in software or programmed to cause an interrupt.

SCON : Serial Port CONtrol Register (098h)

SM0	SM1	SM2	REN	TB8	RB8	T1	R1

Bit	*Name*	*Bit Address*	*Explanation of Function*
7	SM0	9Fh	Serial port mode bit 0
6	SM1	9Eh	Serial port mode bit 1.
5	SM2	9Dh	Multiprocessor Communications bit
4	REN	9Ch	Receiver Enable. This bit must be set in order to receive characters.
3	TB8	9Bh	Transmit bit 8. The 9th bit to transmit in mode 2 and 3.
2	RB8	9Ah	Receive bit 8. The 9th bit received in mode 2 and 3. Mode 0 : Not used.Mode 1 : Stop bit. Mode 2, 3 : Ninth data bit.
1	TI	99h	Transmit Flag. Set when a byte has been completely transmitted.
0	RI	98h	Receive Flag. Set when a byte has been completely received.

Serial Data Transmission Mode Baud Rate

SM0	SM1	Serial Mode	Explanation	Baud Rate
0	0	Mode 0	8-bit Shift Register *Fixed*	Oscillator / 12
0	1	Mode 1	8-bit UART *variable*	Set by Timer 1 (*)
1	0	Mode 2	9-bit UART *Fixed*	Oscillator / 32 (*)
1	1	Mode 3	9-bit UART *variable*	Set by Timer 1 (*)

(*) Note: The baud rate indicated in this table is doubled if PCON.7 (SMOD) is set.

Mode 0		: Not used.
Mode 1	If SM2 = 0	: Normal Operation.
	If SM2 = 1	: Ignore bytes with no stop bit.
Modes 2 & 3	If SM2 = 0	: Set RI (receive interrupt) on all bytes.

SERIAL INTERFACE MODES OF OPERATION

MODE 0: 8-Bit Shift Register Mode. Mode 0 operation can be summarized as:

- In this mode RXD line is used for both input and output while TXD line serves as the clock.
- Eight bits are transmitted and received with the LSB first. Baud Rate is fixed at 1/12 of on-chip oscillator frequency.
- Transmission is initiated by any instruction that writes data to SBUF. Data are shifted out on RXD line with clock pulses sent out by the TXD line. Each transmitted bit is valid on the RXD pin for one machine cycle. E.g., MOV SBUF, A
- Reception is initiated when the REN is 1 and the RI is 0. REN is set at the beginning of the program, and then clear RI to begin a data input operation. The clocking of data into serial port occurs on the positive edge of TXD.

Data transmission/reception in mode-0 is shown in fig. 4.14.

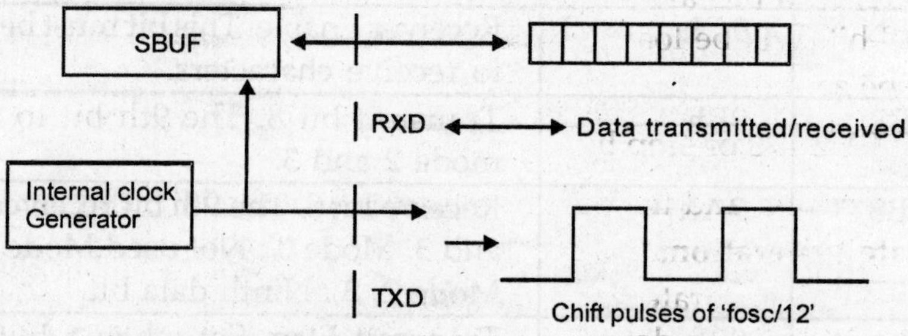

Figure 4.14 Data transmission/reception in Mode-0

MODE 1: Serial port operates as an 8-bit UART with a variable baud rate. Mode 1 operation can be summarized as:

- 10-bits are transmitted on TXD or received on RXD. Start bit (always 0), 8 data bits (LSB first), and a stop bit (always 1). For a receive operation, the stop bit goes into RB8 in SCON. Baud Rate Clock is variable using Timer 1 overflow or external count input.
- Transmission is initiated by writing data to SBUF. Shifted data are outputted on the TXD line beginning with the start bit. The transmit interrupt flag (TI) is set as soon as the stop bit appears on TXD.
- Reception is initiated by a 1-to-0 transition on RXD.

Data transmission/reception in mode-1 is shown in fugure 4.15.

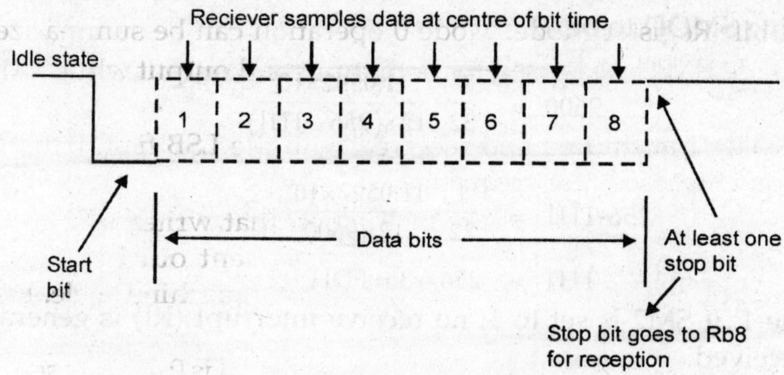

Figure 4.15 Data transmission/reception in mode-1

Bit time = $1/f_{baud}$

In receiving mode, data bits are shifted into the receiver at the programmed baud rate. The data word (8-bit) will be loaded to SBUF if the following conditions are true.

1. RI must be zero. (i.e., the previously received byte has been cleared from SBUF)
2. Mode bit SM2 = 0 or stop bit = 1.

After the data is received and the data byte has been loaded into SBUF, RI become one.

Mode-1 baud rate generation:

Time-1 is used to generate baud rate for mode-1 serial communication by using overflow flag of the timer to determine the baud frequency. Timer-1 is used in timer mode-2 as an auto-reload 8-bit timer. The data rate is generated by timer-1 using the following formula.

$$f_{baud} = \frac{2^{SMOD}}{32} \times \frac{fosc}{12\times[256-(TH1)]}$$

Where.

SMOD is the 7th bit or PCON register

f_{OSC} is the crystal oscillator frequency of the microcontroller

It can be noted that $f_{OSC}/(12 \times [256 - (TH1)])$ is the timer overflow frequency in timer mode-2, which is the auto-reload mode.

If timer-1 is not urn in mode-2, then the baud rate is,

$$f_{baud} = \frac{2^{SMOD}}{32} \times \text{(timer-1 overflow frequency)}$$

Timer-1 can be run using the internal clock, fosc/12 (timer mode) or from any external source via pin T1 (P3.5) (Counter mode).

Example: If standard baud rate is desired, then 11.0592 MHz crystal could be selected. To get a standard 9600 baud rate, the setting of TH1 is calculated as follows.

Assuming SMOD to be '0'

or, $$9600 = \frac{2^0}{32} \times \frac{11.0592 \times 10^6}{12 \times (256 - TH1)}$$

or, $$256\text{-}TH1 = \frac{1}{32} \times \frac{11.0592 \times 10^6}{12 \times 9600} = 3$$

$$TH1 = 256 - 3 = FDH$$

In mode-1, if SM2 is set to 1, no receive interrupt (RI) is generated unless a valid stop bit is received.

MODE 2: Serial port operates as a 9-bit UART with a fixed baud rate. Mode 2 operation can be summarized as:

- 11-bits are transmitted or received. Start bit (always 0), 8 data bits (LSB first), a programmable 9th bit, and a stop bit (always 1).
- On transmission, the 9th bit whatever has been put in TB8 in SCON (may be a parity bit).
- On reception, the 9th bit is placed in RB8 in SCON.
- Baud Rate is programmable to either 1/32 or 1/64 of the on-chip oscillator frequency.

$$f_{baud} = (2^{SMOD}/64)\ f_{OSC}$$

MODE 3: Serial port operates as a 9-bit UART with a variable baud rate. 11-bits are transmitted or received. Baud Rate is programmable and provided by the Timer 1 overflow or external input.

Mode-3 is same as mode-2, except the fact that the baud rate in mode-3 is variable (i.e., just as in mode-1).

$$f_{baud} = (2^{SMOD}/32) * (f_{OSC}/12\,(256 - TH1))$$

This baudrate holds when Timer-1 is programmed in Mode-2.

Note: In summary

Baud rate: Fixed in modes 0 & 2, variable in modes 1 & 3

Data Bits: Eight in mode 1, nine in modes 2 & 3

INITIALIZATION OF SERIAL PORT

Receiver Enable Bit (REN)

Must be set by software to enable the reception of characters at the beginning of a program when the serial port, timers, etc. are initialized. The instructions are

```
SETB REN
or
MOV SCON, #xxx1xxxxB
```

The 9th Bit

The 9th bit transmitted must be loaded into TB8 by software and received is placed in RB8.

ADDING A PARITY BIT

This is a common use of 9th bit. e.g., if communication requires 8 data bits plus even parity then the following line of code will do the same

```
MOV     C, P        ; Put even parity bit in C flag
MOV     TB8, C      ; This becomes the 9th data bit in TB8
MOV     SBUF, A     ; Move 8 bits from ACC to SBUF
```

And if communication requires 8 data bits plus odd parity then the line of code will be

```
MOV     C, P        ; Put even parity bit in C flag
CPL     C           ; Convert to odd parity
MOV     TB8, C      ; This becomes the 9th data bit in TB8
MOV     SBUF, A     ; Move 8 bits from ACC to SBUF
```

Parity can be used in mode 1 also if the 7 data bits are used. e.g., 7-bit ASCII code with even parity can be transmitted as follows:

```
CLR     ACC.7       ; Ensure MSB is clear
MOV     C, P        ; Put even parity bit in C flag
MOV     ACC.7, C    ; Copy even parity bit into MSB
MOV     SBUF, A     ; Send character
```

INTERRUPT FLAGS (RI &TI)

RI & TI in SCON play an important role in serial communications. Both bits are set by hardware but must be cleared by software.

Receive Interrupt Flag (RI)

- RI is set at the end of character reception and indicates "receive buffer full".
- This condition is tested in software or programmed to cause an interrupt.
- If software wishes to input a character from the device connected to the serial port, it must wait until RI is set, then clear RI and read the character from SBUF.

```
WAIT:   JNB RI, WAIT    ; Check RI until set
        CLR RI          ; Clear the flag
        MOV A, SBUF     ; Read character
```

TRANSMIT INTERRUPT FLAG (RI)

- TI is set at the end of character transmission and indicates "transmit buffer empty".
- If software wishes to send a character to the device connected to the serial port, it must wait until TI is set (means previous character was sent, wait until transmission is finished before sending the next character), then clear TI and send the character.

```
WAIT:    JNB TI, WAIT     ; Check TI until set
         CLR TI           ; Clear the flag
         MOV SBUF, A      ; Send character
```

SETTING THE BAUD RATES

Timer/Counter 1 provides the serial port baud rate clock. Usually the 8-bit auto reload operation (Timer/Counter mode 2) is used. Baud rate is also affected by a bit in the PCON register. PCON.7 is SMOD bit. If SMOD = 1, baud rate will be doubled in modes 1, 2 and 3. e.g., mode 2 baud rate is the $1/64^{th}$ the oscillator frequency (SMOD = 0) and can be doubled to $1/32^{nd}$ the oscillator frequency with SMOD = 1.

PCON is not bit-addressable, setting SMOD without altering the other bits requires a "read-modify-write" operation as follows:

```
MOV     A, PCON      ; Get current value of PCON
SETB    ACC.7        ; Set SMOD
MOV     PCON, A      ; Write value back to PCON
```

USING TIMER 1 AS BAUD RATE CLOCK

For specific baud rate usually the timer is used in auto-reload mode and TH1 is loaded with a proper reload value.

Formula for the baud rate in modes 1 and 3 is

Baud Rate = Timer 1 Overflow Rate / 32

e.g., For 1200 baud

1200 = Timer 1 Overflow Rate / 32

Timer 1 Overflow Rate = 1200 * 32 = 38400 Hz

That is ,timer must overflow at a rate of 38.4 kHz and the timer is clocked at a rate of 11.0592 /12=.921,600 MHz (921.6 kHz), overflow required every 921.6/38.4 = 24 clocks, so **MOV TH1, #–24**

The table below shows some values defined for the TH1 register to achieve some of the more common baud rates. The values shown assume a processor clock rate of 11.0592MHz.

Baud rate	*Timer/Counter1 TH1 value*	*PCON.7 (SMOD)*
300	–96 (A0)	0
1200	–24 (E8)	0
2400	–12 (F4)	0
4800	–6 (FA)	0
9600	–3 (FD)	0

Note. The most significant bit of the PCON register is assumed to be at 0. If this were set to 1 the baud rate value would be doubled.

MULTIPROCESSOR COMMUNICATION

8051 operates in multiprocessor mode for serial communication Mode-2 and Mode-3. In multiprocessor mode, a Master processor can communicate with than one slave processors. SM2, is a flag for "Multiprocessor communication." Generally, whenever a byte has been received the 8051 will set the "R1" (Receive Interrupt) flag. This lets the program know that a byte has been received and that it needs to be processsed. However, when SM2 is set the "R1" flag will only be triggered if the 9th bit is clear, the RI flag will never be set. This can be useful in certain advanced serial applications. Normally 9th bit is kept clear so that the flag is set upon reception of any character. Serial Communication Modes 2 and 3 allow one "Master" 8051 to control several "Slaves" 8051. The TXD outputs of the slaves are tied together and to the RXD input of the master. The RXD inputs of the slaves are tied together and to the TXD output of the master. Each slave is assigned an address. Address bytes transmitted by the master have the 9th bit = 1 & data bytes have it = 0.

When the master transmits an address byte, all the slaves are interrupted. The slaves then check to see if they are being addressed or not. The addressed slave will clear its SM2 bit and prepare to received the data bytes that follows and the slaves that weren't addressed leave their SM2 bits set and go about their business, ignoring the incoming data bytes. They will be interrupted again when the next address byte is transmitted by the master processor.

The connection diagram of processors communicating in Multiprocessor mode is given in fig. 4.16.

The Master communicates with one slave at a time. 11 bits are transmitted by the Master, viz, One start bit (usually '0'), 8 data bits (LSB first), TB8 and a stop bit (usually '1'). TB8 is '1' for an address byte and '0' for a data byte.

If the Master wants to communicate with certain slave, it first sends the address of the slave with TB8 = 1. This address is received by all the slaves. Slaves initially have their SM2 bit set to '1'. All slaves check this address and the slave who is being addressed, responds by clearing its SM2 bit to '0' so that the data bytes can be received.

It should be noted that in Mode 2&3, receive interrupt flag RI is set if REN = 1, RI = 0 and the following condition is true.

1. SM2 = 1 and RB8 = 1 and a valid stop bit is received. Or
2. SM2 = 0 and a valid stop bit is received.

After the communication between the Master and a slave has been established, the data bytes are sent by the Master with TB8 = 0. Hence other slaves do not respond/get interrupted by this data as their SM2 is pulled high (1).

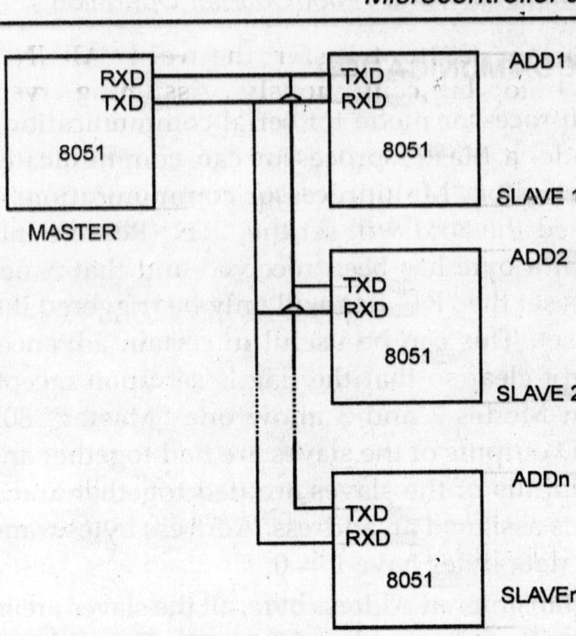

Figure 4.16 8051 in Multiprocessor communication

Example 1: Write a program to initialize the serial port to operate as an 8-bit UART at 2400 baud. Assuming crystal frequency 11.0592 MHz.

Solution:

```
ORG     0000h
MOV     SCON,#50h       ; serial port mode 1
MOV     TMOD,#20h       ; timer 1, mode 2
MOV     TH1, #–12       ; reload count for 2400 baud
SETB    TR1             ; start timer 1
END
```

Example 2: A program for 8051 to transfer serially letter "A" at 9600 baud, continuously. Assuming crystal frequency 11.0592 MHz.

Solution:

```
        MOV     TMOD,#20h       ;timer 1, mode 2 (auto reload)
        MOV     TH1,#–3         ;9600 baud rate at 11.0592 MHz
        MOV     SCON,#50h       ;8-bit, 1 stop, REN enabled
        SETB    TR1             ;start timer 1
AGAIN:  MOV     SBUF,# "A"      ;letter "N" to be transferred
NEXT:   JNB     TI,NEXT         ;wait for the last bit
CLR     TI                      ;clear TI for next char
        SJMP    AGAIN           ;keep sending A
```

Example 3: A program for 8051 to transfer the word "ARUN" at 4800 baud, 8-bit data and 1 stop bit ,continuously . Assuming crystal frequency 11.0592 MHz.

Solution:

```
MOV      TMOD,#20h          ;timer 1, mode 2
MOV      TH1,#–6            ;4800 baud
MOV      SCON,#50h          ;8-bit, 1 stop bit, REN enabled
SETB     TR1                ;start timer 1
REPEAT:  MOV  A,# "A"       ;transfer "A"
         ACALL TRANS
         MOV  A,#"R"        ;transfer "R"
         ACALL TRANS
         MOV  A,#"U"        ;transfer "U"
         ACALL TRANS
         MOV  A,#"N"        ;transfer "N"
         ACALL TRANS
         SJMP REPEAT        ;keep doing it
                            ;serial data transfer subroutine
TRANS: MOV  SBUF,A          ;load SBUF
NEXT:  JNB  TI,NEXT         ;wait for last bit to transfer
       CLR  TI              ;get ready for next byte
       RET
```

Example 4: Write program to receive bytes of data serially, and put them in P1. Set the baud rate at 2400,8-bit data, and 1 stop bit. Assuming crystal frequency 11.0592 MHz.

Solution:

```
       MOV  TMOD, #20h   ;timer1, mode 2 (auto reload)
       MOV  TH1, #–12    ;2400 baud
       MOV  SCON, #50h   ;8-bit, 1 stop, REN enabled
       SETB TR1          ;start timer 1
NEXT:  JNB RI, NEXT      ;wait for char to come in
       MOV  A, SBUF      ;save incoming byte in A
       MOV  P1, A        ;send to port 1
       CLR  RI           ;get ready to receive next byte
       SJMP NEXT         ;keep getting data
```

Example 5: Assuming oscillator freq = 11.0592 MHz, compute (a) the timer 1 frequency used to set the baud rate (b) the baud rate of the data transfer.

```
MOV  A,PCON      ;A=PCON
SETB ACC.7       ;make D7=1
```

```
        MOV  PCON,A         ;SMOD=1,double baud ratewith same osc. freq.
        MOV  TMOD,#20h      ;Timer 1, mode 2,auto reload
        MOV  TH1,-3         ;19200(57,600/3 =19200 baud rate ,since SMOD = 1)
        MOV  SCON,#50h      ;8-bit data,1 stop bit, RI enabled
        SETB TR1            ;start Timer 1
        MOV  A,#"B"         ;transfer letter B
T_1:    CLR  TI             ;make sure TI=0
        MOV SBUF,A          ;transfer it
        S_1 ;JNB  TI S_1    ;stay here until the last bit is gone
        SJMP T_1            ;keep sending "B" again and again
```

Solution:

(a) With Oscillator Frequency = 11.0592 MHz and SMOD = 1 we have11.0592/12=921.6 kHz machine cycle frequency.

921.6/16=57,600 Hz frequency used by timer 1 to set the baud rate.

(b) baud rate = 57,600/3 = 19,200.

4.3 INTERRUPTS

An interrupt is the occurrence of an event that causes temporary suspension of a program while the condition is serviced by another program. It is like a sub-routine. CPU cannot execute more than one instruction at a time; but it can temporarily suspend execution of one program, execute another, then return to the first program.

Difference in *interrupt* and *subroutine* is that in an interrupt-driven system, the interruption occur *asynchronously* with the main program, and it is not known when the main program will be interrupted. Program that deals with the interrupt is called as ISR (Interrupt Service Routine).

INTERRUPT SYSTEM

There are *Five interrupt sources* for the 8051 as shown in Fig. 4.17, (six including the system reset) in order of polling (priority) sequence are:

(System reset)

External Interrupt 0

Timer 0

External Interrupt 1

Timer 1

Serial Port

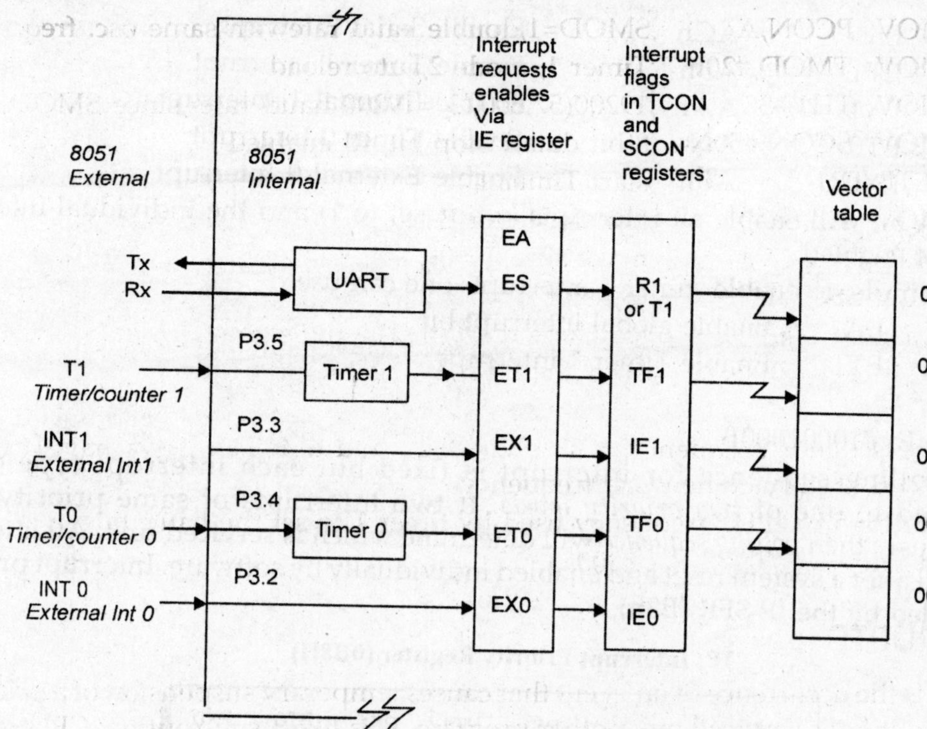

Figure 4.17 8051 Interrupt Sources

We can configure the 8051 so that on interrupt, the appropriate interrupt handler routines are called. Obviously we need to be able to distinguish between various interrupts and executing different code depending on what interrupt was triggered. This is accomplished by jumping to a fixed address (*interrupt vector address)* when a given interrupt occurs. That is, each interrupt type has a separate *vector address.*

By default at power up, all interrupts are disabled. Program must specifically tell the 8051 that it wishes to enable interrupts and specifically which interrupts it wishes to enable.

Program may enable and disable interrupts by modifying the IE SFR (0A8h).

IE : Interrupt Enable Register (0A8H)

EA	----	----	ES	ET1	EX1	ET0	EX0

(1 = Enabled, 0 = Disabled)

Bit	Name	Bit Address	Explanation of Function
7	EA	AFh	Global Interrupt Enable/Disable
6	-	AEh	Undefined
5	-	ADh	Undefined

4	ES	ACh	Enable Serial Interrupt
3	ET1	ABh	Enable Timer 1 Interrupt
2	EX1	AAh	Enable External 1 Interrupt
1	ET0	A9h	Enable Timer 0 Interrupt
0	EX0	A8h	Enable External 0 Interrupt

The EA bit will enable all interrupts (when set to 1) and the individual interrupts must also be enabled.

For example, to enable timer 1 interrupt one can use:

```
SETB    EA     ; Enable global interrupt bit
SETB    ET1    ; Enable Timer 1 interrupt
Or
MOV IE, #10001000B
```

The polling sequence for interrupt is fixed but each interrupt type can be programmed to one of *two priority levels*. If two interrupts of same priority occur simultaneously then *polling sequence* will determine which is serviced first. All interrupts are disabled after a system reset and enabled individually by software. Interrupt priorities are controlled by the IP SFR (B8h).

IP: Interrupt Priority Register (0B8H)

------	------	------	PS	PT1	PX1	PT0	PX0

(1 = High priority, 0 = Low priority)

Bit	Name	Bit Address	Explanation of Function
7	-	-	Undefined
6	-	-	Undefined
5	-	-	Undefined
4	PS	BCh	Serial Interrupt Priority
3	PT1	BBh	Timer 1 Interrupt Priority
2	PX1	BAh	External 1 Interrupt Priority
1	PT0	B9h	Timer 0 Interrupt Priority
0	PX0	B8h	External 0 Interrupt Priority

IP is cleared after a system reset to place all interrupts at the lower priority level by default.

PROCESSING INTERRUPTS

When an interrupt occurs and is accepted by CPU, the following actions occur:

- Current instruction's complete execution
- PC is saved on the stack
- PC is loaded with the vector address of the ISR
- ISR executes and takes action in response to interrupt

- ISR finishes with a RETI instruction
- PC is loaded with its old value from the stack
- Execution of main program continues where it left off

INTERRUPT VECTOR

When an interrupt is accepted, the value loaded into the PC is called the interrupt vector. It is the address of the start of the ISR for the interrupting source. The flag (condition) that caused the interrupt is automatically cleared by microcontroller (system) when an interrupt is vectored.

Interrupt Vector Addresses

Interrupt	Flag	Vector Address	SFR & Bit Position
System Reset	RST	0000H	
External 0	IE0	0003H	TCON.1
Timer 0	TF0	000BH	TCON.5
External 1	IE1	0013H	TCON.3
Timer 1	TF1	001BH	TCON.7
Serial Port	RI or TI	0023H	SCON.0 or SCON.1

• Each one is 8 byte in size.

EXTERNAL INTERRUPTS

If we want to enable the two external interrupts we could use the instruction:

MOV IE, #10000101B

External interrupts can be programmed for *edge or level* sensitivity. Each of the two external interrupt sources can be defined to trigger on the external signal, either on a negative going edge or on a logic low level state. The negative edge trigger is usually preferred as the interrupt flag is automatically cleared by hardware, in this mode. Two bits in the TCON register are used to define the trigger operation.

The TCON register is another SFR register and is located at location 88h in Internal RAM.

TCON : Counter/Timer CONtrol Register (088H)

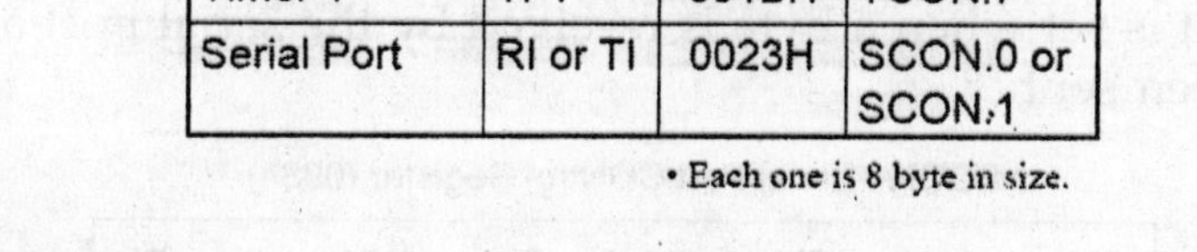

Bit	Name	Explanation of Function
7	TF1	Overflow flags for Timer 1
6	TR1	Run control bits for Timer 1 (Set to run, reset to hold)

5	TF0	Overflow flags for Timer 0
4	TR0	Run control bits for Timer 0 (Set to run, reset to hold)
3	IE1	Edge flag for external interrupts 1 (Set by interrupt edge, cleared when interrupt is processed)
2	IT1	Type bit for External 0 interrupt (Set for falling edge interrupts, reset for 0 level interrupts)
1	IE0	Edge flag for external interrupts 0 (Set by interrupt edge, cleared when interrupt is processed)
0	IT0	Type bit for External 1 interrupt (Set for falling edge interrupts, reset for 0 level interrupts)

For example, to define negative edge triggering for the two external interrupts use instructions as follows:

```
SETB IT0        ; negative edge trigger for interrupt 0
SETB IT1        ; negative edge trigger for interrupt 1
```

SERIAL INTERRUPTS

Serial Interrupts are slightly different than the rest of the interrupts. This is due to the fact that there is two interrupt flags: RI and TI. If either flag is set, a serial interrupt is triggered. The RI bit is set when a byte is received by the serial port and the TI bit is set when a byte has been sent.

SCON : Serial Port CONtrol Register (098h)

SM0	SM1	SM2	REN	Tb8	RB8	TI	RI

Serial Interrupts (TI, RI)

Bit	Name	Bit Address	Explanation of Function
7	SM0	9Fh	Serial port mode bit 0
6	SM1	9Eh	Serial port mode bit 1.
5	SM2	9Dh	Multiprocessor Communications Enable
4	REN	9Ch	Receiver Enable. This bit must be set in order to receive characters.
3	TB8	9Bh	Transmit bit 8. The 9th bit to transmit in mode 2 and 3.
2	RB8	9Ah	Receive bit 8. The 9th bit received in mode 2 and 3.
1	TI	99h	Transmit interrupt flag. Set at the end of character transmission; cleared by software.
0	RI	98h	Receive interrupt flag. Set at the end of character reception; cleared by software.

Figure 4.18 shows the flow of operation when a system is interrupted. In the example it is assumed that some program, say the main program, is executing when the external interrupt INT0 occurs. The 8051 hardware will automatically complete the current machine level (assembler level) instruction and save the Program Counter to the stack. The IE register is also saved to the stack. The IE0 flag is disabled (cleared) so that another INT0 interrupt will be inhibited while the current interrupt is being serviced. The Program Counter is now loaded with the vector location 0003h. This vector address is a predefined address for interrupt INT0 so that program execution will always trap to this address when an INT0 interrupt occurs. Other interrupt sources have uniquely defined vector addresses for this purpose. The set of these vector addresses is referred to as the interrupt vector table.

Program execution is now transferred to address location 0003h. In the example a LJMP instruction is programmed at this address to cause the program to jump to a predefined start address location for the relevant ISR (Interrupt Service Routine) routine. The ISR routine is a user written routine, which defines what action is to occur following the interrupt event. It is good practice to save (PUSH) to the stack any registers used during the ISR routine and to restore (POP) these registers at the end of the ISR routine, thus preserving the registers' contents, just like a register is preserved within a subroutine program. The last instruction in the ISR routine is a RETI (RETurn from Interrupt) instruction and this instruction causes the 8051 to restore the IE register values, enable the INT0 flag, and restore the Program Counter contents from the stack.

Since the Program Counter now contains the address of the next instruction which was to be executed before the INT0 interrupt occurred, the main program continues as if it had never being interrupted. Thus only the temporal behavior of the interrupted program has been affected by the interrupt; the logic of the program has not been otherwise affected.

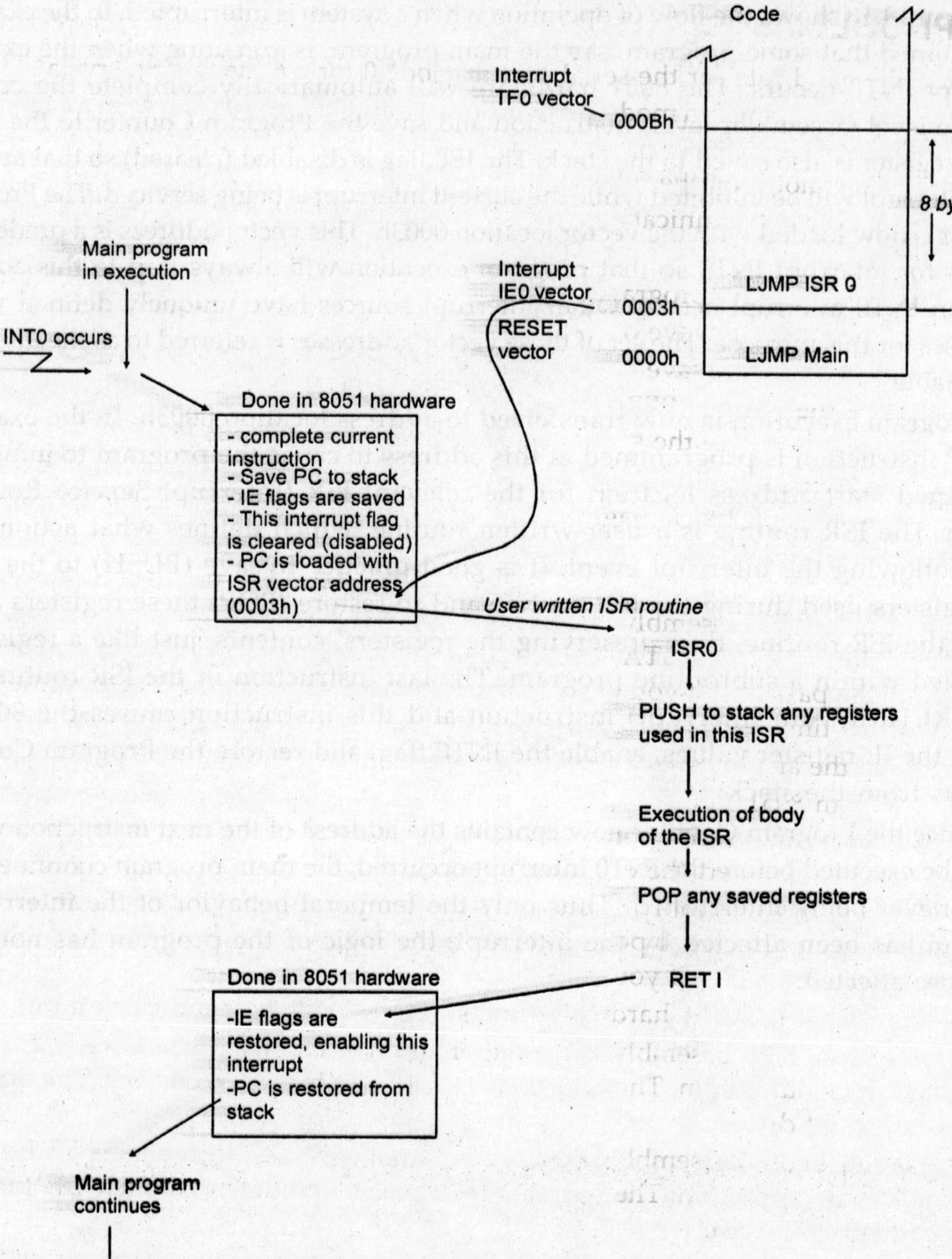

Figure 4.18 : Interrupt operation example

4.4 PROBLEMS

1. Find the baud rate for the serial port in mode 0 for a 6 megahertz crystal.
2. Find the time a timer in mode 1to overflow if initially set to 03Aeh with a 6 megahertz crystal.
3. Write short notes on the following:
   - Serial data communication
   - Interrupts
4. Write the following programs.

   (a) Create a square wave of 50% duty cycle on bit 0 of port 1.

   (b) Create a square wave of 60% duty cycle on bit 3 of port 1.
5. What are the various SFRs required while programming the serial port?Write a program to initialize the serial port of 8051 in mode1.
6. Explain interrupt polling in 8051.
7. (a) Draw a simple block diagram for the transmitter section of an 8051 UART which supports 9-bit data transmission. Briefly explain the function of each block in your diagram.

   (b) Write an 8051 assembly language program to send a block of 256 bytes from the external memory (XDATA) out through the serial port UART. You can choose to ignore the parity bit if you wish. Include the necessary code to configure the UART, baud rate timer etc.
8. (a) With the aid of a block diagram explain the operation of an 8051 UART device.

   b) Write an 8051 assembly language subroutine which will transmit an 8-bit data character via the serial port. A ninth bit is to be used as an even parity bit. Your program must insert the correct parity bit.

   Write an 8051 assembly language subroutine which will receive an 8-bit data character via the serial port. The subroutine is to be interrupt driven but it can ignore receive parity if you choose.
9. Assume that the 8051 hardware timers have a 1 microsecond clock input.

   (a) Write an 8051 assembly language program which will generate a 50 Hz square wave at an output pin. The program is to use a 16 bit timer/counter. The timer is to be interrupt driven.

   (b) Write an 8051 assembly language program which will generate a 5 KHz square wave at an output pin. The program is to use an 8 bit timer/counter. The timer is to be interrupt driven.
10. An 8051 based system constantly outputs a square wave at some frequency through an I/O port bit. The frequency is timed based on an 8-bit timer (assume a 1 microsecond timer input). The 8051 is connected to a PC via the serial port. When an 8-bit data character is received from the PC it interrupts the 8051 through the 8051's serial port interrupt and the received 8-bit data value is passed to the timer

so as to respecify the frequency. Thus a PC programmabale frequency generator is achieved. Write an 8051 assembly language program to implement this system. Assume a serial data baud rate of 9,600 baud. Show all configuration of the UART, timer etc. Calculate the programmable frequency range for your system, showing all calculations.

Chapter 5

Interfacing with 8051

5.1 INTRODUCTION

Communication to and from the microprocessor occurs through I/O devices connected to the bus. External computer peripheral I/O devices include keyboards, printers, displays, modems, and network devices. For mechatronic applications, analog-to-digital (A/D), digital-to-analog (D/A) and digital I/O (D/D) devices provide interfaces to switches, sensors, and actuators.

In industry the 8051 is the most frequently used microcontroller. This chapter looks at some real –world applications of 8051 and discusses the 8051 interfacing with LED, seven segment display, keyboard, LCD, ADC and DAC devices and besides looking into different interface considerations and techniques. For better understanding one should explore this chapter after reading chapter 2, 3 and 4 on 8051.

5.2 I/O PORT CONFIGURATION

The 8255 PPI is interface adapter used for I/O configuration. The 8255 contains an internal mode register to which control words are written by the host computer. These control words determine the action of 8255 PORTs, named A, B, C, act as input port and output ports, or some combination of both. 8255 is considered for illustration of I/O port configuration due to it's simplicity.

There are two ways for I/O configurations these are:

- Memory mapped I/O
- Memory address decoding

5.2.1 MEMORY MAPPED I/O

In ***memory mapped I/O***, expanding I/O in this manner causes reduction in the speed that occurs due to overhead time needed to write control bits Port 1 & Port 3 before the resulting I/O lines selected can be accessed. The advantage of I/O expansion is that entire range of 8051 instruction can be accessed. The added ports via Port 1 & 3 but with memory mapped I/O has the advantage of not using any of the 8051 ports. Disadvantage includes the loss of memory space for the RAM that is used by I/O address space. Programming overhead is same for both cases. The port chip can be addressed anytime

A15 is high (8000H or above) and the 32K RAM can be addressed whenever A15 is low (7FFFH and below). This decoding scheme requires only the addition of the Inverter to decode the memory space for the RAM and I/O. The Fig. 5.1(a) shows the 8255 connections for memory mapped I/O.

5.2.2 MEMORY ADDRESS DECODING

In **memory address decoding technique**, a memory address decoder is used if an additional external RAM above 32K is to be added. Decorder is a combinational logic circuit having multiple outputs. At any time only one of the outputs is activated according to the binary data feeded to it, and remaining outputs are deactivated. Generally activated output is active low and deactivated outputs are active high.

In order to design decorder, first we find out which memory addresses are to be used to enable I/O chips, and then a decoder circuitry is designed. Let us assume that a total of 80H (or 128) addresses are required for I/O chip, and we want to divide it into 4, 20H address spaces. Let I/O chips are assigned would be FF80H to FFFFH. Thus less wastage of upper 32K RAM memory address is achieved. The decoder circuitry to achieve this configuration is shown in Fig. 5.1(b), which have 11 binary inputs and 5 outputs. The 11 input to decoder are address lines (A_{15}–A_5) of 8051. Remaining 5 address lines (A_4–A_0) can be used to access any address from 20H I/O address space ($2^5 = 32 = 20H$). The address bit map for connection is in below table.

Input											Output					
A_{15}	A_{14}	A_{13}	A_{12}	A_{11}	A_{10}	A_9	A_8	A_7	A_6	A_5	Y_0	Y_1	Y_2	Y_3	Y_4	
1	1	1	1	1	1	1	1	1	0	0	0	1	1	1	1	
I/O																
1	1	1	1	1	1	1	1	1	0	1	1	0	1	1	1	address
1	1	1	1	1	1	1	1	1	1	0	1	1	0	1	1	
1	1	1	1	1	1	1	1	1	1	1	1	1	1	0	1	
....											....					
....											....					
For all other address combinations											1	1	1	0	1	RAM address
Note. Output $Y_4 = (Y_0 \text{ NAND } Y_1 \text{ NAND } Y_2 \text{ NAND } Y_3)$																

The memory address range for achieved decoding scheme is :

RAM Memory Address Range (hex)	Active output
FFBO–FF9F	Y_0
FFAO–FFBF	Y_1
FFCO–FFDF	Y_2
FFEO–FFFF	Y_3
OOOO–FF7F	Y_4

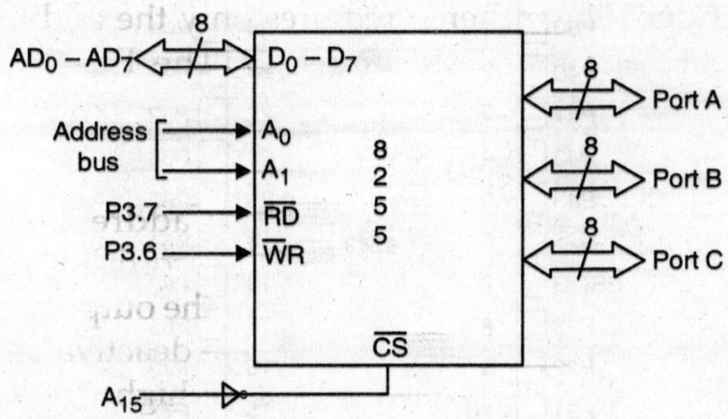

Figure 5.1 (a) 8255 connections for memory mapped I/O.

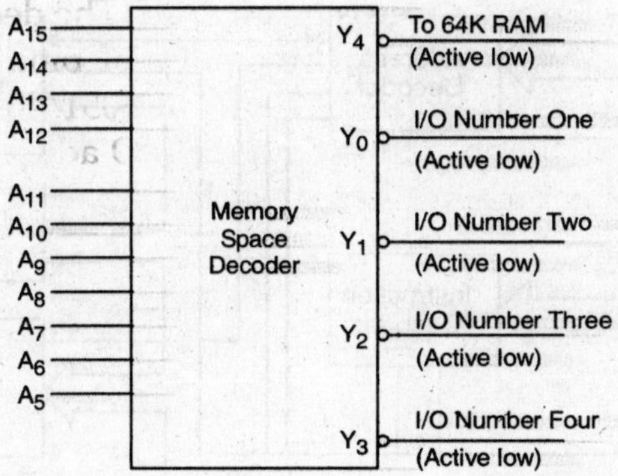

Figure 5.1 (b) Memory space decorder

5.2.3 8243 INTERFACING

The 8243 contains four 4-bit I/O ports as shown in Fig. 5.2, which serve as an extension of the on-chip I/O and are addressed as ports 4.7. The following operations may be performed on these ports:

- Transfer Accumulator to Port
- Transfer Port to Accumulator
- AND Accumulator to Port
- OR Accumulator to Port

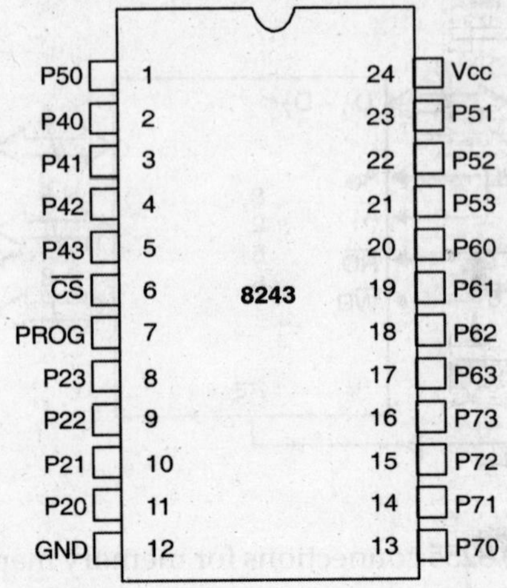

Figure 5.2 (a) PIN diagram of 8243

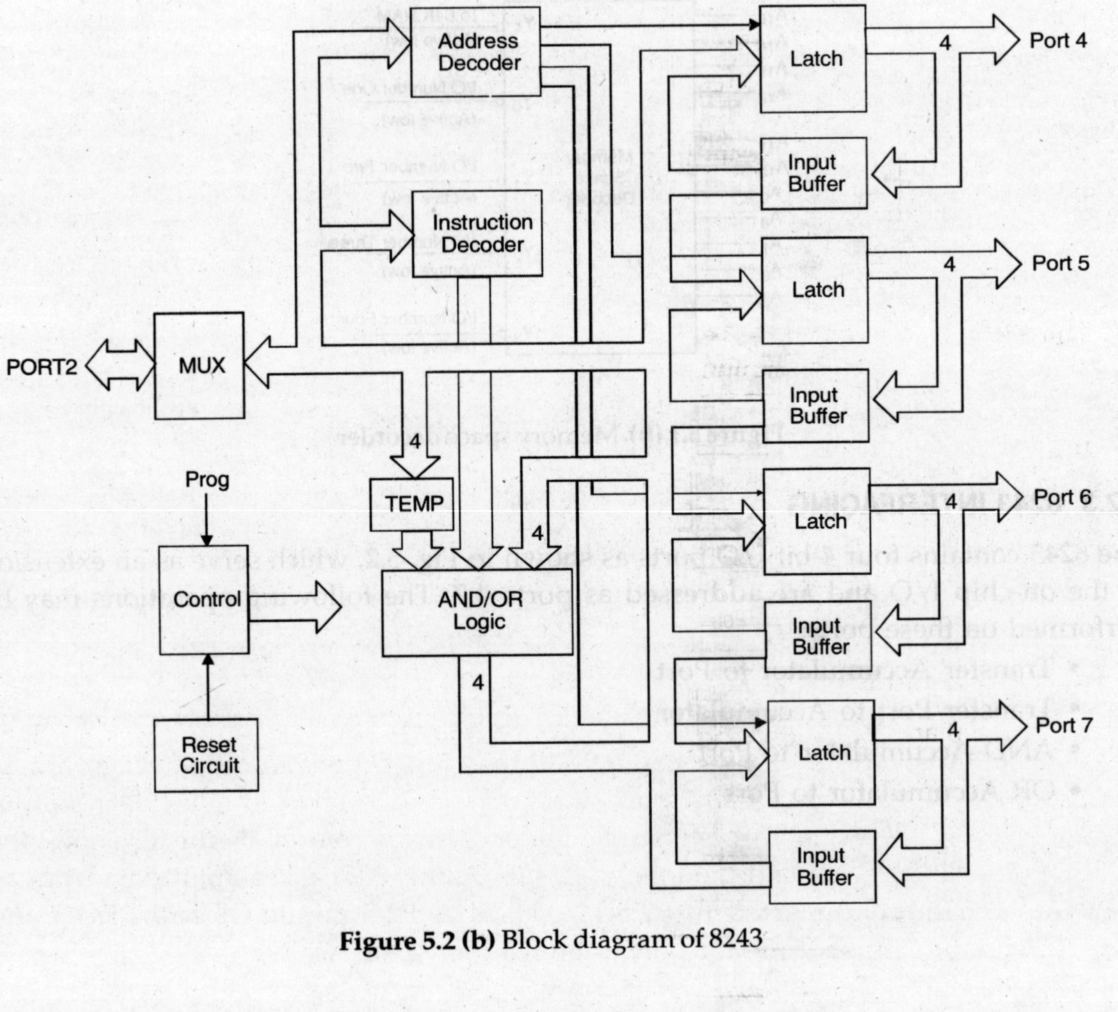

Figure 5.2 (b) Block diagram of 8243

Pin description

Symbol	Pin No	Function
PROG	7	Clock input. A high to low transition of the PROG line indicates that the address is present while low to high transition indicates the presence of data on P20-P23.
CS	6	Chip select input. A high on Cs inhibits any change of output or internal status.
P20-P23	11-8	Four(4) bit bi-directional port contains address and control bits/data. A high to low transition of the PROG line indicates that the address is present while low to high transition indicates the presence of data
GND	12	0V supply
P40-P43	2-5	Four(4) bit-directional I/O ports
P50-P53	P60-P63	Input (during read), low impedance latched output (after write), or
P70-P73	1,23-21	tri-state (after read)
20-17	13-16	
VCC	24	+5V supply

All communication between the 8048 and the 8243 occurs over Port 2 (P20-P23) with timing provided by the output pulse on the PROG pin of the processor. Each transfer consists of 4-nibbles.

The first containing the "op-code" and port address and the second containing the actual 4-bits of data. A high to low transition of the PROG line indicates that the address is present while low to high transition indicates the presence of data. The opcode and port address are given according to below table:

P21	P20	Address code	P23	P22	Instruction code
0	0	Port 4	0	0	Read
0	1	Port 5	0	1	Write
1	0	Port 6	1	0	ORLD
1	1	Port 7	1	1	ANLD

Although the 8051 does not include 8048-type instructions for interfacing with an 8243, the 8051's quasi-bidirectional port structure lets each I/O pin input data, output data, or serve as a test pin or output strobe under software control. Figure 5.3 shows the 8051 and 8043 interfacing and the following subroutine, 8051 takes input data from an 8243 I/O expander connected to P2.0-P2.3, P2.4 & P2.5 mimic CS and PROG and P2.6–P2.7 used as inputs code for port to be read in Acc.0–Acc.1.

```
8243_in:  ORL   A,#11010000B   ;set prog and pins used as input
          MOV   P2,A           ;output port code and operation code
          CLR   P2.4           ;latch address
          ORL   P2,#00001111B  ;set low order pins for input
          MOV   A,P2           ;read in port data
          ORL   P2,#00110000B  ;set prog and cs high
```

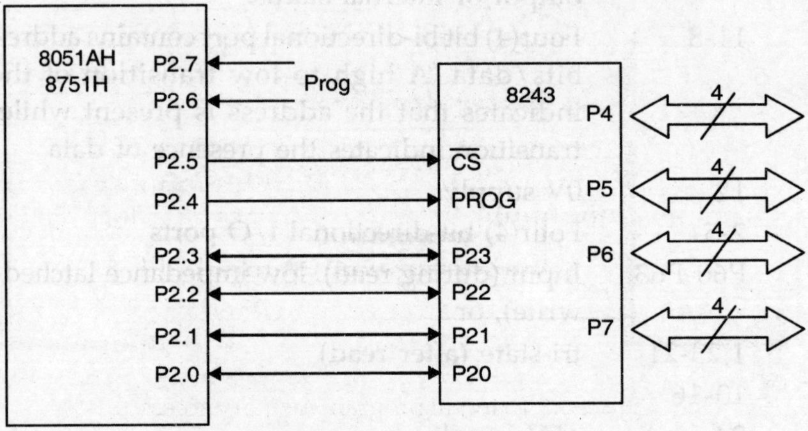

Figure 5.3 The 8243 and 8051 Interfacing

5.3 MEMORY INTERFACING

The 8051 has three types of memory. As shown in Fig. 5.4 they are

- On-Chip Memory
- External Code Memory (ROM)
- External Data Memory (RAM).

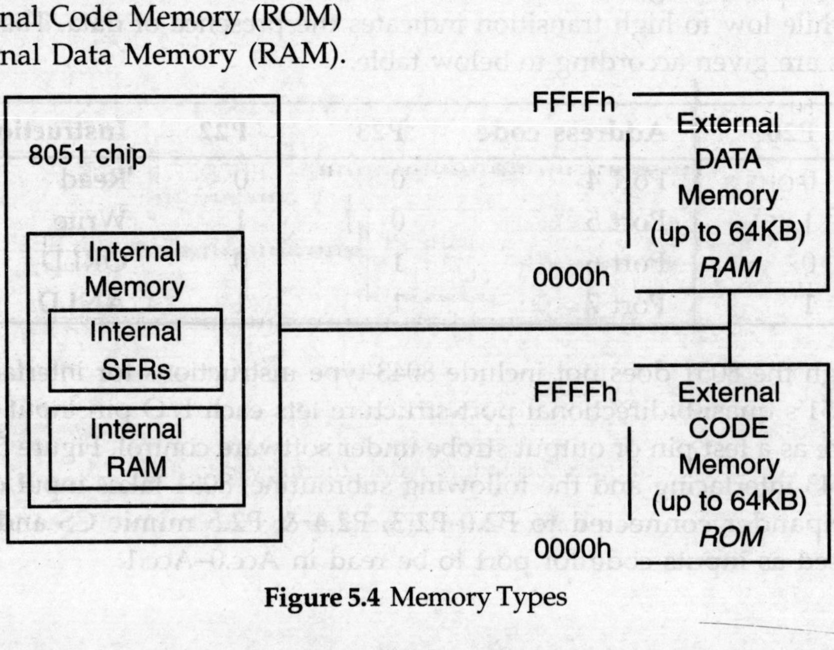

Figure 5.4 Memory Types

5.3.1 INTERFACING EXTERNAL CODE MEMORY (ROM)

The executable program code is stored in this code memory. The code memory size is limited to 64K Bytes (in a standard 8051). The code memory is *read-only* in normal operation and is programmed under special conditions e.g. it is a PROM or a Flash type of memory. However, code memory is most commonly implemented as off-chip EPROM, especially in low-cost development systems. The access of external program (code) memory is shown in Fig. 5.5, which is enabled by PSEN signal.

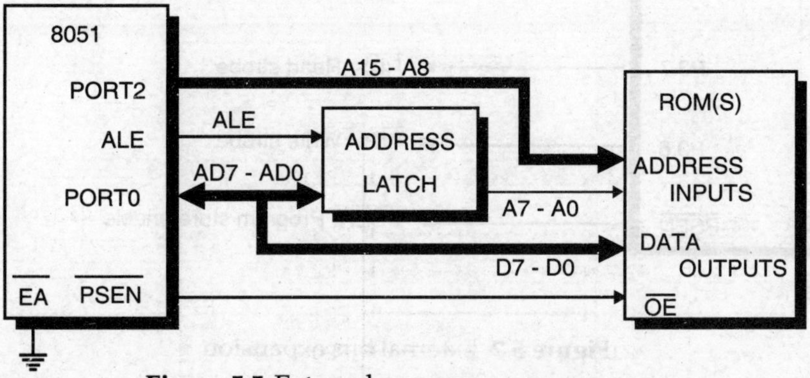

Figure 5.5 External program memory access

5.3.2 INTERFACING EXTERNAL DATA MEMORY (RAM)

This *is read-write* memory and is available for storage of data. Up to 64KBytes of external RAM data memory is supported (in a standard 8051).

While internal RAM is limited to 128 bytes, the 8051 supports external RAM up to 64K. Figure 5.6 shows how to use the External Data Memory.

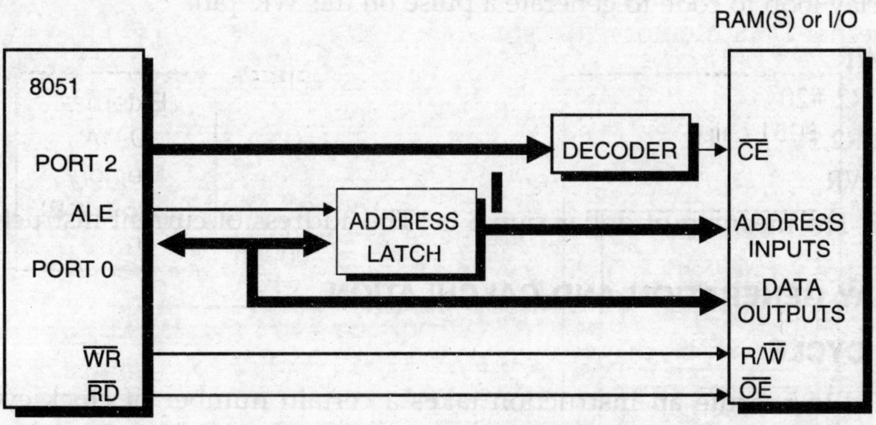

Figure 5.6 External data memory access

Note: Figure 5.7 shows bus expansion for external memory access. The memory organisation of 8051 is already discussed in detail in article 2.5.

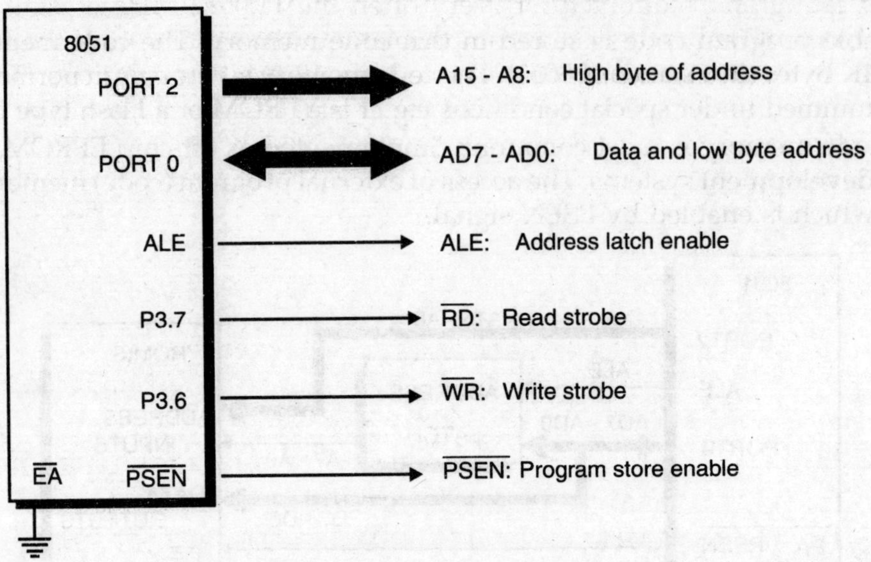

Figure 5.7 External bus expansion

5.4 SOFTWARE DELAY TIMING

Many 8051 application involve exact control over output timing. A software-generated output strobe, for instance, might have to be exactly.50 µsec. wide. The DJNZ operation can insert an one instruction software delay into a piece of code, adding a moderate delay of two instruction cycles per iteration. For example, two instructions can add a 49-µsec software delay loop to code to generate a pulse on the $\overline{WR}$ pin.

```
CLR WR
MOV R2 #20
DJNZ R2,$
SETB WR
```

NOTE: The meaning of dollar sign $ is "The address of current instruction".

TIME DELAY GENERATION AND CALCULATION

MACHINE CYCLE

For the CPU to execute an instruction takes a certain number of clock cycles. In the 8051 family, these clock cycles are referred to as machine cycles. To calculate a time delay, we use this list. In the 8051 family, the length of the machine cycle depends on the frequency of the crystal oscillator connected to the 8051 system. The crystal oscillator, along with on-chip circuitry, provide the clock source for the 8051 CPU. The frequency of the crystal connected to the 8051 family can vary from 4 MHz to 30 MHz, depending on the chip rating and manufacturer. Very often the 11.0592 MHz crystal oscillator is used to make the 8051-based system compatible with the serial port of the IBM PC (see chapter 10). In the 8051, one machine cycle lasts 12 oscillator periods. Therefore, to calculate the machine cycle, we take 1½ of the crystal frequency, then take its inverse.

DELAY CALCULATION

A delay subroutine consists of two parts:

- setting a counter,
- a loop.

Most of the time delay is performed by the body of the loop.

For three different 8051-based systems period of machine cycle is calculated on the basis of crystal frequency as follows

(a) 11.0592/12 = 921.6 kHz; machine cycle is 1/921.6 kHz = 1.085 μs (microsecond)
(b) 16 MHz/12 = 1.333 MHz; machine cycle (MC) = 1/1.333 MHz = 0.75 μs
(c) 20 MHz/12 = 1.66 MHz; MC = 1/1.66 MHz = 0.60 μs

We will now see that how long it takes to execute each of the following instruction.

The machine cycle for the system of 11.0592 Mhz is 1.085 μs as already discussed above.

Instruction	Machine Cycles	Time to execute
(a) MOV r3, #55	1	1 × 1.085 μs = 1.085 μs
(b) DEC R3	1	1 × 1.085 μs = 1.085 μs
(c) DJNZ r2, target	2	2 × 1.085 μs = 2.17 μs
(d) LJMP	2	2 × 1.085 μs = 2.17 μs
(e) SJMP	2	2 × 1.085 μs = 2.17 μs
(f) NOP	1	1 × 1.085 μs = 1.085 μs
(g) MUL AB	4	4 × 1.085 μs = 4.34 μs

Most of the time delay is performed by the body of the loop as described below; shows the delay if crystal frequency is 11.0592 MHz

```
            MOV A, #55H
REPEAT:     MOV P1,A
            ACALL DELAY
            CPL A
            SJMP REPEAT
------------------------------Time delay ------------------------------------
DELAY:      MOV R3, #100
NEXT:       DJNZ R3,NEXT
            RET
```

Total delay offered by subroutine DELAY is = [(100*2) + 1 + 1]*1.085 μs = 219.17 μs.

We have seen how to calculate delays using 11.0592 MHz crystal. Now we will see software based timing delay routines for an 8051 clocked at 12 MHz (for simplicity of delay calculation).The examples introduce the useful programming concept of sub-routines.

For an 8051 microcomputer a single instruction cycle is executed for every 12 clock cycles of the processor clock. Thus, for an 8051 clocked at 12 MHz. The instruction cycle time is one microsecond, as follows:

$$\text{Instruction cycle time} = \frac{12 \text{ clock cycles}}{12 \times 106 \text{ cycles/sec.}} = 10^{-6} \text{ seconds, or } 1\ \mu\text{sec.}$$

The shortest instructions will execute in one instruction cycle, i.e. 1 μsec. Other instructions may take two or more instruction cycle times to execute.

SOME EXAMPLE ROUTINE TO INTRODUCE DELAY IN PROGRAM

1. Sample routine to delay 1 millisecond: ONE_MILLI_SUB

Consider a software routine called 'ONE_MILLI_SUB', written as a subroutine program, which takes a known 1000 instructions cycles (approx.) to execute. Thus it takes 1000 μsecs, or 1 millisecond, to execute. The program is written as a subroutine since it may be called on frequently as part of some longer timing delay routines. The flow chart for the routine is shown in Fig. 5.8 along with the source code for the subroutine. Note, register R7 is used as a loop counter. It is good practice in writing subroutines to save to the stack (PUSH) any registers used in the subroutine and to restore (POP) such registers when finished. See how R7 is saved and retrieved in the program. We say that R7 is 'preserved'. This is important as the program which called the subroutine may be using R7 for another purpose and a subroutine should not be allowed to 'accidentally' change the value of a register used elsewhere.

When calling a subroutine the Program Counter (PC) is automatically pushed onto the stack, so the SP (Stack Pointer) is incremented by 2 when a subroutine is entered. The PC is automatically retrieved when returning from the subroutine, decrementing the SP by 2.

In the ONE_MILLI_SUB subroutine a tight loop is executed 250 times. The number of instruction cycles per instruction is known, as published by the 8051 manufacturer.

The tight loop is as follows:

NOP	takes 1 instruction cycle to execute
NOP	takes 1 instruction cycle to execute
DJNZ R7, LOOP_1_MILLI	takes 2 instruction cycle to execute

Total instruction cycles = 4

So, it takes 4 instruction cycles, or 4 μsecs, to execute the loop. Thus, if we execute the loop 250 times it will take a 1000 μsecs (250 x 4), i.e. 1 millisecond, to complete the loops.

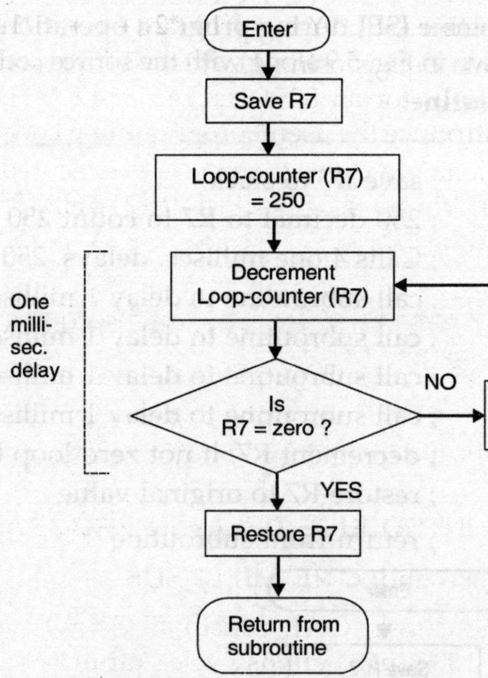

Figure 5.8 ONE_MILLI_SUB flow chart

Program for ONE_MILLI_SUB routine:

```
ONE_MILLI_SUB:
PUSH 07h                  ; save R7 to stack
MOV R7, #250d             ; 250 decimal to R7 to count 250 loops
LOOP_1_MILLI:             ; loops 250 times
NOP                       ; inserted NOPs to cause delay
NOP                       ;
DJNZ R7, LOOP_1_MILLI     ; decrement R7, if not zero loop back
POP 07h                   ; restore R7 to original value
RET                       ; return from subroutine
```

2. Sample routine to delay 1 second: ONE_SEC_SUB

The ONE_SEC_SUB subroutine, when called, causes a delay of ONE second. This subroutine calls the ONE_MILLI_SUB subroutine and is structured so that the ONE_MILLI_SUB subroutine is called exactly 1000 times, thus causing a total delay of 1000 milli. seconds, i.e. ONE second. (There are some small inaccuracies, which will be ignored for now). Note, R7 is used again as the loop counter (we could have used another register). Since R7 is preserved in the ONE_SEC_SUB subroutine, its value is not corrupted within the ONE_SEC_SUB subroutine. This example shows how one subroutine can call another subroutine, demonstrating the concept of subroutine nesting. It is interesting to track the value of the Stack Pointer (SP) during program operation. The flow chart for the ONE_SEC_SUB routine is shown in Fig. 5.9 along with the source code for the subroutine.

Program for ONE_SEC_SUB routine:

```
ONE_SEC_SUB:
PUSH 07h                ; save R7 to stack
MOV R7, #250d           ; 250 decimal to R7 to count 250 loops
LOOP_SEC:               ; Calls 4 one millisec. delays, 250 times
LCALL ONE_MILLI_SUB     ; call subroutine to delay 1 millisecond
LCALL ONE_MILLI_SUB     ; call subroutine to delay 1 millisecond
LCALL ONE_MILLI_SUB     ; call subroutine to delay 1 millisecond
LCALL ONE_MILLI_SUB     ; call subroutine to delay 1 millisecond
DJNZ R7, LOOP_SEC       ; decrement R7, if not zero loop back
POP 07h                 ; restore R7 to original value
RET                     ; return from subroutine
```

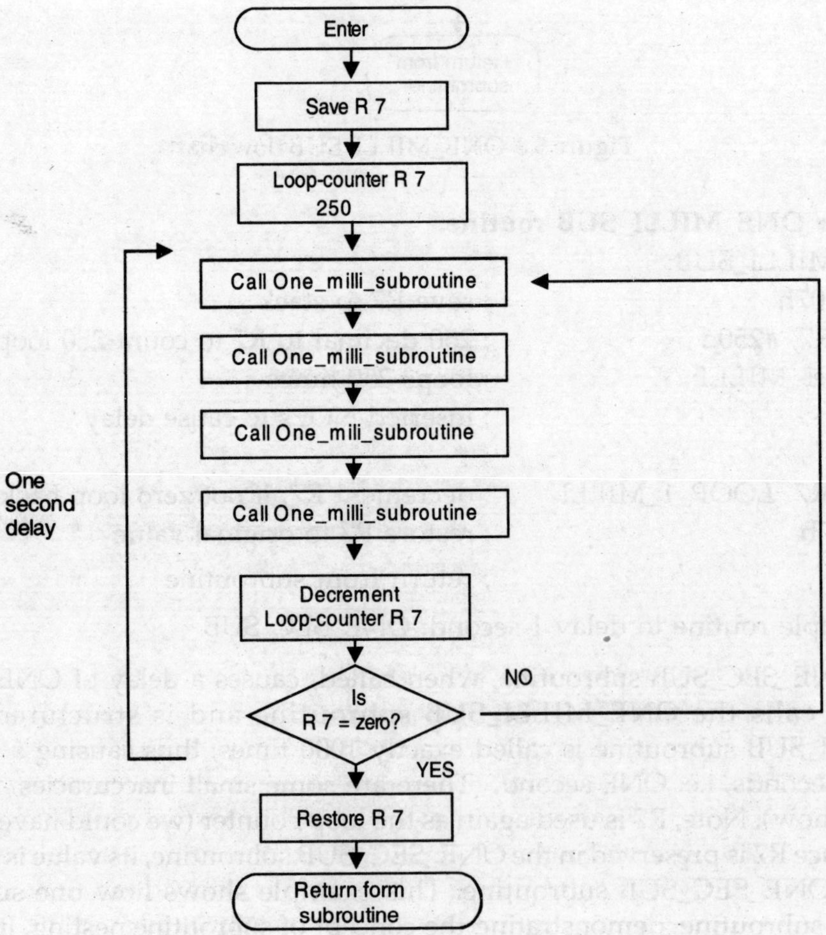

Figure 5.9 ONE_SEC_SUB flow chart

3. Sample routine to delay N seconds: PROG_DELAY_SUB

PROG_DELAY_SUB is a subroutine, which will cause a delay for a specified number of seconds. The subroutine is called with the required number, N, of delay seconds specified in the accumulator. The subroutine calls the ONE_SEC_SUB subroutine, which in turn calls the ONE_MILLI_SUB subroutine. Here is a further example of nesting subroutines. The PROG_DELAY_SUB subroutine preserves the accumulator value. The subroutine also checks to see if it has been called with a zero value in the accumulator. If this is the case the subroutine returns immediately without causing further delay. A maximum delay of 255 seconds can be specified, i.e. accumulator can have a maximum value of 0FFh (255 decimal). The program provides a simple example of passing a parameter to a subroutine where the accumulator is used to pass a number N into the subroutine. The flow chart for the PROG_DELAY_SUB routine is shown in Fig. 5.10 along with the source code for the subroutine.

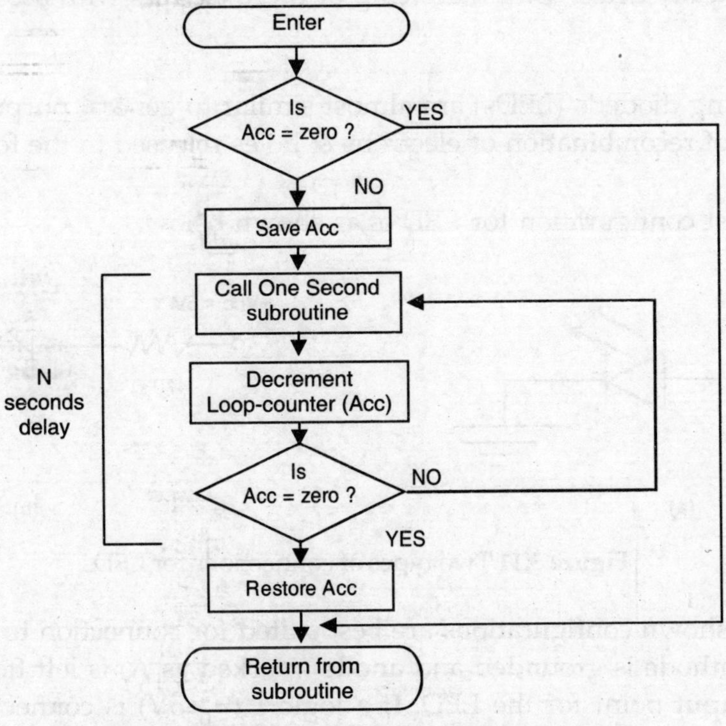

Figure 5.10 PROG_DELAY_SUB flow chart

Program for PROG_DELAY_SUB routine:

```
PROG_DELAY_SUB:
        CJNE A, #00h, OK        ; if A=0 then exit
        LJMP DONE               ; exit
OK:     PUSH Acc                ; save A to stack
```

```
LOOP_N:                              ; calls one second delay, no. of times in A
        LCALL ONE_SEC_SUB            ; call subroutine to delay 1 second
        DJNZ Acc, LOOP_N             ; decrement A, if not zero loop back
        POP Acc                      ; restore Acc to original value
DONE:
        RET                          ; return from subroutine
```

5.5 LEDs, PUSH BUTTONS, RELAY AND LATCH CONNECTIONS

In real life applications, one have encountered many electrical as well as electromechanical devices such as LED, Push Button, latch & electromechanical relays etc. It is therefore important to know how to connect these devices to microcontrollers. This section basically deals with interfacing of these devices with 8051 microcontroller.

5.5.1 LEDs

The Light emitting dioded (LEDs) are almost similar to general purpose diodes except that the energy of recombination of electrons & holes released in the form of photons in case of LEDs.

The simplest configuration for LED is as shown below.

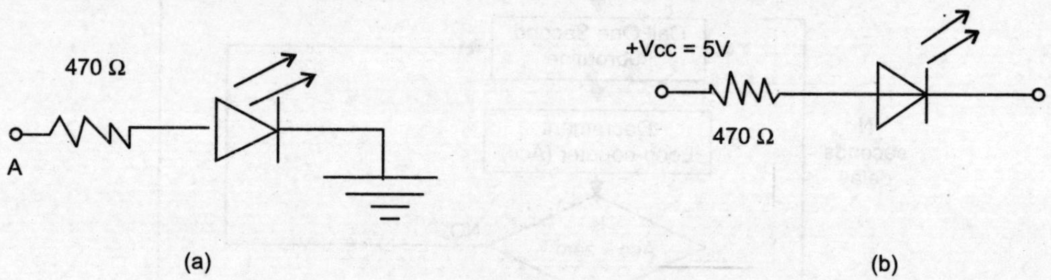

Figure 5.11 Two types of connections for LEDs

The above shown configurations are best suited for connection to microcontrollers. In Fig. 5.11(a) cathode is grounded and anode (marked as A) is left floating. In fact the anode acts as input point for the LED. If a logic 1 (= +5V) is connected at this anode input then LED will glow and if logic 0 is connected then LED will not glow. When this anode is connected to the port of microcontroller as shown in Fig. 5.12(a), then microcontroller has to make the port line HIGH to glow the LED.

In Fig. 5.11(b) anode is connected to +5V and cathode is left floating. If cathode is connected to logic 0 (i.e. gnd) LED will glow. Fig. 5.12(b) shows its connection to a microcontroller.

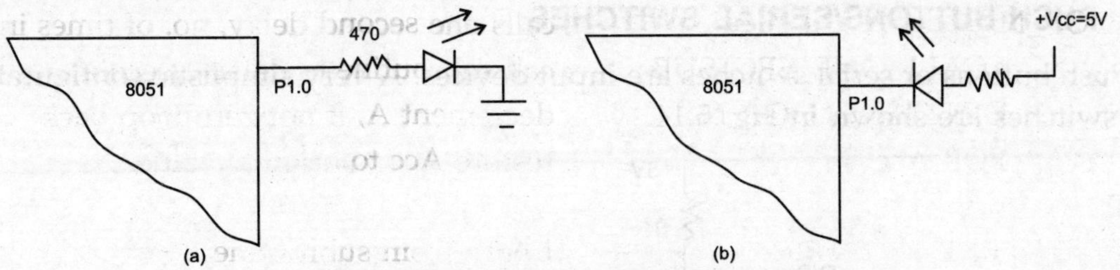

Figure 5.12 Connections of LEDs to 8051

Example: Connect 8 LEDs to port 1 of 8051. It is required to glow the LEDs sequentially. Successive LEDs must be turned ON after 1 msec. Show connections and write assembly language programs.

Sol: To write the program we assume that a software routine named "DELAY" is available which provides a delay of 1 msec. This routine will be similar to the delay routines explained in section 5.4.

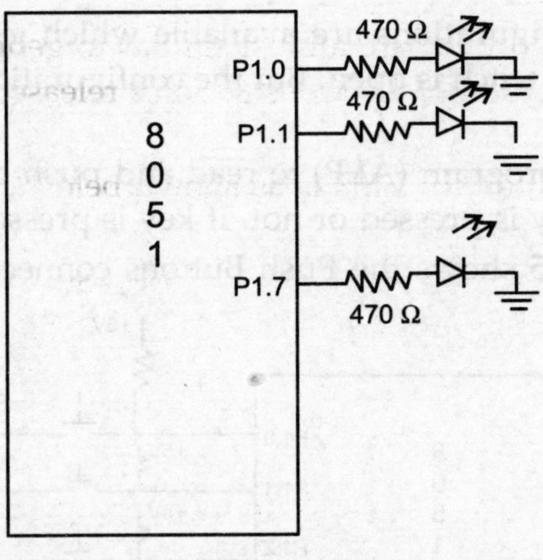

Figure 5.13 LEDs connection to 8051

From Fig. 5.13 it is clear that a logic 1 at any port bit will turn ON the LED. For programming first define all bits of port 1 as output and then write logic 1 sequentially at these bits after 1 msec (i.e. ONE_MILLI_SUB).

```
        CLR A
        MOV A, # 0000 000 1B    ; command to write logic 1 at p 1.0
REPT:   MOV P1, A               ; write command at port 1
        A CALL MILLI_SUB        ; Delay of 1 msec.
        RL  A                   ; Rotate accumulator left to glow next LED in
                                  sequence.
        AJMP REPT               ; Repeat the process to glow the LEDs.
                                  continuosly.
```

5.5.2 PUSH BUTTONS/SERIAL SWITCHES

The Push buttons or serial switches are input devices. A very simplistic configuration of such switches are shown in Fig. 5.14.

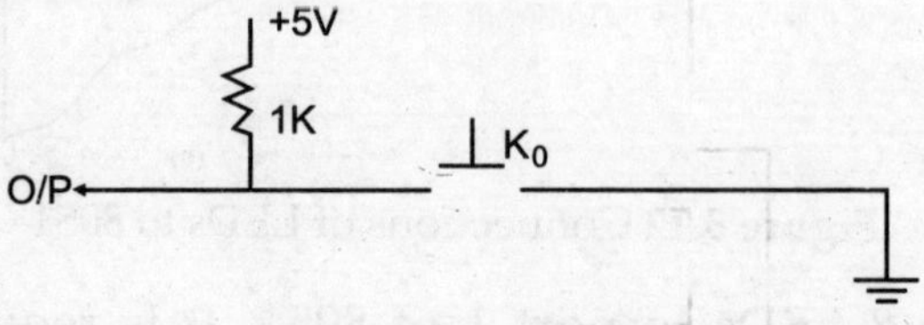

Figure 5.14 Simple configuration of push button

When the button/switch (K_0) is pressed or closed ground is connected directly to the output. Hence output is 0V. When switch (K_0) is not pressed or open +5V is connected to output. Thus whenever logic 0 appears at the output it means switch is pressed and if logic 1 (+5V) appears at output switch is open.

However switch configurations are available which gives logic 1 when switch is pressed and logic 0 when switch is open. But the configuration of Fig. 5.14 is choosen for simplicity.

Prob: Write an 8051 program (ALP) to read and push buttons connected at port 1, and check weather any key is pressed or not. If key is pressed store data in register R3.

Solution: The Fig. 5.15 shows the Push Buttons connection to 8051.

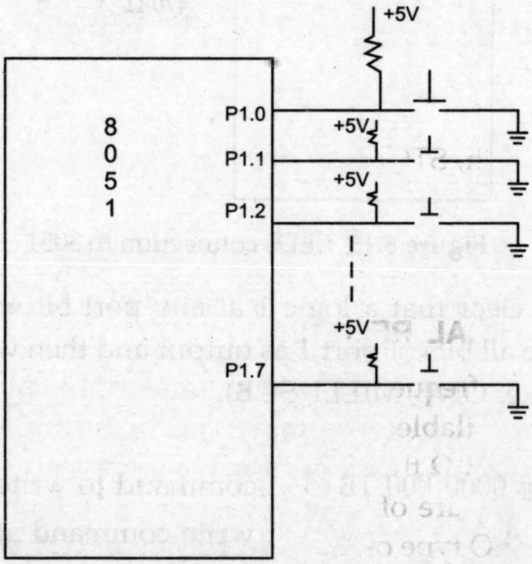

Figure 5.15 Push buttons connection to 8051

Flow chart for the problem is given in Fig. 5.16.

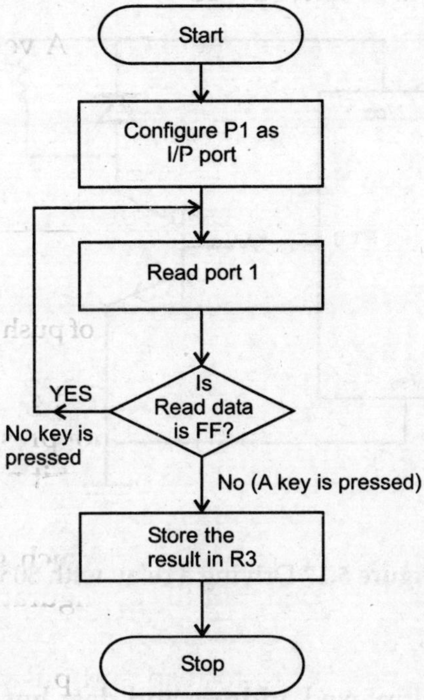

Figure 5.16

```
        CLR A
        MOV A, # FFh
        MOV P1, A             ; Configure port 1 as input port
REPT:   MOV A, P1             ; Read port 1 contents
        CJNE A, # FFh, STORE  ; Keep checking for FFh (key pressed)
        AJMP REPT             ;
STORE:  MOV R3, A             ; Store the value
```

5.5.3 ELECTROMECHANICAL RELAYS

Electromechanical relays are frequently used in industrial and control applications. There are two types of relays available. The relay coil operating at 5V. Normally the coil resistance having value of 50 Ω therefore it can stands a current of normally 100 mA. The electromechanical relays are of normally open (NO) type or normally closed (NC) type. When energised the NO type of relay closed while NC type of relay become open to connect/disconnect the device. For example, to Start or Stop a 230-50V AC motor using a microcontroller a relay is used. The simple connection of a electromechanical relay with 8051 microcontroller is shown in Fig. 5.17. In this, a relay is connected as pin 1.0 of 8051.

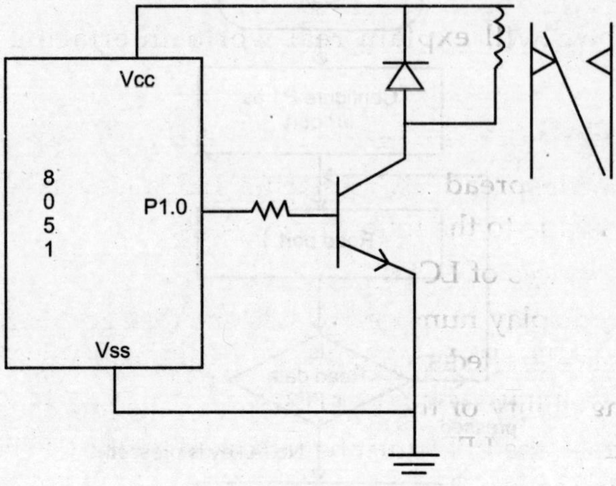

Figure 5.17 Driving a relay with 8051

5.5.4 LATCH

In 8051, port 0 is used as multiplexed address and data bus while port 2 as address bus. Since data and address are mutiplexed at port 0 we need an external device to hold address information externally. For this purpose we use an external latch. To latch the address information the ALE signal of 8051 is connected to enable input of external latch.

The Fig. 5.18 shows the external address latch connection of 8051.

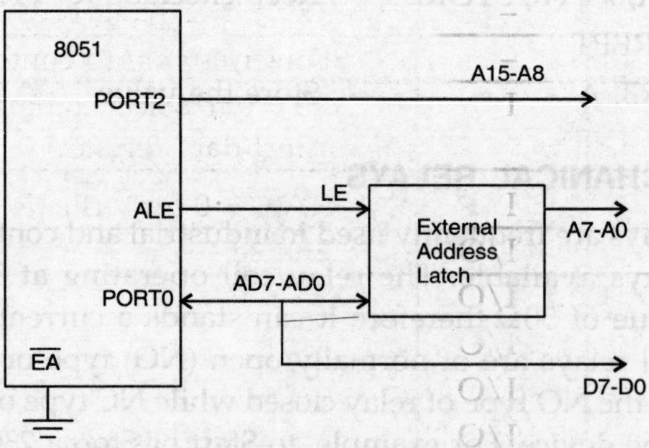

Figure 5.18 Interfacing latch with an 8051 microcontroller

One such generally used latch is 74LS573.

5.6 INTERFACING

In solved examples we will explain real world interfacing problems with 8051 microcontroller.

5.6.1 LCD INTERFACING

The LCD is finding widespread use replacing LEDs (seven segment LEDs or other multisegment LEDs), is due to the following reasons:

- The declining prices of LCDs
- The ability to display numbers, characters, and graphics. This is in contrast to LEDs, which are limited to numbers and a few characters.
- Self refreshing ability of the LCD, thereby relieving the CPU to refreshing the LCD. In contrast, the LED must be refreshed by the CPU (or in some other way) to keep displaying the data.
- Ease of programming for characters and graphics.

LCD Pin Descriptions

The LCD discussed in this section has 14 pins. The functions of each pin is given in Table 5.1.

Pin Descriptions for LCD

Table 5.1

Pin	Symbol	I/O	Description
1	VSS	–	Ground
2	VCC	–	+5V power supply
3	VEE	–	Power supply to control contrast
4	RS	I	RS = 0 to select command register, RS = 1 to select data register
5	$R/\overline{W}$	I	$R/\overline{W}$ = 0 for write, $R/\overline{W}$ = 1 for read
6	E	I/O	Enable
7	DBO	I/O	The 8-bit data bus
8	DB1	I/O	
9	DB2	I/O	
10	DB3	I/O	
11	DB4	I/O	
12	DB5	I/O	
13	DB6	I/O	
14	DB7	I/O	

VCC, VSS and VEE

While VCC and VSS provide +5V and ground, respectively, VEE is used for controlling LCD contrast.

RS, register select

There are two important registers inside the LCD, the instruction command code and data register. The RS pin is used for their selection as follows.

If RS=0, the instruction command code register is selected, allowing the user to send a command such as clear display, cursor at home, etc.

If RS=1, the data register is selected, allowing the user to send data to be displayed on the LCD.

$R/\overline{W}$, read/write

$R/\overline{W}$ input allows the user to write information to the LCD or read information from it. $R/\overline{W}=1$ when reading, $R/\overline{W}=0$ when writing.

E, enable

The enable pin is used by the LCD to latch information presented to its data pins. When data is supplied to data pins, a high-to-low pulse must be applied to this pin in order for the LCD to latch in the data present at the data pins. This pulse must be a minimum of 450 ns wide.

D0-D7

The 8-bit data pins, D0 – D7, are used to send information to the LCD or read the contents of the LCD's internal registers.

To display letters and numbers, we send ASCII codes for the letters A–Z, a–z, and numbers 0–9 to these pins while making RS = 1.

There are also instruction command codes that can be sent to the LCD to clear the display or force the cursor to the home position or blink the cursor.

We also use Rs=0 to check the busy flag bit to see if the LCD is ready to receive infomation. The busy flag is D7 and can be read when R/W=1 and RS=0. When D7 = 1 (busy flag = 1), the LCD is busy taking care of internal operations and will not accept any new information. When D7 = 0, the LCD is ready to receive new information. Note: It is recommended to check the busy flag before writing any data to the LCD.

LCD COMMAND CODES

Code (Hex)	Command to LCD Instruction Register
1	Clear display screen
2	Return home
4	Decrement cursor (shift cursor to left)
6	Increment cursor (shift cursor to right)
5	Shift display right

7	Shift display left
8	Display off, cursor off
A	Display off, cursor on
C	Display on, cursor off
E	Display on, cursor blinking
F	Display on, cursor blinking
10	Shift cursor position to left
14	Shift cursor position to right
18	Shift the entire display to the left
1C	Shift the entire display to the right
80	Force cursor to beginning to 1st line
C0	Force cursor to beginning to the 2nd line
38	2 lines and 5 × 7 matrix

LCD DATA SHEET

In the LCD, one can put data at any location. The following shows address locations and how they are accessed.

RS	$R/\overline{W}$	DB7	DB6	DB5	DB4	DB3	DB2	DB1	DB0
0	0	1	A	A	A	A	A	A	A

where AAAAAAA = 0000000 to 0100111 for line 1 and AAAAAAA = 1000000 to 1100111 for line 2.

LCD Addressing

	DB7	DB6	DB5	DB4	DB3	DB2	DB1	DB0
Line 1 (min)	1	0	0	0	0	0	0	0
Line 1 (max)	1	0	1	0	0	1	1	1
Line 2 (min)	1	1	0	0	0	0	0	0
Line 2 (max)	1	1	1	0	0	1	1	1

The upper address range can go as high as 0100111 for the 40-character-wide LCD while for the 20-character-wide LCD it goes up to 010011 (19 decimal = 10011 binary). Notice that the upper range 0100111 (binary) = 39 decimal which corresponds to locations 0 to 39 for the LCDs of 40 × 2 size.

From the above discussion we can get the addresses of cursor positions for various sizes of LCD's. Note that all the addresses are in hex. Previous table provides a detailed list of LCD commands and instructions. Given table is extracted from previous table.

16 × 2 LCD	80	81	82	83	84	85	86 through 8F
	C0	C1	C2	C3	C4	C5	C6 through CF
20 × 1 LCD	80	81	82	83	through 93		
	C0	C1	C2	C3	through D3		
20 × 2 LCD	80	81	82	83	through 93		
	C0	C1	C2	C3	through D3		
20 × 4 LCD	80	81	82	83	through 93		
	C0	C1	C2	C3	through D3		
	94	95	96	97	through A7		
	D4	D5	D6	D7	through E7		
40 × 4 LCD	80	81	82	83	through A7		
	C0	C1	C2	C3	through E7		
Note: All data is in hex.							

SENDING COMMANDS AND DATA TO LCDS WITH A TIME DELAY

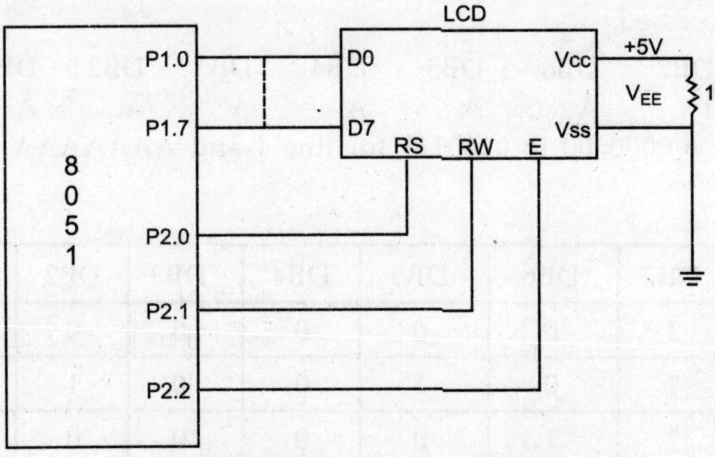

Figure 5.19 LCD-8051 Interfacing

; calls a time delay before sending next data/command

; P1.0-P1.7 are connected to LCD data pins D0-D7

; P2.0 is connected to RS pin of LCD

; P2.1 is connected to R/$\overline{W}$ pin of LCD

; P2.2 is connected to E pin of LCD

```
          ORG
          MOV       A,#38h          ;init. LCD 2 lines, 5 × 7 matrix
          ACALL     LCD_COM         ;call command subroutine
          ACALL     LCD_DELAY       ;give LCD sometime
          MOV       A,#OEh          ;display on, cursor on
          ACALL     LCD_COM         ;call command subroutine
          ACALL     LCD_DELAY       ;give LCD sometime
          MOV       A,#01           ;clear LCD
          ACALL     LCD_COM         ;call command subroutine
          ACALL     LCD_DELAY       ;give LCD sometime
          MOV       A,#06h          ;shift cursor right
          ACALL     LCD_COM         ;call command subroutine
          ACALL     LCD_DELAY       ;give LCD sometime
          MOV       A,#84h          ;cursor at line l,pos. 4
          ACALL     LCD_COM         ;call command subroutine
          ACALL     LCD_DELAY       ;give LCD sometime
          MOV       A,#'N'          ;display letter N
          ACALL     LCD_DATAWRT     ;call display subroutine
          ACALL     LCD_DELAY       ;give LCD sometime
          MOV       A,#'O'          ;display letter O
          ACALL     LCD_DATAWRT     ;call display subroutine
AGAIN: SJMP AGAIN                   ;stay here
LCD_COM:                            ;send command to LCD
          MOV       Pl,A            ;copy reg A to portl
          CLR       P2.0            ;RS=0 for command
          CLR       P2.1            ;R/W=0 for write
          SETB      P2.2            ;E=1 for high pulse
          CLR       P2.2            ;E=0 for H-to-L pulse
          RET                       E=0 for H-to-L pulse
LCD_DATAWRT:                        ;write data to LCD
          MOV       Pl,A            ;copy reg A to port 1
          SETB      P2.0            ;RS=1 for DATA
          CLR       P2.1            ;R/W=0 for write
          SETB      P2.2            ;E=1 for high pulse
          CLR       P2.2            ;E=0 for H to L pulse
          RET
   LCD_DELAY: MOV R3, #50           ;50 or higher for fast CPUs
   HERE2: MOV       ;R4,#255        ;R4 = 255
   HERE: DJNZ R4, HERE              ;stay until R4 becomes 0
   DJNZ R3, HERE2
   RET
   END
```

Sending code or data to the LCD with checking busy flag

```
;Check busy flag before sending data, command to LCD
;P1=data pin
;P2.0 connected to RS_pin
;P2.1 connected to R/ W pin
;P2.2 connected to E pin
    ORG
    MOV         A,#38h              ;init. LCD 2 lines, 5 × 7 matrix
    ACALL       LCD_COMMAND         ;issue command
    MOV         A,#0Eh              ;LCD on, cursor on
    ACALL       LCD_COMMAND         ;issue command
    MOV         A,#01h              ;clear LCD command
    ACALL       LCD_COMMAND         ;issue command
    MOV         A,#06h              ;shift cursor right
    ACALL       LCD_COMMAND         ;issue command
    MOV         A,#86h              ;cursor: line 1, pos. 6
    ACALL       LCD_COMMAND         ;command subroutine
    MOV         A,#'N'              ;display letter N
    ACALL       LCD_DISPLAY
    MOV         A,#'O'              ;display letter O
    ACALL       LCD_DISPLAY
HERE: SJMP HERE                     ;STAY HERE
LCD_COMM.AND: ACALL READY           ;is LCD ready?
    MOV         Pl,A                ;issue command code
    CLR         P2.0                ;RS=0 for command
    CLR         P2.1                ;R/ W =0 to write to LCD
    SETB        P2.2                ;E=1 for H-to-L pulse
    CLR         P2.2                ;E=O,latch in
    RET
LCD_DISPLAY:
    ACALL       READY               ;is LCD ready?
    MOV         Pl,A                ;issue data
    SETB        P2.0                ;RS=1 for data
    CLR         P2.1                ;R/ W =0 to write to LCD
    SETB        P2.2                ;E=1 for H-to-L pulse
    CLR         P2.2                ;E=0, latch in
    RET
PEADY:
    SETB        P1.7                ;make P1.7 input port
```

```
    CLR          P2.0               ;RS=0 access command reg
    SETB         P2.1               ;R/W=1 read command reg
;read command reg and check busy flag
RETURN1:  CLR P2.2                  ;E=1 for H-to-L pulse
    SETB         P2.2               ;E=0 H-to-L pulse
    JB           P1.7, RETURN1      ;stay until busy flag=0
    RET
    END
```

5.6.2 8051: INTERFACING TO THE KEYBOARD

Keyboards and LCDs are the most widely used input/output devices of the 8051. We first discuss keyboard fundamentals, along with key press and key detection mechanisms. Then we show how a keyboard is interfaced to an 8051.

KEYBOARD INTERFACING

At the lowest level, keyboards are organized in a matrix of rows and columns. The CPU accesses both rows and columns through ports; therefore, with two 8-bit ports, an 8 × 8 matrix of keys can be connected to a microprocessor. When a key is pressed, a row and a column make a contact; otherwise, there is no connection between rows and columns.

SCANNING AND IDENTIFYING THE KEY

A 4×4 matrix connected to two ports. The rows are connected to an output port and the columns are connected to an input port. If no key has been pressed, reading the input port will yield 1s for all columns since they are all connected to high (VCC). If all the rows are grounded and a key is pressed, one of the columns will have 0 since the key pressed provides the path to ground. It is the function of the microcontroller to scan the keyboard continuously to detect and identify the key pressed.

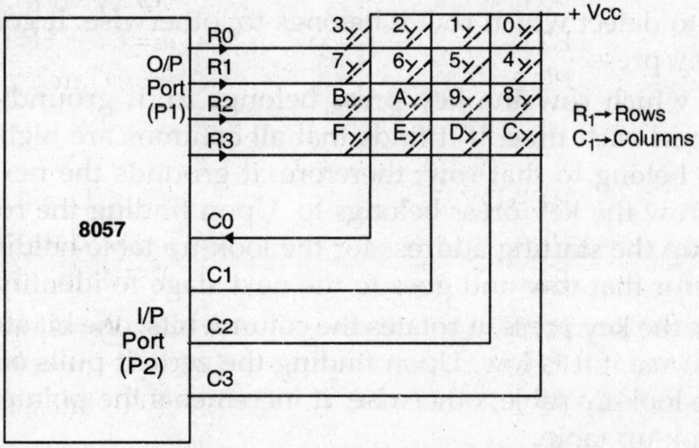

Figure 5.20 4×4 Matrix Keyboard

Ground Rows and Reading the Columns

To detect a pressed key, the microcontroller grounds all rows by providing 0 to the output latch, then it reads the columns. If the data read from the columns is C3–C0 = 1111, no key has been pressed and the process continues until a key press is detected. However, if one of the column bits has a zero, this means that a key press has a occured. For example, if C3—C0 = 1101, this means that a key in the C1 column has been pressed. After a key press is detected, the microcontroller will go through the process of identifying the key. Starting with the top row, the microcontroller grounds it by providing a low to row R0 only; then it reads the columns. If the data read is all 1s, no key in that row is activated and the process is moved to the next row. It grounds the next row, reads the columns, and checks for any zero. This process continues until the row is identified. After identification of the row in which the key has been pressed, the next task is to find out which column the pressed key belongs to. This should be easy since the microcontroller knows at any time which row and column are being accessed.

8051 Assembly language program for detection and identification of key activation. In this program, it is assumed that P1 and P2 are initialized as output and input, respectively. This program have four major stages:

- To make sure that the preceding key has been released, 0s are output to all rows at once, and the column are read and checked repeatedly until all the column are high. When all columns are found to be high, the program waits for a short amount of time before it goes to the next stage of waiting for a key to be pressed.
- To see if any key is pressed, the columns are scanned over and over in an infinite loop until one of them has a 0 on it. Remember that the output latches connected to rows still have their initial zeroes (provided in stage 1), making them grounded. After the key press detection, it waits 20 ms for the bounce and then scans the columns again. This serves two functions: (a) it ensures that the first key press detection was not an erroneous one due to a spike noise, and (b) the 20-ms delay prevents the same key press from being interpreted as a multiple key press. If after the 20-ms delay the key is still pressed, it goes to the next stage to detect which row it belongs to; otherwise, it goes back into the loop to detect a real key press.
- To detect which row the key press belongs to, it grounds one row at a time, reading the columns each time. If it finds that all columns are high, this means that the key press cannot belong to that row; therefore, it grounds the next row and continues until it finds the row the key press belongs to. Upon finding the row that the key press belongs to, it set up the starting address for the look-up table holding the scan codes (or the ASCII value) for that row and goes to the next stage to identify the key.
- To identify the key press, it rotates the column bits, one bit at a time, into the carry flag and checks to see if it is low. Upon finding the zero, it pulls out the ASCII code for that key from the look-up table; otherwise, it increments the pointer to point to the next element of the look-up table.

While the key press detection is standard for all keyboards, the process for determining which key is pressed varies.

There are IC chips such as National Semiconductor's MM74C923 that incorporate key board scanning and decoding all in one chip. Such chips use combinations of counters and logic gates (no microcontroller) to implement the underlying concepts presented in above discussion and below program. The program assumes the system setup as shown in Fig. 5.20.

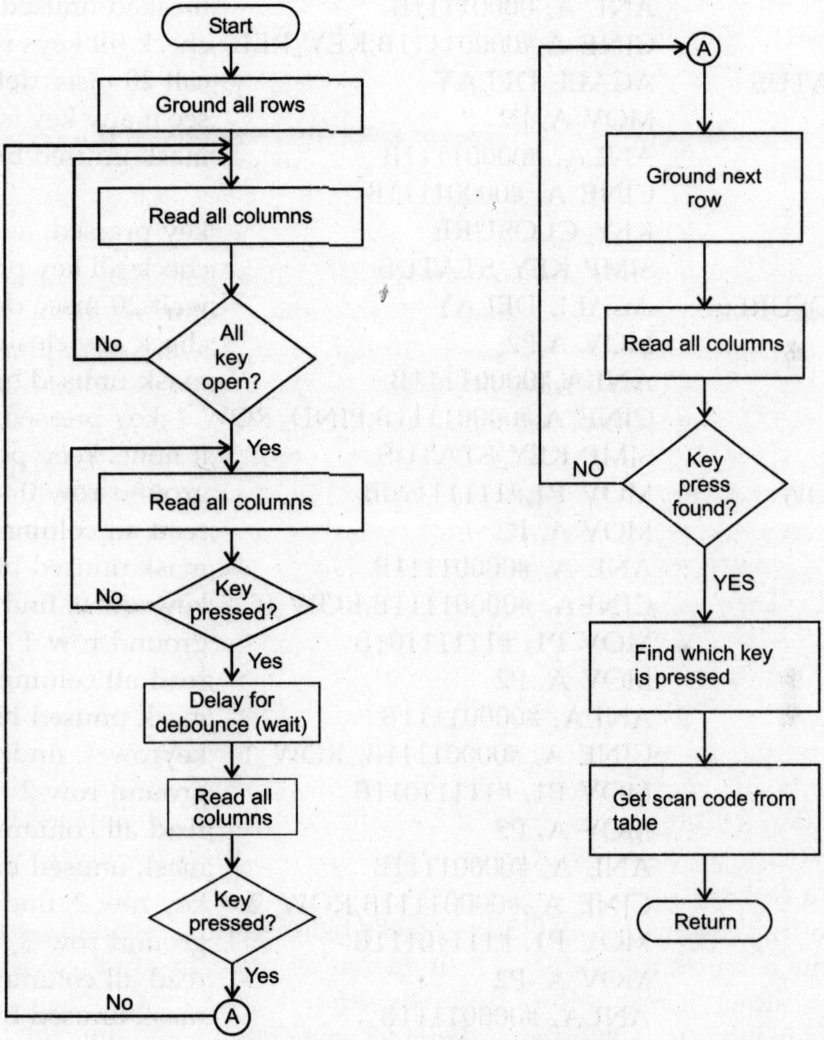

Figure 5.21 Flow chart for keyboard interfacing program

The Fig. 5.21 provides the flowchart of keyboard interfacing procedure for the given program.

```
; Keyboard subroutine. This program sends the ASCII code
; for pressed key to P0.1
; P1.0–P1.3 connected to rows P2.0-P2.3 connected to columns
```

```
              MOV P2, #0FFh                ;make P2 an input port
KEY_REL;      MOV P1, #0                   ;ground all rows at once
              MOV A, P2                    ;read all col. (ensure all keys
                                           open)
              ANL A, 00001111B             ;masked unused bits
              CJNE A,#00001111B,KEY_REL    ;check till keys released
KEY_STATUS:   ACALL DELAY                  ;call 20 msec delay
              MOV A, P2                    ;see if any key is pressed
              ANLA, #00001111B             ;mask unused bits
              CJNE A; #00001111B
              KEY_CLOSURE                  ;key pressed, await closure
              SJMP KEY_STATUS              ;check till key pressed
KEY CLOSURE:  ACALL DELAY                  ;wait 20 msec debounce time
              MOV A,P2                     ;check key closure
              ANLA,#00001111B              ;mask unused,bits
              CJNE A,#00001111B,FIND_ROW   ;key pressed, find row
              SJMP KEY_STATUS              ;if none, keep polling
FIND_ROW:     MOV P1,#11111110B            ;ground row 0
              MOV A, P2                    ;read all columns
              ANL A, #00001111B            ;mask unused bits
              CJNEA, #00001111B,ROW_0      ;key row 0, find the col.
              MOV P1, #11111101B           ;ground row 1
              MOV A, P2                    ;read all columns
              ANLA, #00001111B             ;mask unused bits
              CJNE A, #00001111B, ROW_1    ;keyrow 1, find the col.
              MOV P1, #11111011B           ;ground row 2
              MOV A, P2                    ;read all columns
              ANL A, #00001111B            ;mask unused bits
              CJNE A ,#00001111B,ROW_2     ;key row 2, find the col.
              MOV P1, #11110111B           ;ground row 3
              MOV A, P2                    ;read all columns
              ANLA, #00001111B             ;mask unused bits
              CJNEA, #00001111B,ROW_3      ;keyrow 3, find the col.
              LJMP KEY_STATUS              ;if none, false input, repeat
ROW_0:        MOV DPTR,#KCODE0             ;set DPTR=start of row 0
              SJMP FIND_COL                ;find col. key belongs to
ROW_1:        MOV DPTR, #KCODE1            ;set DPTR=start of row 1
              SJMP FIND_COL                ;find col. key belongs to
ROW_2:        MOV DPTR, #KCODE2            ;set DPTR=start of row 2
              SJMP FIND_COL                ;find col. key belongs to
```

```
ROW_3:          MOV DPTR, #KCODE3       ;set DPTR=start of row 3
FIND_COL:       RRC A                   ;see if any CY bit low
                JNC GET_ASCII           ;if zero, get the ASCII code
                INC DPTR                ;point to next col. address
                SJMP FIND_COL           ;keep searching
GET_ASCII:      CLR A                   ;set A=0 (match is found)
                MOV A, @A+DPTR          ;get ASCII code from table
                MOV P0,A                ;display pressed key
                LJMP KEY_REL
;ASCII LOOK-UP TABLE FOR EACH ROW
                ORG 300H
KCODE0: DB      '0', '1', '2', '3'      ;ROW 0
KCODE1: DB      '4', '5', '6', '7'      ;ROW 1
KCODE2: DB      '8', '9', 'A', 'B'      ;ROW 2
KCODE3: DB      'C', 'D', 'E', 'F'      ;ROW 3
                END
```

5.6.3 INTERFACING DAC & ADC

DIGITAL-TO-ANALOG (DAC) CONVERTER

The digital-to-analog converter (DAC) is a device widely used to convert digital pulses to analog signals. In this section we discuss the basics of interfacing a DAC to the 8051.

The two methods of making the DAC: binary weighted and R/2R ladder. The vast majority of integrated circuit DACs, including the MC1408 (DAC808) used in this section, use the R/2R method since it can achieve a much higher degree of precision. The principle criterion for a DAC is its resolution, which is a function of the number of binary inputs. The common DACs are 8, 10 and 12 bits. The number of data bit inputs decides the resolution of the DAC since the number of analog output levels is equal to 2^n, where n is the number of data bit inputs. Therefore, an 8-input DAC such as the DAC808 provides 256 discrete voltage (or current) levels of output. Similarly, the 12-bit DAC provides 4096 discrete voltage levels.

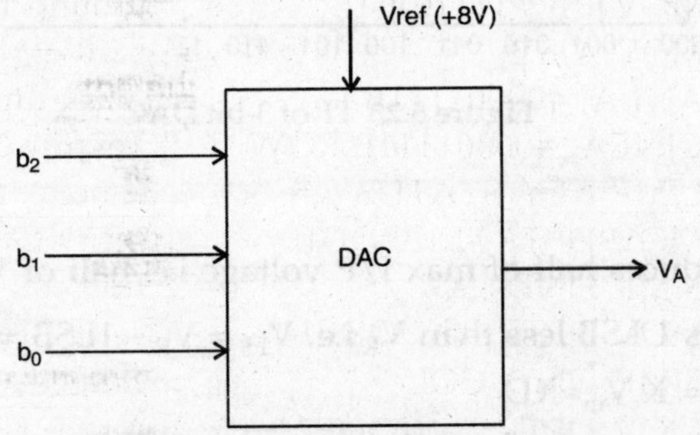

Figure 5.22 Block diagram of DAC

Let i/p range from 0 to 8 V.

It has $2^n = 2^3 = 8$ levels

and $2^n - 1 = 2^3 - 1 = 7$ steps

Since n = 3 the V_{ref} can be divided into 8 equal parts, so a 1 at LSB should produce $\frac{1}{8}$ V_R. So resistive network should be such that the resistance in bit b_0 (or 2^0) position can cause $\frac{1}{8}\times 8 = 1$ V.

Similarly 1 at b1 should cause $2\times\left(\frac{1}{8}V_R\right)$

1 at b2 should cause $2\times\left(2\times\left(\frac{1}{8}V_R\right)\right)$

The TF of 3-bit DAC is shown in Fig. 5.23.

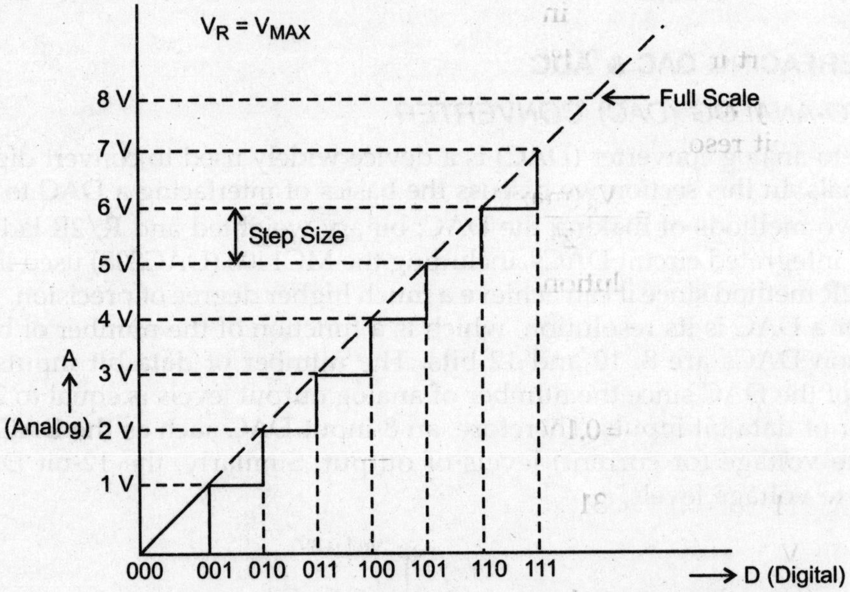

Figure 5.23 TF of 3-bit DAC

From curve note that

(I) A 1 at MSB produces half of max I/P voltage i.e. half of $V_R = \frac{8}{2} = 4$ V.

(II) Full scale O/P is 1 LSB less than V_R i.e. $V_{FS} = V_R - 1LSB = 8 - 1 = 7$ V

(III) $V_o \alpha V_{in}$ i.e. $V_o = K.V_{in} = KD$

where K=1LSB or resolution

(IV) Each successive O/P is $\frac{1}{8}$ V_R higher than the previous.

(V) Slep size is equal to 1 LSB.

DAC PARAMETERS

1. Full Scale O/P: Full scale O/P is the O/P when all the bits of DAC are placed at logic1.

$V_{FS} = K(2^n - 1) = 2^n k - k = V_R - k = V_R - 1\text{LSB}$

2. Resolution: Resolution is the smallest incremental change in O/P voltage as a fraction of the full scale O/P range against the smallest change in I/P.

$$\text{Resolution } K = \frac{V_{FS}}{2^n - 1}$$

$$\text{For } n = 8, 2n - 1 = 255 \text{ so } K = \frac{V_{FS}}{255}$$

It means smallest change in O/P would be $\frac{1}{255\text{th}}$ of the full scale O/P. Hence resolution is 1 part in 255 or 0.4%.

Alternatively no. of bits itself can be defined as resolution. For example an n-bit DAC has an n-bit resolution.

$$\text{Also Resolution} = K = \frac{V_R(\max)}{2^n}$$

Example: Find out resolution and full scale output of 5 bit DAC that produces 0.2 V when I/P is 0010.

Solution: $V_o = KD$

$$K = \frac{V_o}{D} = \frac{0.2}{(0010)_2} = \frac{0.2}{2} = 0.1\ \text{V/LSB}$$

$V_{FS} = K(11111)_2 = 0.1 \times 31$

$V_{FS} = 3.1$ V

Example: Calculate the values of LSB, MSB and full scale O/P voltage for an 8 bit DAC having the range 0 to 10 V.

Solution: $\text{LSB} = \text{Resolution} = \frac{V_R}{2^n} = \frac{10}{256} \cong 39\ \text{mV}$

$$\text{MSB} = \frac{1}{2}V_{\max} = \frac{1}{2}V_R = \frac{1}{2} \times 10 = 5\ \text{V}$$

$V_{FS} = V_R - 1\ \text{LSB} = 10 - 39 \times 10^{-3} = 9.961$ V

3. Linearity: The linearity of DAC is a measure precision with which the linear input-output relationship is satisfied. In a DAC equal increment in numerical value of I/P should result in equal increments in analog O/P.

The linearity error is the difference between the acutual value and expecled value and is generally maintained less than $\frac{1}{2}$ LSB.

4. Accuracy: It is measure of difference between the actual and expected O/P. It is defined as the percentage (%age) of full scale or max O/P voltage. If a DAC have 10 V max O/P voltage and an accuracy of 0.2% then max error = 0.002 × 10 = 20 mV for any O/P voltage.

5. Settling time: Settling time is the time taken by DAC to settle to desired accuracy. The time taken for analog O/P to settle to within $\pm\frac{1}{2}$ LSB of the final value after a change in digital I/P is usually defined as settling time.

The binary weighted DAC is shown in Fig. 5.24.

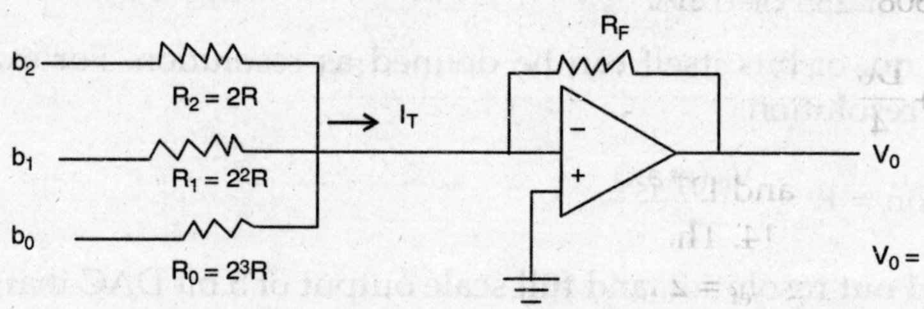

Figure 5.24 3-bit voltage O/P binary weighted DAC

Here $V_o = -I_T R_F$

$$V_o = - I_R R_F \sum_{i=0}^{n-1} \frac{bi}{2^{n-i}}$$

$$V_o = -\frac{V_R}{R} R_F \left(\frac{b_o}{2^n} + \frac{b_1}{2_{n-1}} + - - + \frac{b_{n-1}}{2} \right)$$

In the DAC of Fig. 5.25, the resistive network has value of resistors according to binary weight of digital I/P. The resistive network provide O/P current (I_T) equivalent to digital input and the OP-AMP converts this current into equivalent voltage.

The R/2R ledder DAC is shown in Fig. 5.25.

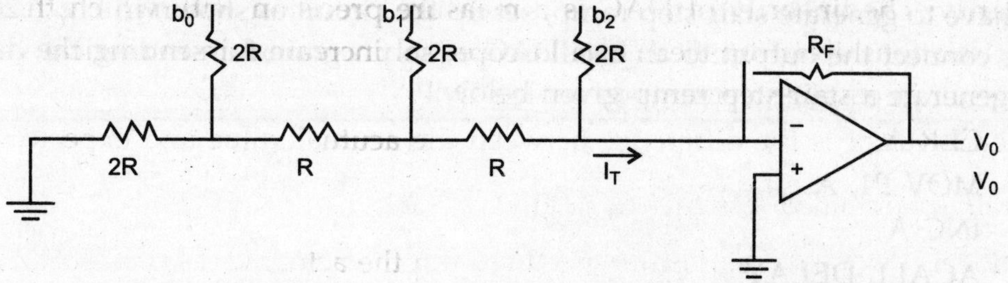

Figure 5.25 3-bit voltage O/P R/2R ladder DAC

In the DAC of Fig. 5.25, the resistive network provide O/P current (I_T) equivalent to digital input and the OP-AMP converts this current into equivalent voltage.

MC1408 DAC (OR DAC 808)

In the MC1408 (DAC808), the digital inputs are converted to current (I_{out}) and by connecting a current to voltage converter to the I_{out} pin, we convert the result to voltage. The total current provided by the Iout pin is a function of the binary numbers at D0–D7 inputs of the DAC808 and the reference current (I_{ref}) and is as follows:

$$I_{out} = I_{ref} \left(\frac{D7}{2} + \frac{D6}{4} + \frac{D5}{8} + \frac{D4}{16} + \frac{D3}{32} + \frac{D2}{64} + \frac{D1}{128} + \frac{D0}{256} \right)$$

Where D0 is the LSB, and D7 is the MSB for the inputs, and I_{ref} is the input current that must be applied to pin 14. The I_{ref} current is generally set to 2.0 mA. The generation of current reference (setting I_{ref} = 2 mA) by using the standard 5 V power supply and 1K, 1.5K ohm standard resistors. Now assuming that I_{ref} = 2mA, if all the inputs to the DAC are high, the maximum output current is 1.99 mA which approximately same as I_{ref}. Thus with R_F= 5 K maximum output voltage = $5 \times 10^3 \times 2 \times 10^{-3}$ = 10 V.

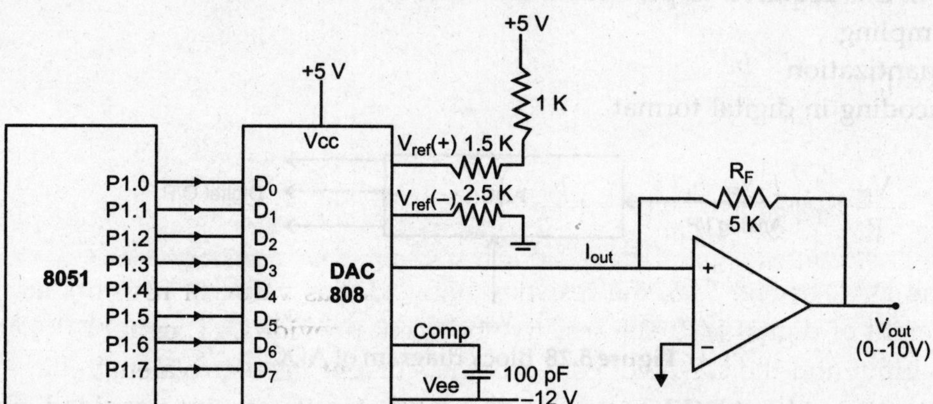

Figure 5.26 8051 connection to DAC

Let we have to generate stair step ramp, set up the circuit as shown in Fig. 5.26 and the output is connect the output to an oscilloscope, so program for sending the data to the DAC to generate a stair-step ramp given below:

```
            CLR A
REPEAT:     MOV P1, A
            INC A
            ACALL DELAY
            SJMP REPEAT
```

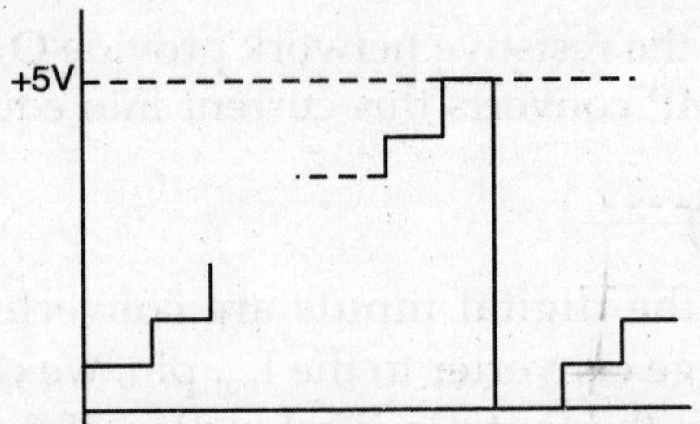

Figure 5.27 Stair-step ramp waveform

The waveform generated (stair-step) is shown in Fig. 5.27.

ANALOG-TO-DIGITAL CONVERTER (ADC)

An ADC is used to convert analog quantity into digital quantity. It is essentially a hardware encoder. The conversion process is the process of dividing (or mapping) the analog input into a set of discrete output levels. It accepts analog I/P with a reference voltage V_R and provides a digital O/P.

An ADC is required to perform three basic functions

- Sampling
- Quantization
- Encoding in digital format

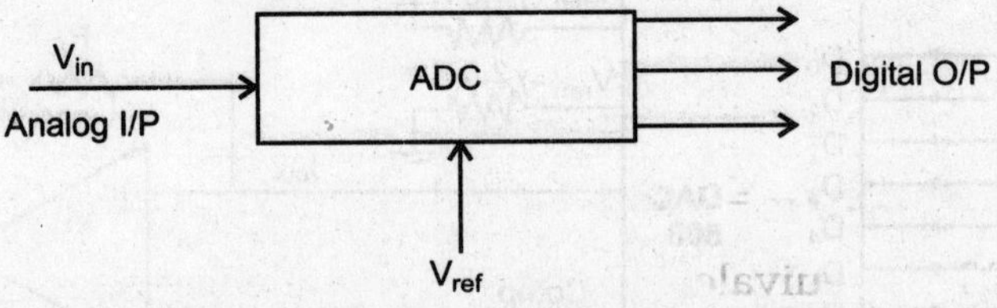

Figure 5.28 Block diagram of ADC

In many popular ADC ICs sample and hold circuits are not provided, so the last two functions are performed by ADCs and an external sampling circuit is to be provided to measure AC or ever varying quantities.

CONVERSION PROCESS

The conversion process is same as weighing anything with a balance scale. Let Wx = 3.25 kg is to be weighed with reference W_R = 1kg. Then no. of reference weights has to be added (one at a time) untill 3 < W_R < 4. But there will an error due to unavailability of smaller reference weights. This is called quantization error in an ADC. If smaller values of reference weights are used more accurate measurements can be achieved.

TF of an ideal ADC is shown in Fig. 5.29. It has an staircase waveform. The size of step in transfer function is called quantum size "Q" or step size Q.

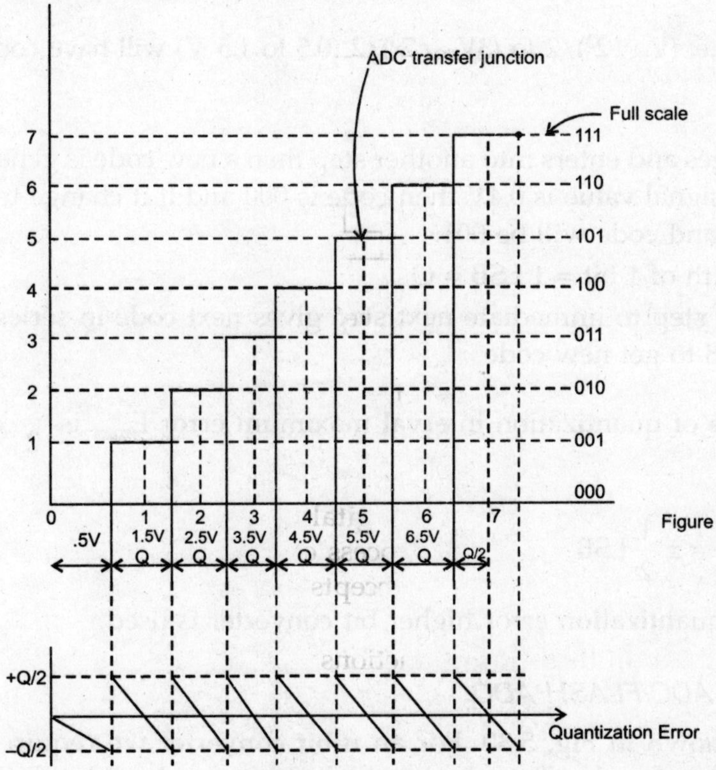

Figure 5.29 (a): TF

Figure 5.29 (b): Quantization Error

Figure 5.29 Transfer function of an Ideal ADC

For an n-bit converter

$$Q = \frac{V_{FS}}{2^n - 1} \cong \frac{V_{FS}}{2^n} \quad \text{where } V_{FS} = \text{Full scale voltage}$$

One step in ADC TF is equivalent to one unit of reference weight W_R. V_{FS} is maximum weight that can be measured.

In the waveform 3-bit ADC is considered. On vertical axis 8 discrete O/P levels are defined and represented by set of 3-bit binary number (000 to 111). The analog signal is represented at horizontal axis. The analog voltage is divided into quanta (i.e. quantized) at decision levels 0.5 V, 1.5 V, 2.5 V etc. at horizontal axis. The decision levels are located at Q/2, 3Q/2, 5Q/2 etc.

For example, for V_{FS} = 8 V, Q = 1 V

$$\text{1st decision level} = \frac{Q}{2} = 0.5 \text{ V}$$

$$\text{2nd decision level} = \frac{3Q}{2} = 1.5 \text{ V and so on.}$$

Thus any voltage ranging between 0 to Q/2V (0 to 0.5V) will have code 000. Any voltage ranging between $\frac{Q}{2}$ to $\frac{3Q}{2}$ i.e. $(V_{FS}/2^3)/2$ to $(3V_{FS}/2^3)/2$ (0.5 to 1.5 V) will have code 001 and so on.

If the signal value changes and enters into another step then a new code is generated for the signal. For example, signal value is 0.4V then code is 000 and if it change to 1.2V then it enters into next step and code will be 001.

Hence 1 step size = width of 1 bit = 1 LSB = Q

Since moving from one step to immediate next step gives next code in series, it is equivalent to add 1bit to LSB to get new code.

On either side of centre of quantization interval maximum error E_{max} is $\frac{1}{2}$ of the interval so

$$E_{max} = \pm \frac{V_{FS}}{2^n} \frac{1}{2} = \pm \frac{Q}{2} = \pm \frac{1}{2} \text{ LSB}$$

In order to reduce the quantization error higher bit converter is used.

PARALLEL COMPARATOR ADC/FLASH ADC

A 3-bit A/D converter is shown in Fig. 5.30. For an n-bit converter we require 2^n-1 Comparators and a resistive networks. The comparator stage provides 7-bit O/P and encoder circuit gives equivalent 3-bit O/P.

The resistive network provide the fraction of reference voltage required for comparision or provides the decision level.

Fraction $V_{R1} = \frac{1}{14} V_R$ is first decision level. If the analog voltage $V_a > V_{R1}$ then comparator O/P $C_1 = 1$. Similarly decisions are made for all the decision or reference level.

$$V_{R1} = \frac{V_{FS}}{2(2^n - 1)} = \frac{V_R}{2(2^3 - 1)} = \frac{V_R}{14}$$

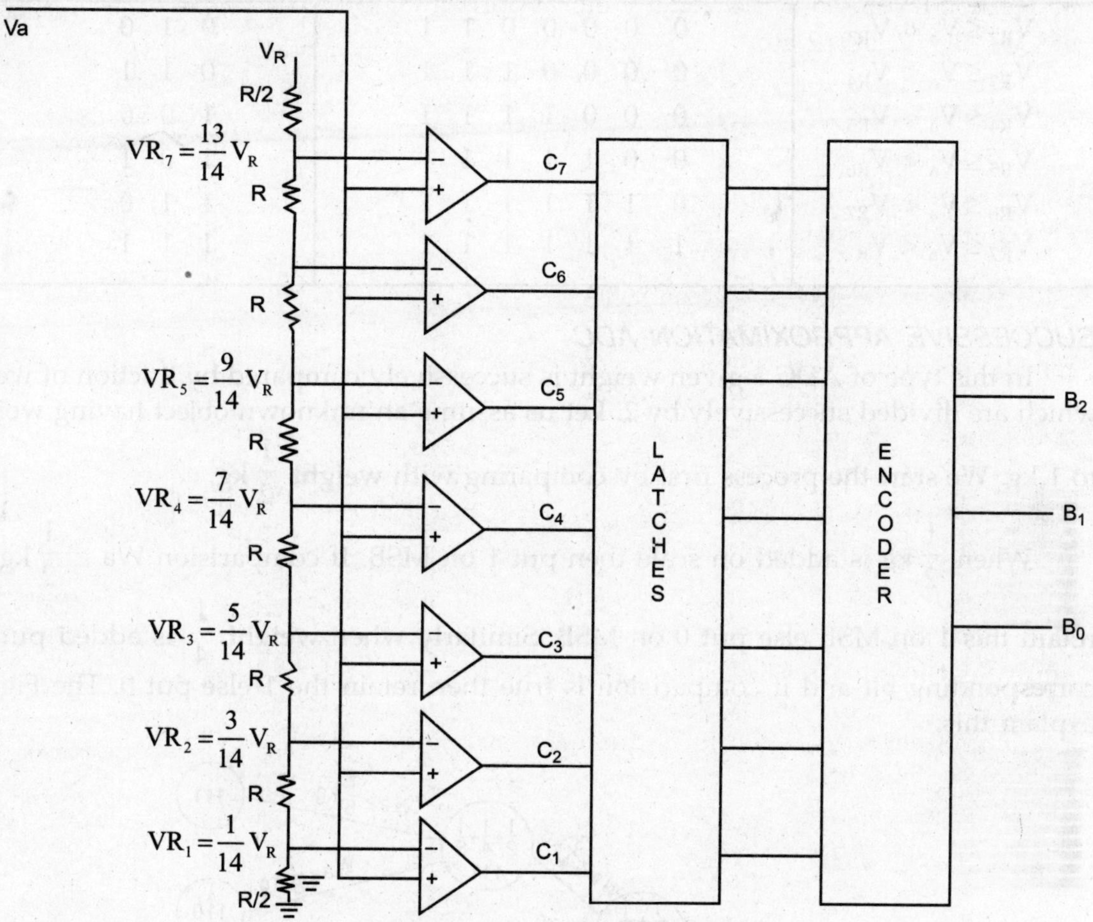

Figure 5.30 3-bit FLASH ADC

Similarly $VR_2 = \dfrac{3V_{FS}}{2(2^n - 1)} = \dfrac{3V_R}{14}$

The value of V_{R1}, V_{R2}, ------ are calculated as per TF of an ideal ADC

The flash ADC output is given in the following table:

Analog I/P	Comparator O/P	Binary O/P
V_a	$C_7\ C_6\ C_5\ C_4\ C_3\ C_2\ C_1$	$B_2\ B_1\ B_0$
$0 \le V_a < V_{R1}$	0 0 0 0 0 0 0	0 0 0
$V_{R1} \le V_a < V_{R2}$	0 0 0 0 0 0 1	0 0 1

(Contd...)

$V_{R2} \le V_a < V_{R3}$	0 0 0 0 0 1 1	0 1 0
$V_{R3} \le V_a < V_{R4}$	0 0 0 0 1 1 1	0 1 1
$V_{R4} \le V_a < V_{R5}$	0 0 0 1 1 1 1	1 0 0
$V_{R5} \le V_a < V_{R6}$	0 0 1 1 1 1 1	1 0 1
$V_{R6} \le V_a < V_{R7}$	0 1 1 1 1 1 1	1 1 0
$V_{R7} \le V_a < V_R$	1 1 1 1 1 1 1	1 1 1

SUCCESSIVE APPROXIMATION ADC

In this type of ADC a given weight is successively compared by fraction of weights which are divided successively by 2. Let us assume an unknown object having weight 0 to 1 kg. We start the process first by comparing with weight $\frac{1}{2}$ kg.

When $\frac{1}{2}$ kg is added on scale then put 1 on MSB. If comparision Wa $\geq \frac{1}{2}$ kg then retain this 1 on MSB else put 0 on MSB. Similarly when weight $\frac{1}{4}$ is added put 1 on corresponding bit and if comparision is true then retain the 1 else put 0. The Fig. 5.31 explain this.

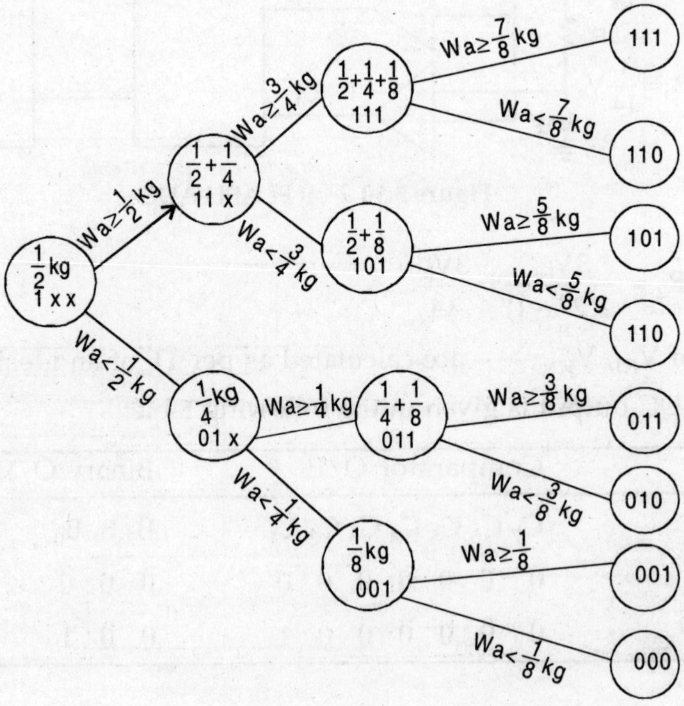

Figure 5.31 3-bit successive approximation ADC

From Fig. 5.31, we see that whenever a weight is added a 1 is placed on the corresponding bit. If after comparision the weight is removed this 1 is replaced by 0.

CALCULATION OF O/P

In this ADC the width of LSB will be $\frac{1}{2^3}$ i.e. LSB $= \frac{1}{8}$kg . It means adding $\frac{1}{8}$kg to scale equivalent to put 1 at LSB. Similarly adding $\frac{1}{2}$ to scale is equivalent to put 1 at MSB.

If binary O/P is 101 then measured weight

$$W_a = 1 \times \frac{1}{2} + 0 \times \frac{1}{4} + 1 \times \frac{1}{8} = \frac{5}{8} \text{kg}$$

So binary 101 = $\frac{5}{8}$ kg

Similary for binary 100

$$W_a = 1 \times \frac{1}{2} + 0 \times \frac{1}{4} + 0 \times \frac{1}{8} = \frac{1}{2} \text{kg}$$

and for binary 011

$$W_a = 0 \times \frac{1}{2} + 1 \times \frac{1}{4} + 1 \times \frac{1}{8} = \frac{3}{8} \text{kg}$$

The block diagram of successive approximation ADC is shown in Fig. 5.32.

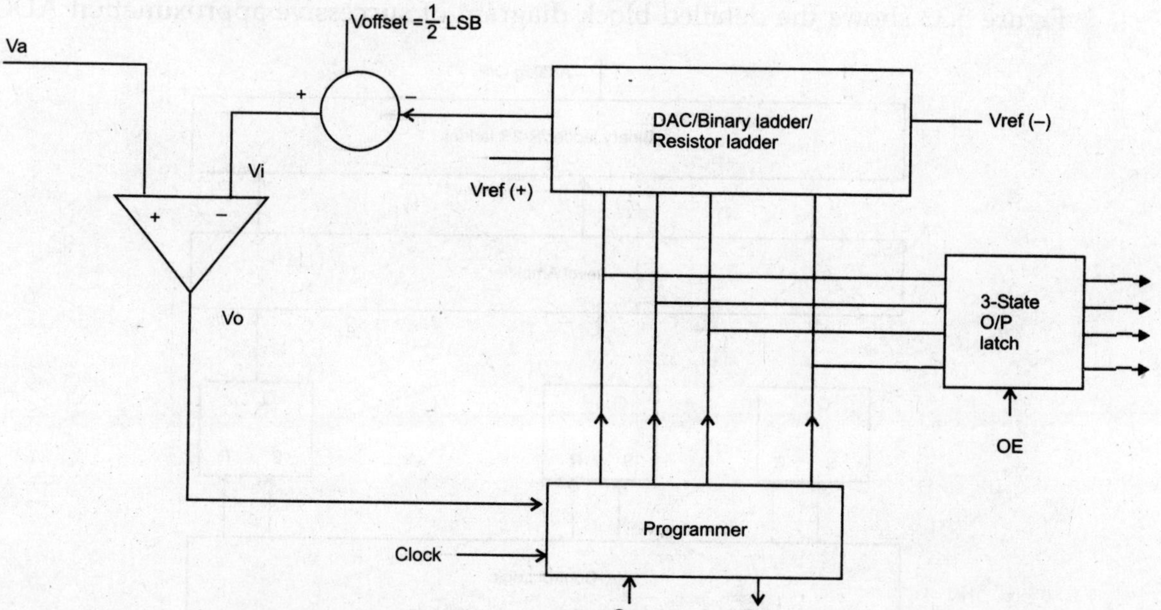

Figure 5.32 Block diagram of successive approximation ADC

The comparator serves the function of scale and its O/P is fed to programmer to set or reset the bits at the output of programmer. The O/P of programmer will change only at arrival of clock pulse. The DAC accepts the digital O/P of the programmer and converts it into the equivalent voltage. The offset voltage is subtracted from the O/P of the DAC and the resultant is applied to inverting input of OP-AMP. The unknown voltage is applied at non inverting I/P of op-amp.

As soon as SOC is applied the programmer is reset i.e. all the bits of programmer are set to 0. On the arrival of 1st clock pulse MSB of the programmer is set to 1, and the data is applied to DAC. DAC produces equivalent analog voltage which compared to the unknown I/P after offset is subtracted from DAC O/P. If $V_a > V_1$, comparator voltage V_0 goes HIGH and sets the next bit of the programmer to 1. If $V_a < V_i$ the O/P of comparator goes LOW which sets the MSB of programmer to 0 and sets the next bit to 1 for next successive approximation. Thus a 1 is tried at each bit of DAC untill the binary equivalent of analog voltage is obtained. For an N-bit converter, N clock pulses are required and hence it is slower than flash ADCs. As soon as conversion is completed EOC signal goes HIGH. To read the data 3-state O/P latches must be enabled by providing a HIGH on OE signal.

Note 1: Here the OP-AMP is used as comparator, which compares voltage present at its input terminals. If the voltage at noninverting I/P is higher than the voltage at inverting I/P then O/P of comparator is HIGH otherwise it goes LOW.

2: The offset adjustment is to tilt the scale towards unknown voltage; To do this we must add the offset from the O/P of DAC (i.e. subtracted from known weight side) to get the equivalent effect.

Figure 5.33 shows the detailed block diagram of successive approximation ADC

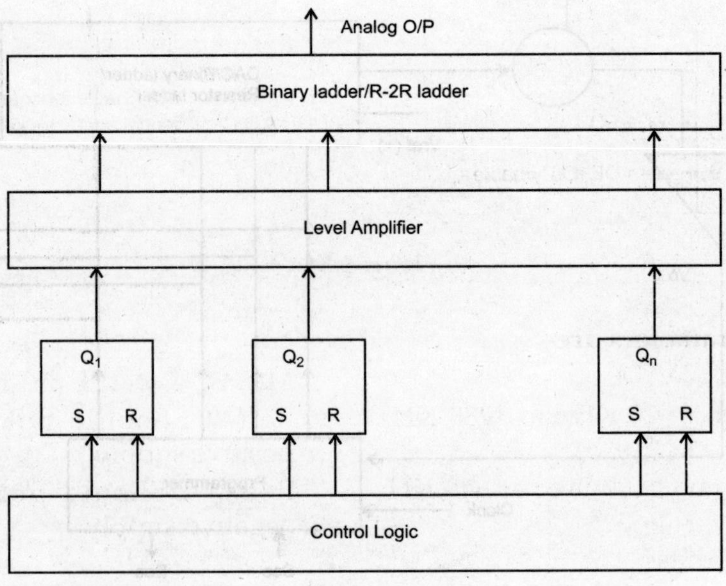

Figure 5.33 Detailed block diagram of successive approximation ADC

ADC INTERFACE

Earlier we have discussed two type of ADC, the Flash ADC and successive approximation ADC-For the purpose of measurement and instrumentation successive approximation ADCs can easily be used under the control of micro controller. Here in particular we take ADC 0808/0809 an 8-bit, 8 channel successive approximation ADC of National and semiconductor make. This is a monolithic CMOS device that does not require external full scale and zero scale adjustments.

Figure 5.34 below shown are pin diagram and timing diagram of ADC 0808/0809.

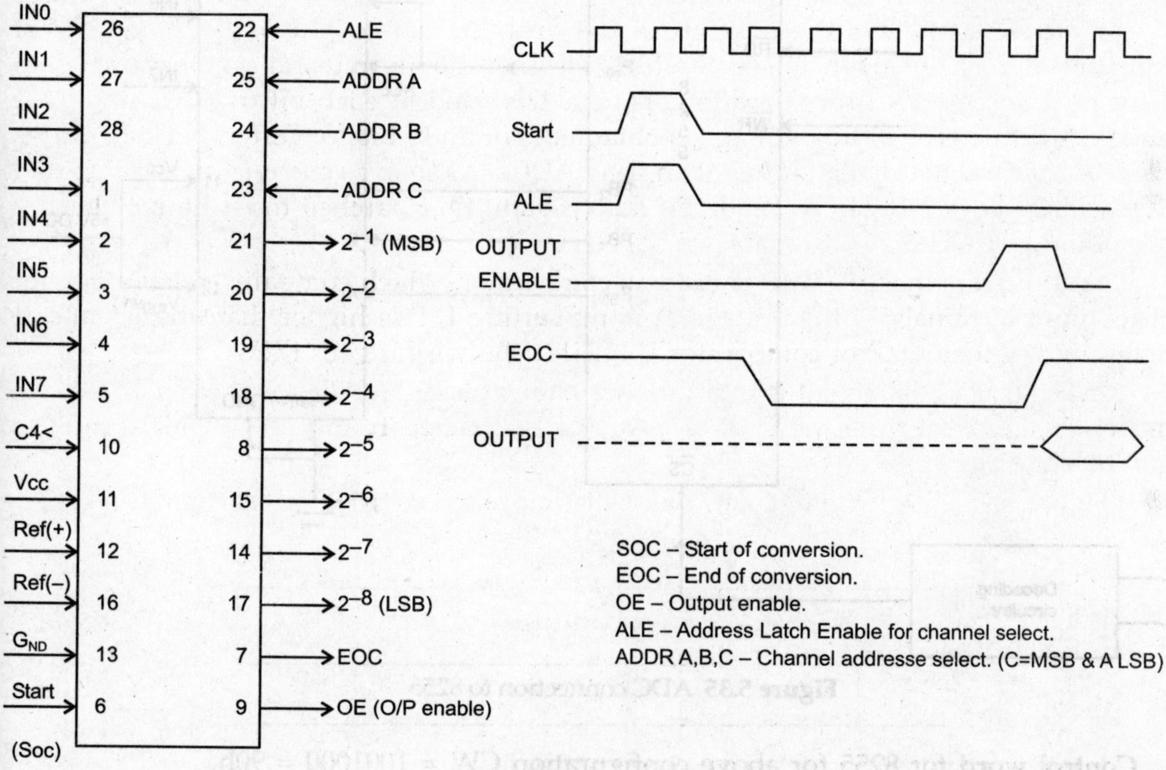

Figure 5.34

Some critical parameters are–

Supply (Vcc) : 5V DC.

Clock frequency: 10 KHz to 1280 KHz

Conversion time : 100 µsec at 640 KHz

Resolution : 8-bits

Error : ± 1-bit

Max SOC & ALE pulse with : 100 µsec

Ref(+) : Should not be more than positive supply

Ref(–) : Should not be less than negative supply

The below figure (Fig. 5.35) shows interfacing of ADC 0808/0809 to microcontroller through 8255.

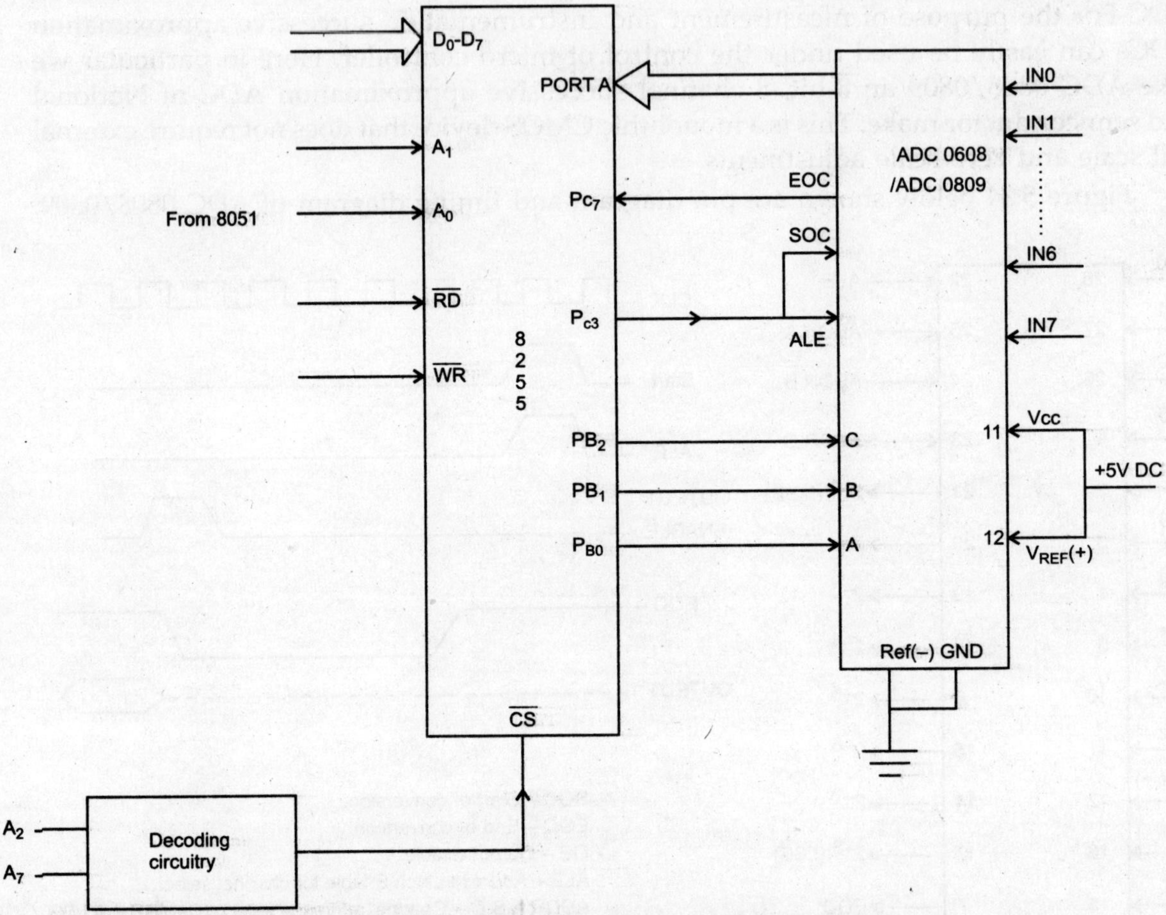

Figure 5.35 ADC connection to 8255

Control word for 8255 for above configuration CW = 1001000 = 90h.

Data table for above configuration for digital output for a given analog input for 0 to 5V analog input.

Analog input voltage (mV)	Digital O/P of ADC (in hex)
0	00
1	34
2	6D
3	9A
4	CE
5	FF

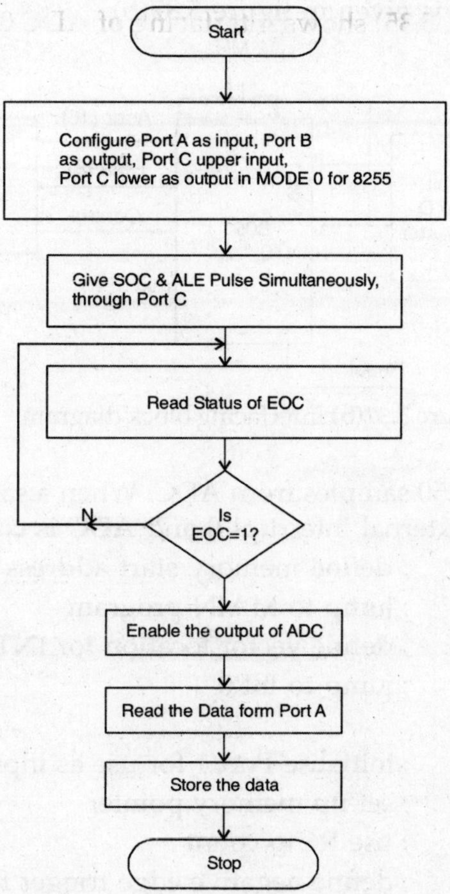

Figure 5.36 Flowchart for ADC interface

The flowchart of Fig. 5.36 show ADC interfacing. On the basis of this flowchart one can write program (ALP) for 8051. It is left as an excercise for reader.

Example: A simple 8-bit analog to digital converter device as shown in Fig. 5.37(a) is to be interfaced to an 8051 microcontroller. The READY line goes low when conversion data is available. The READY line should be used to interrupt the 8051 microcontroller.

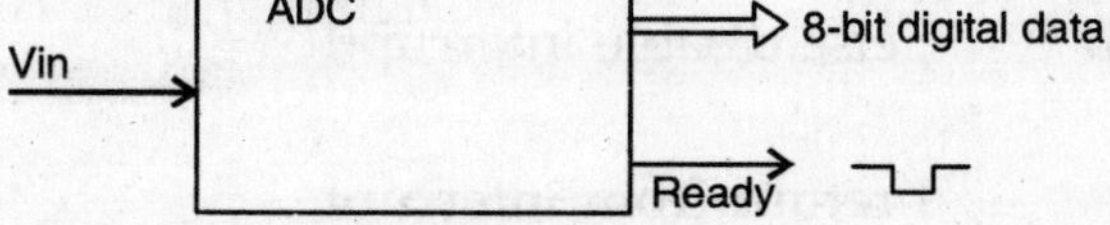

Figure 5.37 (a)

Write an ALP which will capture 250 data samples from the A/D converter and store this data in external data memory. The program is to be interrupt driven.

Solution: Interfacing of ADC is given in figure 5.37(b)

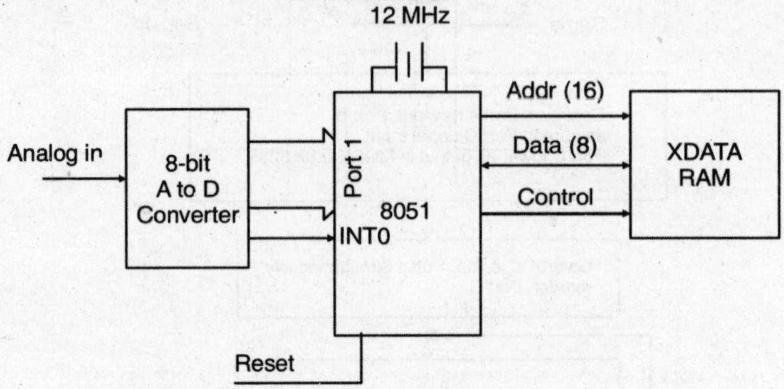

Figure 5.37(b) Interfacing block diagram

The given ALP capture 250 samples from ADC. When a sample is ready the 8051 is interrupted. This ALP uses External interrupt 0 and ADC is connected to Port 1.

```
    ORG 0000h                 ; define memory start address 0000h
    LJMP MAIN                 ; jump to MAIN program
    ORG 0003h                 ; define vector location for INT0
    LJMP ISR0                 ; jump to ISR0
MAIN:
    MOV P1, #0FFh             ; initialise Port 1 for use as input
    MOV DPTR, #2000h          ; set up memory pointer
    MOV R6, #250d             ; use R6 to count
    SETB IT0                  ; define negative edge trigger for int 0
    MOV IE, #10000001b        ; enable Interrupt 0
LOOP:
    LJMP LOOP                 ; just loop around!
ISR0:
    MOV A, P1                 ; read the ADC
    MOVX @DPTR, A             ; save to memory location
    INC DPTR                  ; increment memory pointer
        R6, AGAIN             ; decrement R6 count: if not 0 go again
    MOV IE, #00000000b        ; else disable interrupt!
AGAIN:
    RETI                      ; return from interrupt
```

5.6.4 SEVEN SEGMENT DISPLAY INTERFACING

The LEDs can be used to make 7-segment display digit. This is a very popular alphanumeric display. The block diagram is shown in Fig. 5.38. As shown, actually there are 8-display segments, but first seven segments are

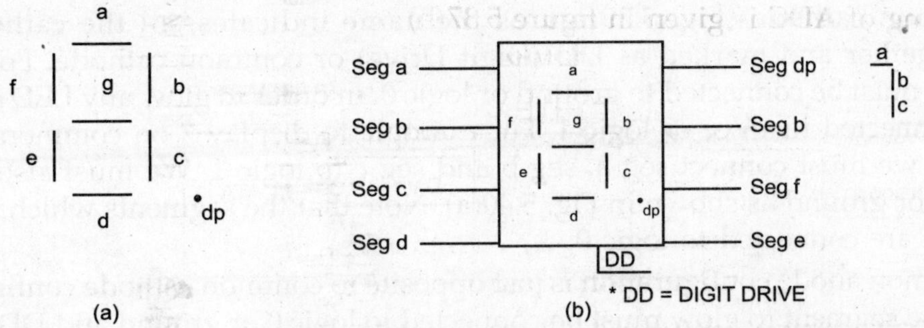

Figure 5.38 Construction of 7-seg

used to display a character and hence the name 7-seg. The 8th segment named dp is used to diaplay a decimal point. Internally there is an LED corresponding to each of segments. Whenever LED is turned ON the corresponding segment glows. Thus in order to display a character we must find which segments to glow and which not to glow. For example to display 7, segments a, b, and c should be turned on and rest of the segments should be turned OFF. The resulting display is shown in Fig. 5.38(c). The segment connection is brought out as shown in Fig. 5.38(b). On these pins logic levels to turn ON or turn OFF, are applied. Earlier shown that there may be two types of LED connections. One is in which logic 1 turns ON the LED and the other is in which logic 0 turns ON the LED. Depending upon these two facts we have two types of 7-segment configuration, namely common cathode and common anode display as show below in Fig. 5.39.

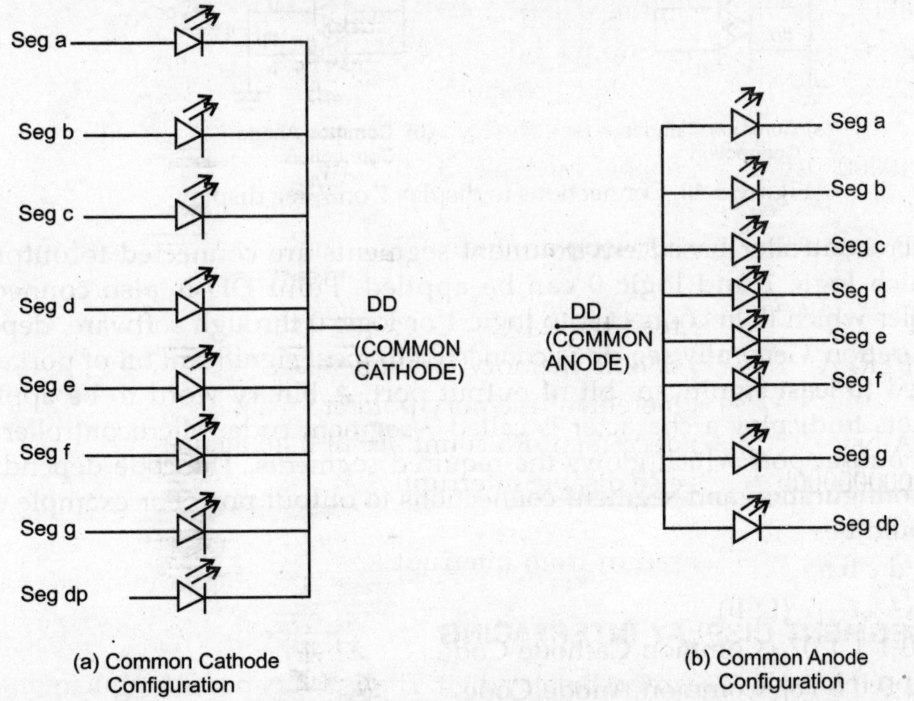

Figure 5.39 7-Segment configuration

In common cathode (Fig. 5.39(a)), as the name indicates, all the cathodes are connected together and marked as DD (Digit Drive) or common cathode. For proper operation DD must be connected to ground or logic 0. In order to glow any LED segment, it must be connected to +Vcc or logic 1. For example to display 7 on common cathode configuration we must connect seg a, seg b and seg c to logic 1. We must also connect DD to logic 0 or ground as shown in Fig. 5.40(a). Note that the segments which are to be switched OFF are connected to logic 0.

The common anode configuration is just opposite to common cathode configuration. In this case, the segment to glow must be connected to logic 0 or ground and DD must be connected to logic 1 or +Vcc. Connections to display 7 on common anode configuration is shown in Fig. 5.40(b).

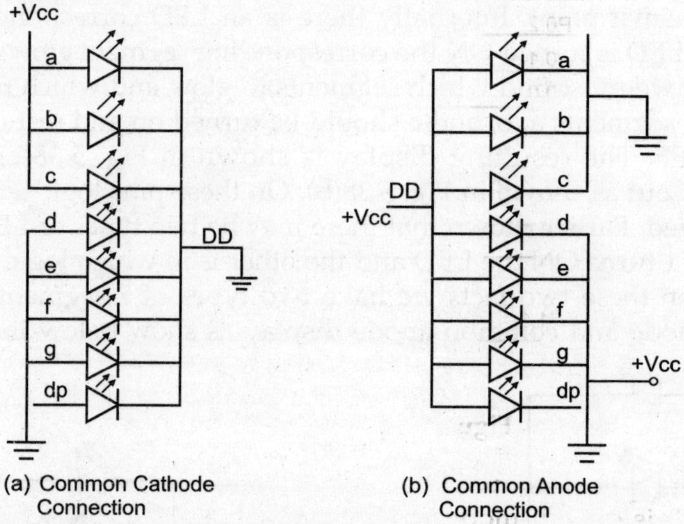

Figure 5.40 Connections to display 7 on 7-seg display

In a microcontroller based environment segments are connected to output port through which logic 1 and logic 0 can be applied. Point DD is also connected to microcontroller which then connect it to logic 1 or logic 0 through software, depending upon configuration. Generally seg dp is connected to most significant bit of port and seg a is connected to least significant bit of output port. A binary word to be applied on segment inputs to display a character is called 7-segment code. Microcontroller writes this code on output port which glows the required segments. The code depends upon the display configuration and segment connections to output port. For example code to display 7 would be.

dp g f e d c b a
(MSB) (LSB)
0 0 0 0 0 1 1 1 07_H Common Cathode Code
1 1 1 1 1 0 0 0 $F8_H$ Common Anode Code

Following example will demonstrate interface of 7-segment display device.

Example: Inter face two common cathode 7-segment display digits to 8051 and display EC continuously on it.

Solution: Below Fig. 5.41 shows connections between 8051 and 7-segments.

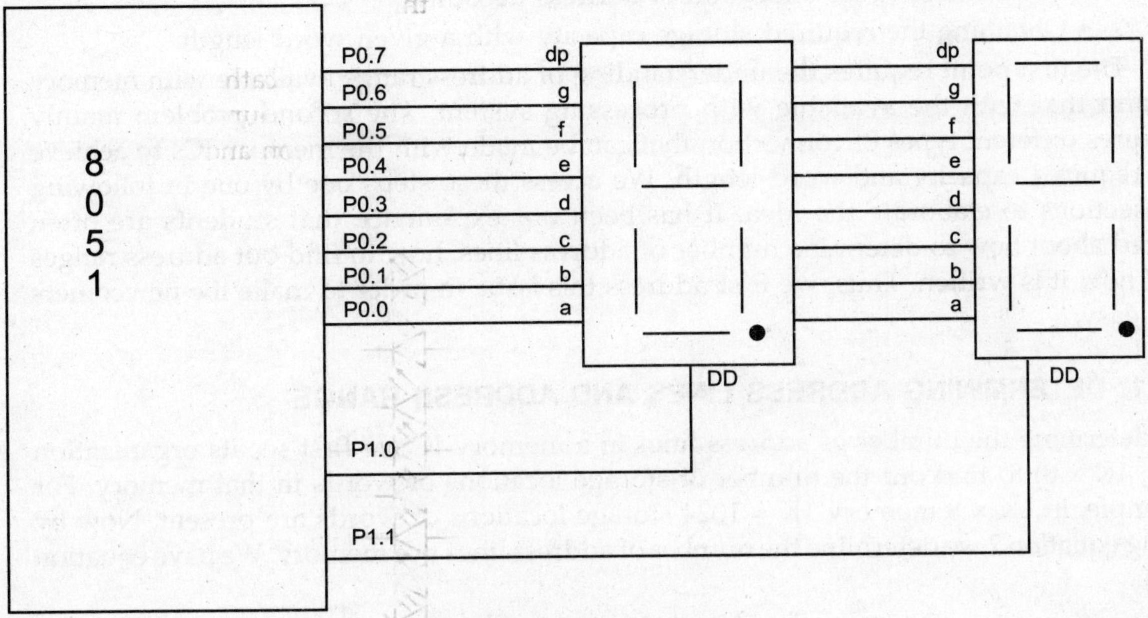

Figure 5.41 Segment interface

Here port 0 and port 1 are used for interfacing and are required to be configured as output port (which is default mode in 8051). Below are 7 Segments codes.

Common Cathode Codes for EC

dp g f e d c b a

0 1 1 1 1 0 0 1 = 79_H Code for "E"

0 0 1 1 1 0 0 1 = 39_H Code for "C"

Below is the program to display EC continuously.

```
REPT:   MOV A, #79h     ; Load 7-seg code of E into A.
        MOV PO, A       ; Out code of E on port 0.
        MOV A, #FEh     ; Word make P1.0=0, all others HIGH.
        MOV P1, A       ; Make P1.0=0 or DD of 1st 7-segment to ground.
        MOV A, #39h     ; Load 7-segment Code of C into A.
        MOV P0, A       ; Out code of C on port 0.
        MOV A, #FDh     ; Word to make P1.1=0, and all others HIGH.
        MOV P1, A       ; Make P1.1=0 or DD of 2nd 7-segment to ground
        AJMP REPT       ; Repeat the process continuously.
```

5.7 DESIGN EXAMPLE OF MEMORY SYSTEM (MEMORY INTERFACING)

A design engineer is suppose to design a memory system that meets number of required storage words and the word length with the available resources. The memory system design mainly involves the two things:

- The address space allocation or address decoding.
- Obtaining the required storage capacity with a given word length.

The first point requires the understanding of address range available with memory IC and that with the available with processing system. The second problem mainly requires different types of connection that can be made with the memory ICs to achieve the required capacity and word length. We access these steps one by one in following subsections to elaborate the idea. It has been our experience that students are often feared about how to determine number of address lines, how to find out address ranges and how it is written. Thus, we first address this issue in order to make the newcomers feel easy.

5.7.1 DETERMINING ADDRESS LINES AND ADDRESS RANGE

To determine the number of address lines in a memory IC we first see its organization (e.g. 1K × 8) to find out the number of storage locations or words in that memory. For example, in 1K × 8 memory 1K = 1024 storage locations or words are present. Now by using equation 2 we determine the number of address lines in a memory. We have equation 2 as

$$2^n \geq \textit{Number of Storage Locations}$$

where n = number of address lines and is always integer.

Address bits ⟶	A_9	A_8	A_7	A_6	A_5	A_4	A_3	A_2	A_1	A_0	*Address In Hex*
Starting Address	0	0	0	0	0	0	0	0	0	0	000_H
Ending Address	1	1	1	1	1	1	1	1	1	1	$3FF_H$

Figure 5.42 Address Bit Map or Address Range for 1K × 8 Memory

So for 1K × 8 memory $2^n \geq 1K = 1024$ results in $n = 10$. i.e. it have 10 address lines. The address bits are written as A_0, A_1... A_{n-1} i.e., for $n = 10$ they are labelled as A_0, A_1... A_9. To determine the address range, we use the fact that addresses are specified as binary bit and each binary bit can have max change from 0 to 1. Thus to determine range we consider this max change for address bits at a time as shown in Fig. 5.42 for 1K × 8 memory. While writing the memory addresses the usual way is to write in hexadecimal instead of binary for the sake of easiness.

Thus the address ranges from 000_H to $3FF_H$ for a 1K × 8 memory. The bitwise representation of memory address as shown in Fig. 5.42 is called as *Address Bit Map.* We will use such type of bit maps in designing problems. From the above *we can conclude that adding* $3FF_H$ *to the initial address will give the last address of 1K memory locations.* The same can be said alternately, that by changing the 10 address bits we traverse through any of the 1K address location.

5.7.2 PARALLEL AND SERIES CONNECTIONS OF MEMORY

In this subsection, we are concerned with how connect more than one memory ICs to get the desired word length and desired number of address location. In general, we can connect the memory in three different configurations. They are:

- Parallel connection
- Series connection
- Series-parallel connection.

The *parallel connection* of memory ICs are used when we need to increase the word length while keeping the address location same. In this case the address lines and control signals are tied together by forming wired-OR and data lines from all the ICs are taken at the output to provide desired word length. Let we have two ICs organized as 1K × 4 and we need a memory of 1K × 8. A parallel connection shown in Fig. 5.43 can solve this issue.

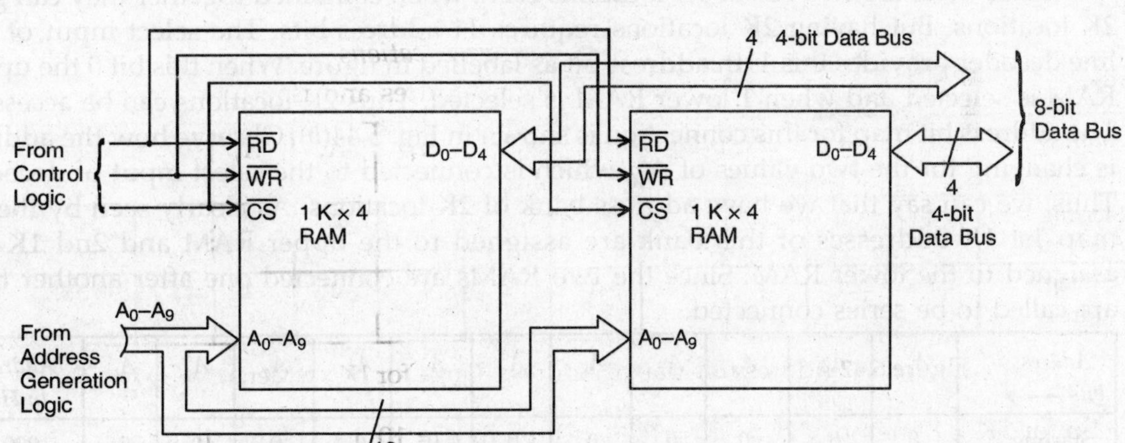

Figure 5.43 Parallel connection of 1024 × 4 RAMS to obtain 1024 × 8 RAM

Observe the figure carefully and notice that 4-bit data bus from two ICs are taken at the output in parallel giving a total of 8-bit data bus, that why it is called parallel connection. Any group of the four bits can be defined least significant or most significant.

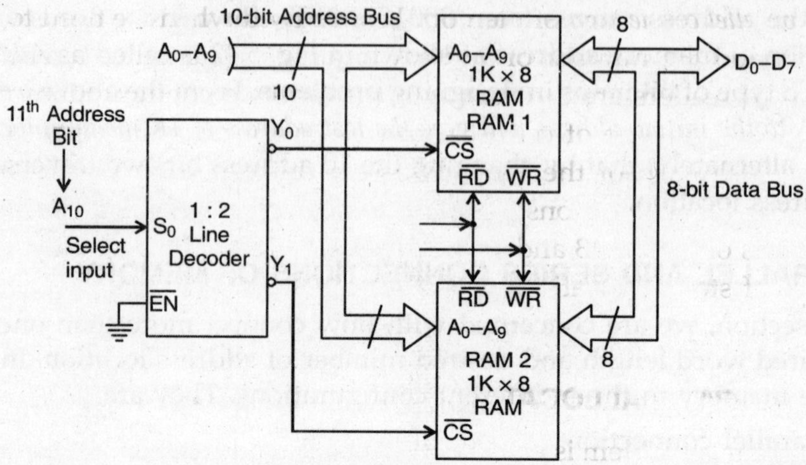

Figure 5.44 (a) Series connection of two 1K × 8 RAM to obtain 0K × 8 RAM

The *series connection* of memory ICs are used when we need to increase the address location while keeping the word length same. In this case the address lines, data lines and control signals are all tied together by forming wired-OR. A decoder can then be used to select one of the ICs. This provides the desired numbers of address locations. Let we have two ICs organized as 1K × 8 and we need a memory of 2K × 8. A series connection shown in Fig. 11.44(*a*) can solve this issue.

Since there are two ICs of 1K locations each, when combined together they can give 2K locations. But having 2K locations requires 11-address bits. The select input of 2:1 line decoder provides this 11th address bit as labelled in figure. When this bit 0 the upper RAM is selected and when 1 lower RAM is selected. Thus 2K locations can be accessed. The address bit map for this connection is shown in Fig. 5.44(*b*). Observe how the address is changing for the two values of A_{10} which is connected to the select input of decoder. Thus, we can say that we have address bank of 2K locations. As clearly seen by the bit map 1st 1K addresses of this bank are assigned to the upper RAM and 2nd 1K are assigned to the lower RAM. Since the two RAMs are connected one after another they are called to be series connected.

Address bits →	A_{10}	A_9	A_8	A_7	A_6	A_5	A_4	A_3	A_2	A_1	A_0	*Address In Hex*
Starting Address	0	0	0	0	0	0	0	0	0	0	0	000_H
Ending Address	0	1	1	1	1	1	1	1	1	1	1	$3FF_H$
Starting Address	1	0	0	0	0	0	0	0	0	0	0	400_H
Ending Address	1	1	1	1	1	1	1	1	1	1	1	$7FF_H$

Figure 5.44 (b) Address Bit Map or Address Range for 1K × 8 Memory

The *series-parallel connection* of memory ICs are used when we need to increase both the word length and the number of address locations. This is the combination of first two connections. If readers are through with the first two configurations this can easily be understood. For this type of connection, we can consider the connection shown in Fig. 5.43(*a*) in which each of the 1K × 8 ICs are derived from Fig. 5.44. Readers are instructed to draw the connections to obtain a memory of 2K × 8 by using the 4-ICs of 1K × 4 on the basis of Figs. 5.43 and 5.43(*a*). In this fashion, the desired word length and desired number of storage locations can be obtained. In fact, it is the connection often required.

5.7.3 ADDRESS SPACE ALLOCATION—THE ADDRESS DECODING

The address-decoding problem is associated with what addresses to be assigned to which memory devices from entire address space available, and what exactly should be the scheme to assign it. In nutshell it is the problem of memory address allocation. In a general microprocessor system the number of address lines are large allowing it to access large amount of memory. Whereas the memory ICs available may be of smaller storage capacities i.e. they can process smaller number of address lines. Now the problem could be which of the ICs are to be given which address. In fact, the problem can be solved by careful analysis of requirement and applying the appropriate decoding scheme.

There are two types of decoding schemes, *Exhaustive Decoding* and *Partial Decoding*. In the exhaustive or fully decoded system all the address lines of processor must be decoded. In case of partial decoding scheme all the address lines of processor are not decoded. But in this case, the addresses may not be unique and more than one address can be assigned to same memory word.

To understand it let us consider a residential colony in which house numbers can be a 4-digit numbers and any of the house can be allotted a number between 0000 to 9999. Now suppose only the numbers from 1000 to 2000 are allotted to houses. In this case saying house numbers 500 or even 3500 or 4500 is same as 1500 as we know that only house numbers are one from 1000 to 2000. Saying just 500 as house number means *Partial Decoding* in case of memory address decoding. Whereas saying house number 1500 is *Exhaustive Decoding*. Now consider the case when allotted house numbers are 1000 to 3000 then saying just 500 to mention same house creates trouble that weather it refers to 1500 or 2500 as both are present. In memories it means two memory ICs are assigned same address. So both the ICs will start working at a time causing *BUS Contention* to occur. *BUS Contention* is a situation in which more than one device attempts to drive the system bus simultaneously in which case busses may be damaged. To avoid all such problems we must give complete house number i.e. 1500 to refer to that house. Thus before saying 500 we must ensure that there is no other house number whose last 3 digits are 500. The same is ensured in memory systems too, to avoid bus contention. Thus irrespective of the decoding schemes the goal of design is to assign unambiguous (or unique) addresses to memory devices. The way two schemes are realized are explained in next subsection.

5.7.4 FORMATION OF MEMORY SYSTEM

In this section, we are concerned with how to deal with the requirements of different systems. Here we must analyze the different requirement given to us and check the resources available and then take the appropriate steps to solve the problem. In fact, a design engineer is supposed to come with the appropriate access circuitry for the memory modules given to him/her in order to obtain the required system. It has our best observation and reading that it is far better if we consider the problems to illustrate the ideas to students. So, we start with the example in this subsection to consider the different situation and its fulfillment. *Note that we illustrate many important facts and make the important conclusions through these examples only.* We first start with the assumption that processing system can be a microprocessor or any other system capable of providing the required number address bits and control signals required for memory. Our job is mainly to find out the decoding circuitry for the circuits.

Example 1: It is required to obtain a memory system of 2K × 8 bits for a certain application. Given that memory ICs available are 1K × 8. Obtain the desired system.

Solution: By reading the problem it is revealed that we have already solved this problem even before saying any thing!!!!. If surprised see Fig. 5.44-(a), it is same as required by problem. Sit comfortably now because we are already through with it. For the reference we reproduce the Figs. 5.44-(a) and 5.44-(b) again.

It's now time to list out the different steps in order to solve these types of problems. Carefully read all steps we take to solve this problem again.

1. > *Determine the total number of address lines required for the memory system to be designed.*
Given total requirement is 2K × 8 means we need a *total of 11 address lines* because $2^{11} = 2048 = 2K$.

2. > *Determine the number of address bits available with the given memory ICs.*
Given ICs are 1K × 8 means we have 10 address lines available with the individual ICs because $2^{10} = 1024 = 1K$.

3. > *Determine the number of bits available for the chip decoder.*
Since total required address bits are 11 and individual memories can handle 10-bits of address, we are left with 1 address bit. This extra bit can be feeded to the decoder as shown in the Fig. 5.45 (*a*).

4. > *Draw the Address Bit Map for Entire Memory Space and indicate change in bits for individual memory ICs.* This is needed to assign particular address to individual ICs. The same is shown Fig. 5.45 (*b*).

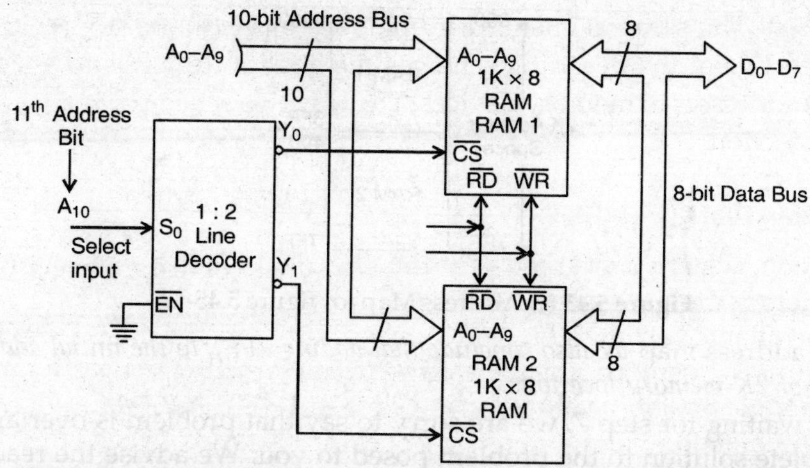

Figure 5.45 (a) Series connection of two 1K × 8 RAMs to obtain 2K × 8 RAM

Decoder bit ← Address bits handled by memory ICs →

	A_{10}	A_9	A_8	A_7	A_6	A_5	A_4	A_3	A_2	A_1	A_0	HEX Addr	IC
Start Addr	0	0	0	0	0	0	0	0	0	0	0	000_H	RAM
End Addr	0	1	1	1	1	1	1	1	1	1	1	$3FF_H$	1
Start Addr	1	0	0	0	0	0	0	0	0	0	0	400_H	RAM
End Addr	1	1	1	1	1	1	1	1	1	1	1	$7FF_H$	2

Figure 5.45 (b) Address Bit Map for Fig. 5.45 (*a*)

Observe that bit A_{10} does not change anywhere within the address range for RAM1 and remains 0 always. The same is true for and RAM2 where bit A_{10} 1 always. This justifies the step 3 to take the left over bits for decoder. As one can *see* that *the decoder bit selects how much memory address (1K in this case) can be selected by each output of the decoder*. In fact, this is the main purpose of drawing address bit maps.

5. > *Draw the Connection diagram for the memory ICs as per Address Bit Map*. This is the one we have done already in Fig. 5.45(*a*). But this done for this example only. We will draw the connection diagram in this step only for the other examples.
6. > *Draw the Address Map*. In step we diagrammatically represents the entire memory address space and show which address is assigned to which IC as shown in Fig. 5.45(*c*).

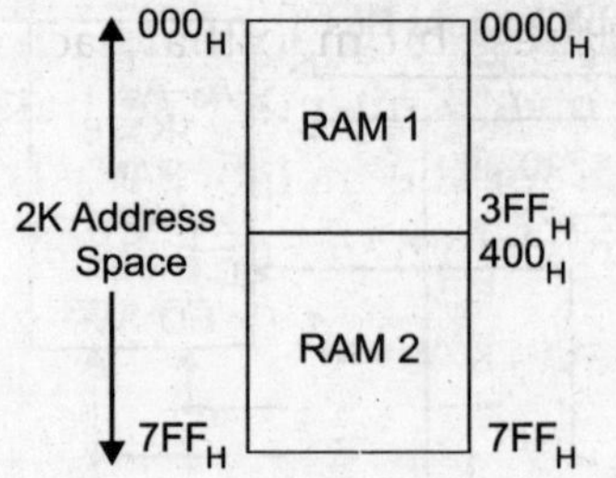

Figure 5.45 (c) Address Map for figure 5.45-(*a*)

From this address map *we also conclude that adding $7FF_H$ to the initial address will give the last address of 2K memory locations.*

If you are waiting for step 7, we are sorry to say that problem is over and you have given the complete solution to the problem posed to you. We advise the readers to go to the beginning of this example and carefully read it again, as these are the findings we would be using in following examples.

Example 2: Given two 2K × 8 ROM ICs and two 2K × 8 RAM ICs obtain a memory system of 8K × 8 bits.

Solution: We start step by step as defined by the previous problem.

1. > Given total requirement is 8K × 8 means we need a *total of 13 address lines* because 2^{13} = 8192 = 8K.
2. > Given ICs are 2K × 8 means we have 11 address lines available with the individual ICs because 2^{11} = 2048 = 2K.
3. > Since total required address bits are 13 and individual memories can handle 11-bits of address, we are left with 2-address bit, which can be feeded to the decoder.
4. > *Draw the Address Bit Map for Entire Memory Space and indicate change in bits for individual memory ICs.* This is needed to assign particular address to individual ICs. The same is shown in Fig. 5.46(*a*).

Decoder bit ← Address bits handled by memory ICs →

	A_{12}	A_{11}	A_{10}	A_9	A_8	A_7	A_6	A_5	A_4	A_3	A_2	A_1	A_0	HEX Addr	IC
Start Addr	0	0	0	0	0	0	0	0	0	0	0	0	0	0000_H	ROM
End Addr	0	0	1	1	1	1	1	1	1	1	1	1	1	$07FF_H$	1
Start Addr	0	1	0	0	0	0	0	0	0	0	0	0	0	0800_H	ROM
End Addr	0	1	1	1	1	1	1	1	1	1	1	1	1	$0FFF_H$	2
Start Addr	1	0	0	0	0	0	0	0	0	0	0	0	0	1000_H	RAM
End Addr	1	0	1	1	1	1	1	1	1	1	1	1	1	$17FF_H$	1
Start Addr	1	1	0	0	0	0	0	0	0	0	0	0	0	1800_H	RAM
End Addr	1	1	1	1	1	1	1	1	1	1	1	1	1	$1FFF_H$	2

Figure 5.46 (a) Address Bit-Map for 8K × 8 Memory System

It is clear from the address bit map that each decoder output (selected by A12 and A11 bits) selects one 2K-memory address space.

5. > Connection diagram for the memory ICs is shown in Fig. 5.46 (*b*).
6. > The Address Map is shown in Fig. 5.46 (*c*).

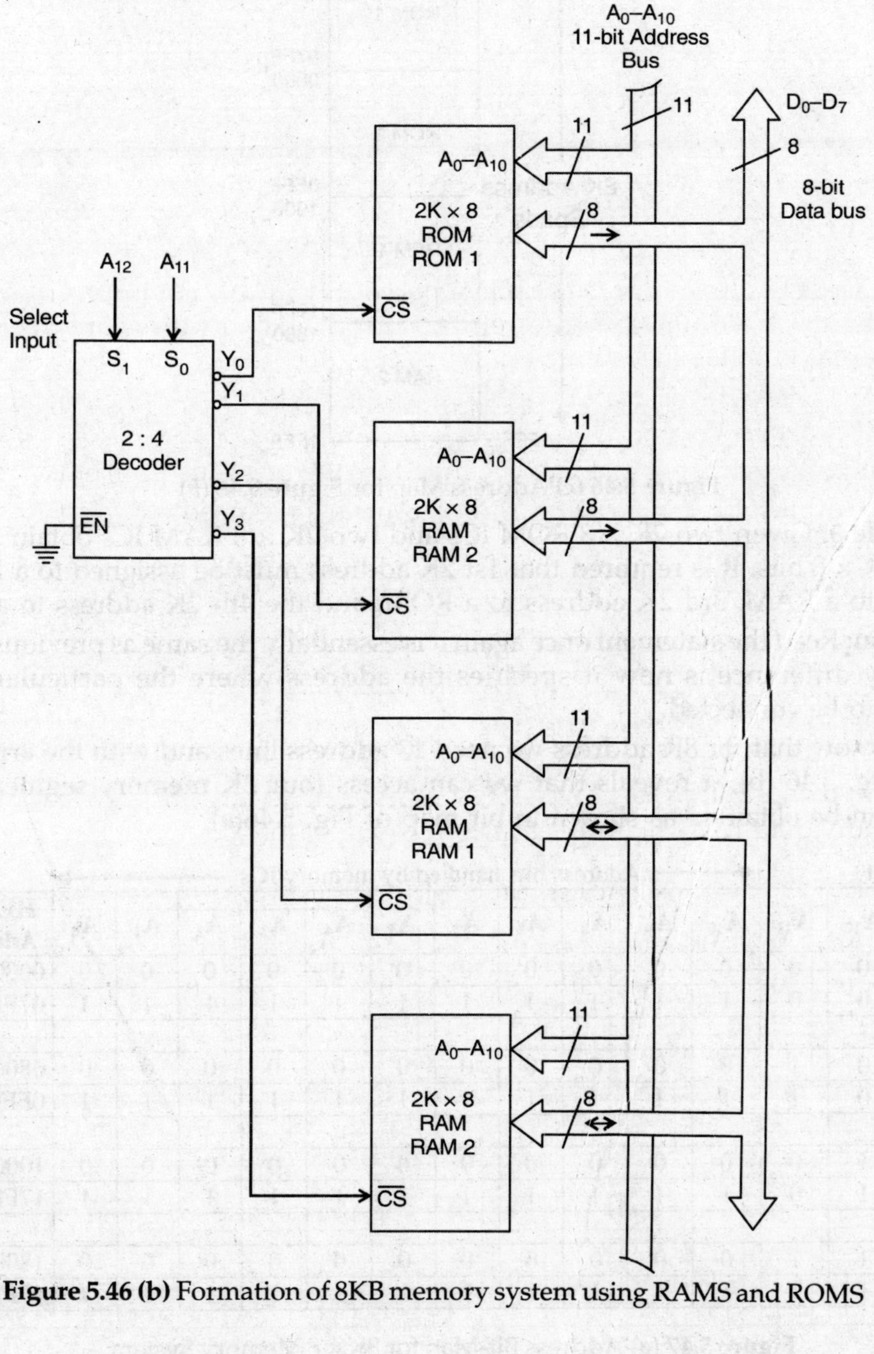

Figure 5.46 (b) Formation of 8KB memory system using RAMS and ROMS

From this address map *we also conclude that adding $1FFF_H$ to the initial address will give the last address of 8K memory locations.* Alternately we can say that we must change 13 address bits at a time to traverse through 8K memory locations.

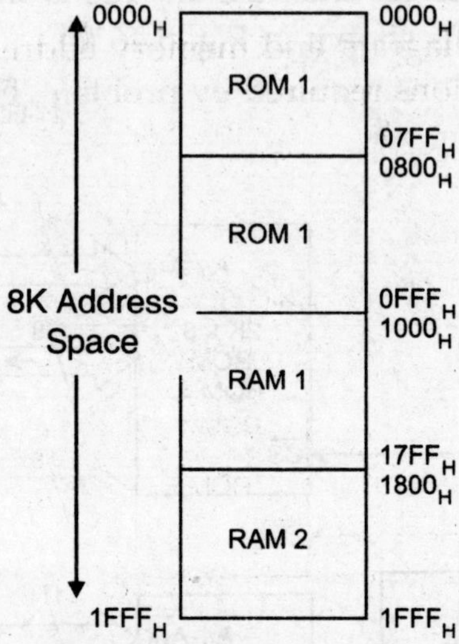

Figure 5.46 (c) Address Map for Figure 5.46 (*b*)

Example 3: Given two 2K × 8 ROM ICs and two 2K × 8 RAM ICs obtain a memory system of 8K × 8 bits. It is required that 1st 2K address must be assigned to a ROM, 2nd 2K address to a RAM, 3rd 2K address to a ROM, and the 4th 2K address to a RAM.

Solution: Read the statement once again it is essentially the same as previous problem, but the only difference is now it specifies the address where the particular memory devices are to be connected.

We know that for 8K address we need 13 address lines and with the arrangement shown in Fig. 5.46 (b), it reveals that we can access four 2K memory segments whose addresses can be obtained as shown in bit map of Fig. 5.46(*a*).

Decoder bit ← Address bits handled by memory ICs →

	A_{12}	A_{11}	A_{10}	A_9	A_8	A_7	A_6	A_5	A_4	A_3	A_2	A_1	A_0	HEX Addr	IC
Start Addr	0	0	0	0	0	0	0	0	0	0	0	0	0	0000_H	ROM
End Addr	0	0	1	1	1	1	1	1	1	1	1	1	1	$07FF_H$	1
Start Addr	0	1	0	0	0	0	0	0	0	0	0	0	0	0800_H	RAM
End Addr	0	1	1	1	1	1	1	1	1	1	1	1	1	$0FFF_H$	1
Start Addr	1	0	0	0	0	0	0	0	0	0	0	0	0	1000_H	ROM
End Addr	1	0	1	1	1	1	1	1	1	1	1	1	1	$17FF_H$	2
Start Addr	1	1	0	0	0	0	0	0	0	0	0	0	0	1800_H	RAM
End Addr	1	1	1	1	1	1	1	1	1	1	1	1	1	$1FFF_H$	2

Figure 5.47 (a) Address Bit-Map for 8K × 8 Memory System

Now the only thing we need to do is to connect the device at correct outputs of the decoder, which can be obtained from bit map shown in Fig. 5.47(*a*). Go through the details of this map carefully.

The similar connection diagram and memory address map would also appear but with the ICs changed to positions required by problem. Figures 5.47(*b*) and 5.47(*c*) show this.

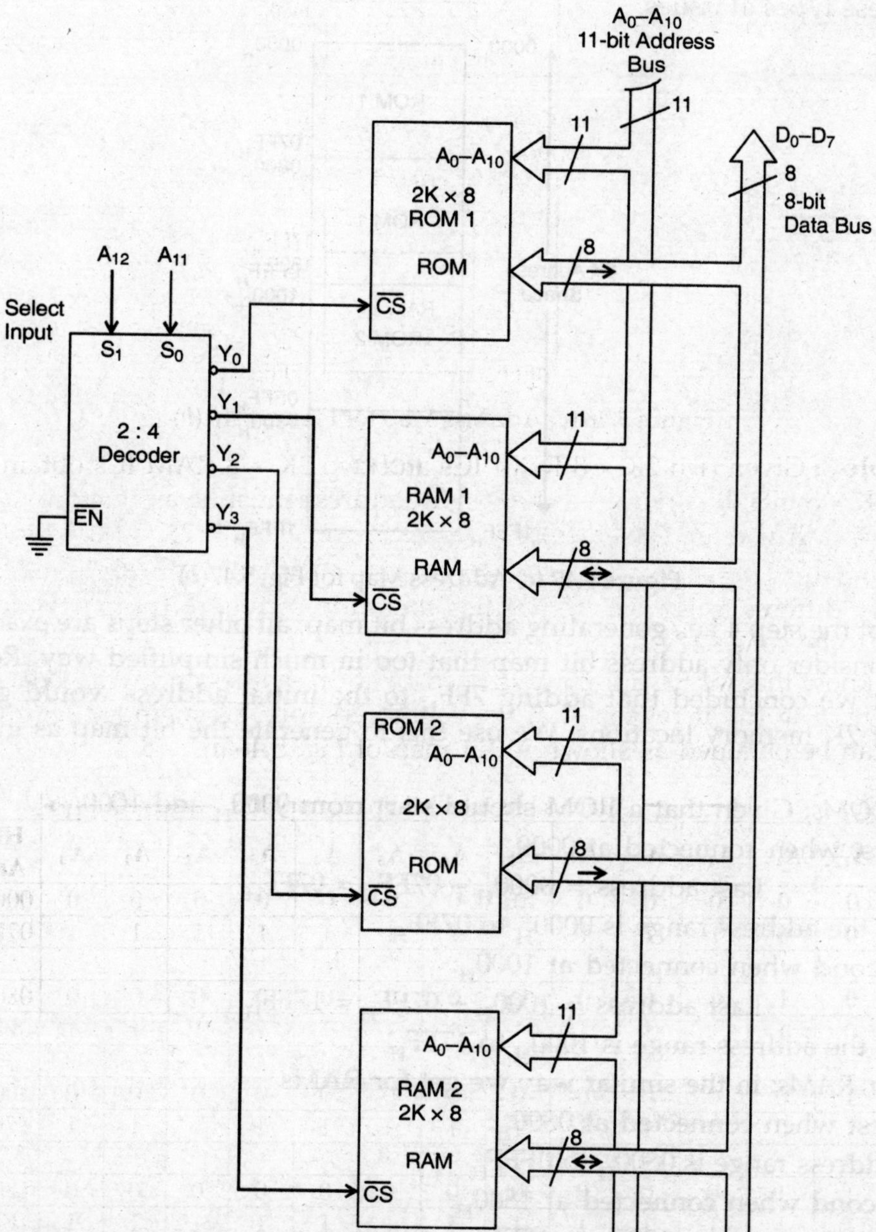

Figure 5.47 (b) Formation of 8KB memory system using RAMS and ROMS

Example 4: Given two 2K × 8 ROM ICs and two 2K × 8 RAM ICs obtain a memory system of 8K × 8. It is required that two ROMs must be connected to addresses beginning from 0000H and 1000H. Also the RAMs should be connected to begin from 0800_H and 1800_H.

Solution: Given example is just another way or giving statement for previous problem. But we will consider it separately to understand that what should be the way to solve these types of issues.

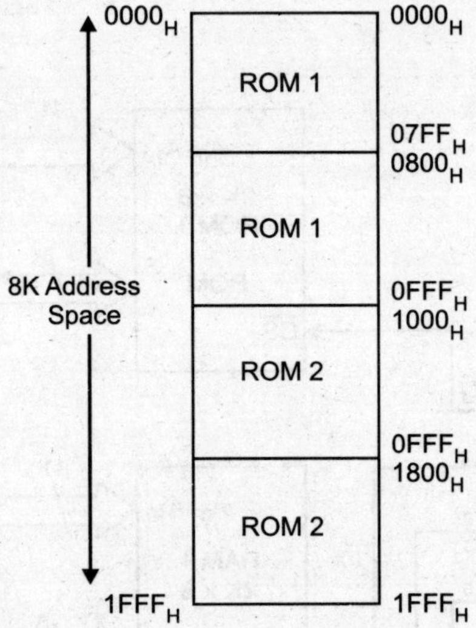

Figure 5.47 (c) Address Map for Fig. 5.47(*b*)

Except the step 4 i.e., generating address bit map, all other steps are exactly same so that we consider only address bit map that too in much simplified way. Recall that in example 1 we concluded that adding $7FF_H$ to the initial address would give the last address of 2K memory locations. We use this to generate the bit map as given ICs are 2K × 8.

For ROMs: Given that a ROM should start from 0000_H and 1000_H

First when connected at 0000_H:

$$\text{Last address} = 0000_H + 07FF_H = 07FF_H$$

So the address range is 0000_H to $07FF_H$

Second when connected at 1000_H:

$$\text{Last address} = 1000_H + 07FF_H = 17FF_H$$

So the address range is 1000_H to $17FF_H$

For RAMs: in the similar way we get for RAMs

First when connected at 0800_H:

Address range is 0800_H to $0FFF_H$

Second when connected at 1800_H:

Address range is 1800_H to $1FFF_H$

Compare these addresses with those shown in the bit map of Fig. 5.47(*a*), you reached the same map. Thus the entire Fig. 5.47 can redrawn.

It is interesting to see that instead of adding 07FF if we would have changed the least 11 significant address bits (as $2^{11} = 2K$) of initial address to 1 even in that case also we could have reached the same point. Either the way we proceed it is same because we found the number 07FFH from the fact that the highest hexadecimal number that can be written by 11 address bits is 07FFH. Many a times you will find that adding a number to initial address is easier because it is less time consuming than case of drawing complete bit map. But this short hand is useful only when you are through with concept and saying a hexadecimal number displays its bit pattern in your mind.

Shadowing or Address Overlapping address overlapping means assigning more than one address space to the memory device. It is the situation similar with a student who has his roll number and university enrolment number unique to him. So that when called by enrolment number or by roll number the same student will respond and none of the other students respond. An example will illustrate this best.

Example 5: A system needs a 4K × 8 memory system. But the requirement is such that a single 2K × 8 RAM IC be used and the two consecutive 2K memory addresses should be overlapped to this device only.

Solution: We know that for 4K system we will have 12 address lines. The 2K devices can process only 11 address bits thus the left over is 1-bit that can be used to access two 2K segments. By address overlapping we mean that both the segments would be referenced for same device. This is shown in Fig. 5.48.

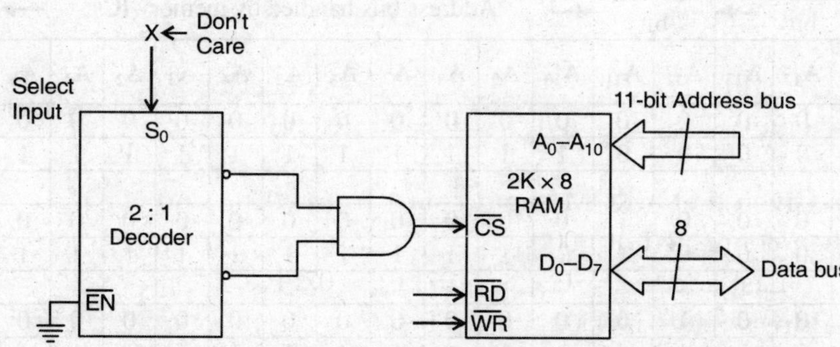

Figure 5.48 Illustration of memory address overlapping with 2K × 8IC

Notice the use of AND gate used to generate chip select for memory device. As shown, upon activation decoder outputs goes low so weather activated output is Y_0 or Y_1 AND gate out output is always low. This means memory is selected irrespective of the status of select input of decoder.

If we draw (readers are instructed to draw) the bit map for 4K as two 2K address block we see that first 2K block is 000 to $7FF_H$ and second 2K block is 800_H to FFF_H. With the configuration shown in Fig. 5.48 both the address blocks refers to the same IC thus address blocks are overlapped to each other and hence the name address overlapping. In the similar way we can overlap any two equal sized address blocks present in entire address map (or space).

We now turn our attention to exhaustive and partially decoded memory system. Read the problem statement carefully as it is going to create the difference.

Example 6: It is required to obtain an 8K × 8 memory system for 8085 microprocessor system that has an addressing capability of 64K locations. Given memories are 2K × 8 ROM ICs and 2K × 8 RAM ICs. Obtain the exhaustive or fully decoded as well as partially decoded system.

Solution: We first determine the number of address lines this processor has. 64K means 2^{16} *i.e.,* the processor has 16 address bits whereas the requirement for memory is just 13-bits. This means 3 address bits of processor will remain unused (or unchanged). This is shown by the address bit maps in Fig. 5.49, which now contains 16 bits instead of 13.

For exhaustive decoding: As stated for this scheme, we must decode all the address bits of microprocessor. The address bit map for this scheme is shown in Fig. 5.49(*a*). It shows that bit A_{13} to bit A_{15} are unchanged for entire 8K-address space. Since in this scheme we must decode all address bits, we can use these 3-bits to generate $\overline{EN}$ signal for Decoder which can also be used enable or disable the memory system by enabling/disabling decoder.

	← Unchanged bit →			Decoder bit		← Address bits handled by memory ICs →												
	A_{15}	A_{14}	A_{13}	A_{12}	A_{11}	A_{10}	A_9	A_8	A_7	A_6	A_5	A_4	A_3	A_2	A_1	A_0	**HEX Addr**	**IC**
Start Addr	0	0	0	0	0	0	0	0	0	0	0	0	0	0	0	0	0000_H	ROM
End Addr	0	0	0	0	0	1	1	1	1	1	1	1	1	1	1	1	$07FF_H$	1
Start Addr	0	0	0	0	1	0	0	0	0	0	0	0	0	0	0	0	0800_H	RAM
End Addr	0	0	0	0	1	1	1	1	1	1	1	1	1	1	1	1	$0FFF_H$	1
Start Addr	0	0	0	1	0	0	0	0	0	0	0	0	0	0	0	0	1000_H	ROM
End Addr	0	0	0	1	0	1	1	1	1	1	1	1	1	1	1	1	$17FF_H$	2
Start Addr	0	0	0	1	1	0	0	0	0	0	0	0	0	0	0	0	1800_H	RAM
End Addr	0	0	0	1	1	1	1	1	1	1	1	1	1	1	1	1	$1FFF_H$	2

Figure 5.49 (a) Address Bit-Map for exhaustive decoded 8K × 8 Memory System of example 6

The diagram for decoder along with enable generation is shown in Fig. 5.49 (*b*). The figure indicates which decoder output to be connected to which IC. In fact connections will be same as Fig. 5.49 (*b*) and the decoder of Fig. 5.49 (*b*) will replace decoder of Fig. 5.49 (*b*).

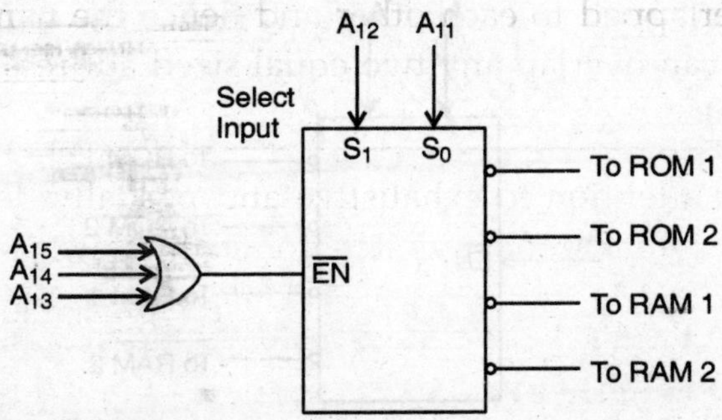

Figure 5.49 (b) Exhaustive decoded system

Notice the use of OR gate. Output of OR gate is low only when all its inputs are low otherwise high. Thus saying an address higher than $1FFF_H$ will not be responded by this system. If we say 8000H it means bit A_{15} goes high and output of OR gate goes high thus disabling the decoder and consequently the entire memory system.

For partial decoding: Here the idea is not to use all the address bits of processor for address decoding. As the 3 most significant address bits A_{15}, A_{14}, A_{13} are unchanged we can say that they are not used i.e. don't care. So it hardly matters if we use them for decoding or not. The address bit map shown in Fig. 5.50 (*a*) show this.

	Unused bits			Decoder bit	Address bits handled by memory ICs												
	A_{15}	A_{14}	A_{13}	A_{12}	A_{11}	A_{10}	A_9	A_8	A_7	A_6	A_5	A_4	A_3	A_2	A_1	A_0	HEX Addr	IC
Start Addr	X	X	X	0	0	0	0	0	0	0	0	0	0	0	0	0	0000_H	ROM 1
End Addr	X	X	X	0	0	1	1	1	1	1	1	1	1	1	1	1	$07FF_H$	
Start Addr	X	X	X	0	1	0	0	0	0	0	0	0	0	0	0	0	0800_H	RAM 1
End Addr	X	X	X	0	1	1	1	1	1	1	1	1	1	1	1	1	$0FFF_H$	
Start Addr	X	X	X	1	0	0	0	0	0	0	0	0	0	0	0	0	1000_H	ROM 2
End Addr	X	X	X	1	0	1	1	1	1	1	1	1	1	1	1	1	$17FF_H$	
Start Addr	X	X	X	1	1	0	0	0	0	0	0	0	0	0	0	0	1800_H	RAM 2
End Addr	X	X	X	1	1	1	1	1	1	1	1	1	1	1	1	1	$1FFF_H$	

Figure 5.50 (a) Address Bit-Map for partially decoded 8K × 8 Memory System of example 6

This means irrespective of the status of A_{15}, A_{14} and A_{13} the memory system can be used. Thus Fig. 5.50 (*b*) is direct implementation of partially decoded system, as it does not include these bits.

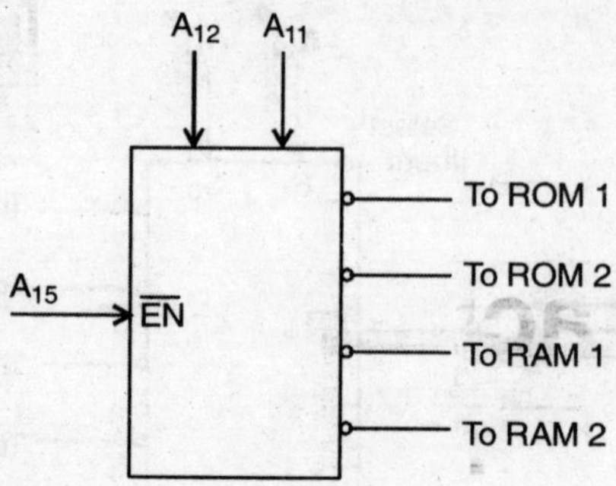

Figure 5.50 (b) Partially decoded system

A variation of implementation is shown in Fig. 5.50 (*b*), which uses A_{15} to enable the address decoder. Since A_{14} and A_{13} are not used it is still a partially decoded system.

5.8 PROBLEMS

1. With a schematic diagram and related program, interface a printer to 8051. Give reasonable details after stating the assumptions.
2. A serial interface of one 8051 is communicating with the serial interface of another 8051. The sampling rate at both the terminals are set to be 32 times the Baud Rate. Find the relationships between transmission and reception clock frequencies so that no framing error occurs. The frame format has 1 start bit, one stop bit, one software generated parity bit and 8 data bits. Deduce any formula used.
3. Assuming a crystal frequency of 12 MHz, find the time delay associated with the loop section of the following DELAY subroutine.

```
DELAY:
          MOV R3, #100
HERE:     NOP
          NOP
          NOP
          DJNZR3, HERE
          RET
```

4. Draw a schematic diagram to explain the controlling temperature of a filament with microcontroller.
5. Interface ADC 0801 analog to digital converter to 8051, through Port1. Pin 2.0 is being used to provide start of conversion signal to ADC. The end of conversion is connected to INTϕ. The interrupt vector address is $(0003)_4$. Program interrupt for edge triggered and keep it at highest priority. Store the 8 bit digital data so received from $(1000)_4$.

Chapter 6

Interfacing the 8051 with 8255 (Programmable I/O Port)

6.1 INTRODUCTION

The 8255 is a programmable peripheral Interface (PPI) device which is designed for use with microcomputer systems. It provides 24 I/O pins which may be individually programmed in 2 groups of 12 and used in 3 major modes (mode 0, mode 1, mode 2) of operation.

In mode 0, each group of 12 I/O pins may be programmed in sets of 4 to be input or output. In mode 1, each group may be programmed to have 8 lines of input or output 3 of the remaining 4 pins are used for handshaking and interrupt control signals. Mode 2 is a strobed bi-directional bus configuration.

6.2 PROGRAMMING THE 8255

6.2.1 8255 FUNCTIONAL DESCRIPTION

The 8255 is a programmable peripheral interface device designed for use in microcomputer systems. Its function is that of a general purpose I/O component to interface peripheral equipment to the microcomputer system bus. The functional configuration of the 8255 is programmed by the system software so that normally no external logic is necessary to interface peripheral devices.

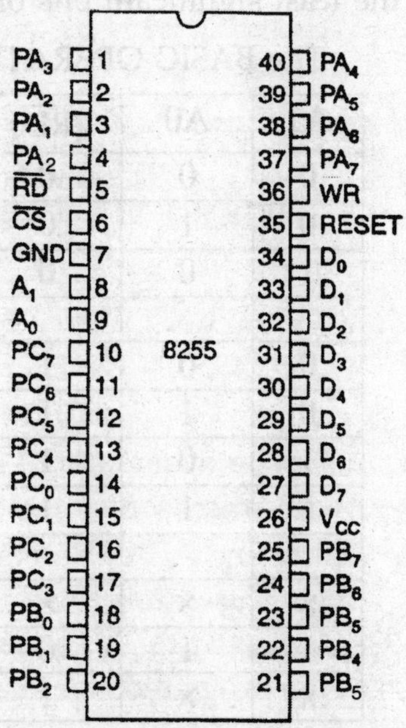

Figure 6.1 Pin configuration of 8255

DATA BUS BUFFER

This 3-state bidirectional 8-bit buffer is used to interface the 8255 to the system data bus. Data is transmitted or received by the buffer upon execution of input or output instructions by the microcontroller. Control words and status information are also transferred through the data bus buffer.

READ/WRITE AND CONTROL LOGIC

The function of this block is to manage all of the internal and external transfers of both Data and Control or Status words. It accepts inputs from the microcontroller Address and Control busses and in turn, issue commands to both of the Control Groups.

($\overline{CS}$) CHIP SELECT. A "low" on this input pin enables the communication between the 8255 and the microcontroller.

($\overline{RD}$) READ. A "low" on this input pin enables the 8255 to send the data or status information to the microcontroller on the data bus.

($\overline{WR}$) WRITE. A "low" on this input pin enables the microcontroller to write data or control words into the 8255.

(A_0 and A_1) PORT SELECT 0 AND PORT SELECT 1

These input signals, in conjunction with the $\overline{\textbf{RD}}$ and $\overline{\textbf{WR}}$ inputs, control the selection of one of the three ports or the control word registers. They are normally connected to the least significant bits of the address bus (A_0 and A_1).

The BASIC OPERATION of 8255 is summarized in table of figure 6.2

A1	A0	($\overline{RD}$)	($\overline{WR}$)	($\overline{CS}$)	INPUT OPERATION (READ)
0	0	0	1	0	PORT A → DATA BUS
0	1	0	1	0	PORT B → DATA BUS
1	0	0	1	0	PORT C → DATA BUS
					OUTPUT OPERATION (WRITE)
0	0	1	0	0	DATA BUS → PORT A
0	1	1	0	0	DATA BUS → PORT B
1	0	1	0	0	DATA BUS → PORT C
1	1	1	0	0	DATA BUS → CONTROL
					DISABLE FUNCTION
×	×	×	×	1	DATA BUS → TRI–STATE
1	1	0	1	0	ILLEGAL CONDITION
×	×	1	1	0	DATA BUS → TRI–STATE

Figure 6.2 8255 basic operation

RESET

A "high" on this input clears the control register and all ports are set to the input mode.

GROUP A AND GROUP B CONTROLS

The functional configuration of each port is programmed by the systems software. In essence, the CPU "outputs" a control word to the 8255. The control word contains information such as "mode", "bit set", etc., that initializes the functional configuration of the 8255.

Each of the Control blocks (Group A and Group B) accepts "commands" from the Read/Write Control Logic, receives "control words" from the internal data bus and issues the proper commands to its associated ports.

Control Group A - Port A and Port C upper (C7-C4)

Control Group B - Port B and Port C lower (C3-C0)

PORTS A, B, AND C

The 8255 contains three 8-bit ports (A, B, and C). All can be configured in a wide variety of functional characteristics by the system software but each has its own special features or "personality" to further enhance the power and flexibility of the 8255.

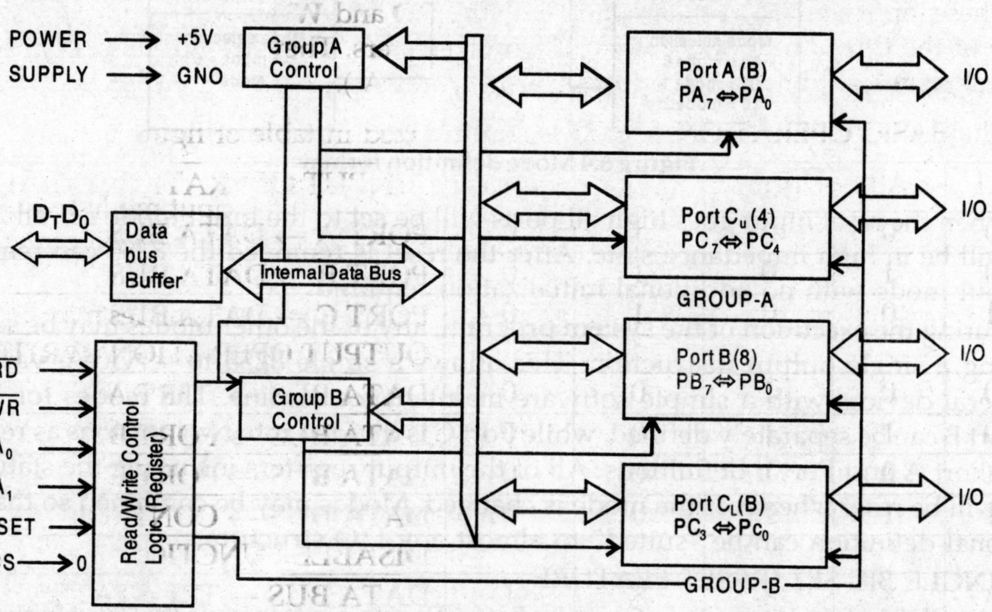

Figure 6.3 8255 Block diagram

Port A. One 8-bit data output latch/buffer and one 8-bit input latch buffer.

Port B. One 8-bit data input/output latch/buffer and one 8-bit data input buffer.

Port C. One 8-bit data output latch/buffer and one 8-bit data input buffer (no latch for input). This port can be divided into two 4-bit ports under the mode control. Each 4-bit port contains a 4-bit latch and it can be used for the control signal outputs and status signal inputs in conjuction with ports A and B.

6.2.2 8255 OPERATIONAL DESCRIPTION

Mode Selection

There are three basic modes of operation that can be selected by the system software:

Mode 0—Basic input/output

Mode 1—Strobed Input/output

Mode 2—Bi-directional Bus

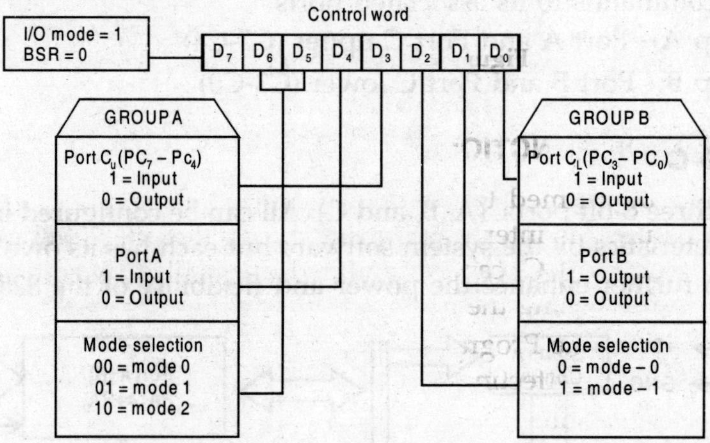

Figure 6.4 Mode definition format

When the reset input goes high all ports will be set to the input mode *i.e.*, all 24 port lines will be in high impedance state. After the reset is removed the 8255 can remain in the input mode with no additional initialization required.

During the execution of the system program, any of the other modes may be selected by using a single output instruction. This allows a single 8255 to service a variety of peripheral devices with a simple software maintenance routine. The modes for Port A and Port B can be separately defined, while Port C is divided into two portions as required by the Port A and Port B definitions. All of the output registers including the status flip-flops, will be reset whenever the mode is changed. Modes may be combined so that their functional definition can be "suited" to almost any I/O structure.

SINGLE BIT SET/RESET FEATURE

Any of the eight bits of Port C can be Set or Reset using a single OUTput instruction. When port C is being used as status/control for Port A or B, these bits can be set or reset by using the Bit Set/Reset operation just as if they were data output ports.

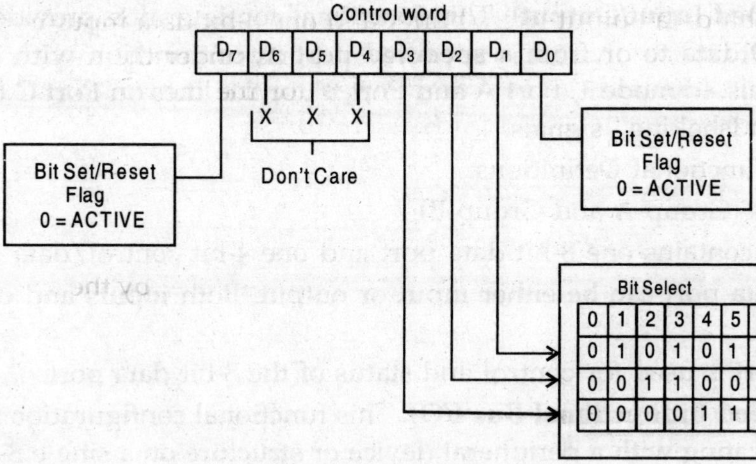

Figure 6.5 Bit set/reset format

INTERRUPT CONTROL FUNCTIONS

When the 8255 is programmed to operate in mode 1 or mode 2, control signals are provided that can be used as interrupt request inputs to the CPU. The interrupt request signals, generated from port C, can be inhibited or enabled by setting or resetting the associated INTE flip-flop, using the bit set/reset function of port C.

This function allows the Programmer to disallow or allow a specific I/O device to interrupt the CPU without affecting any other device in the interrupt structure.

INTE flip–flop definition:

(BIT-SET)–INTE is SET–Interrupt enable

(BIT-RESET)–INTE is RESET–Interrupt disable

Note: All Mask flip-flops are automatically reset during mode selection and device Reset.

OPERATING MODES

Mode 0 (Basic Input/Output). This functional configuration provides simple input and output operations for each of the three ports. No "handshaking" is required, data is simply written to or read from a specified port.

Mode 0 Basic Functional Definitions:

- Two 8-bit ports and two 4-bit ports.
- Any port can be input or output.
- Outputs are latched.
- Inputs are not latched.
- 16 different Input/Output configuration are possible in this Mode.

MODE 1 (Strobed Input/Output). This functional configuration provides a means for transferring I/O data to or from a specified port in conjunction with strobed or "handshaking" signals. In mode 1, Port A and Port B use the lines on Port C to generate or accept these "handshaking" signals.

Mode 1 Basic Functional Definitions:

- Two Groups (Group A and Group B).
- Each group contains one 8-bit data port and one 4-bit control/data port.
- The 8-bit data port can be either input or output. Both inputs and outputs are latched.
- The 4-bit port is used for control and status of the 8-bit data port.

MODE 2 (Strobed Bidirectional Bus I/O). This functional configuration provides a means for communicating with a peripheral device or structure on a single 8-bit bus for both transmitting and receiving data (bidirectional bus I/O). "Handshaking" signals are provided to maintain proper bus flow discipline in a similar manner to MODE 1. Interrupt generation and enable/disable functions are also available.

MODE 2 Basic Functional Definitions:

- Used in Group A only.
- One 8-bit, bidirectional bus port (Port A) and a 5-bit control port (Port C).
- Both inputs and outputs are latched.
- The 5-bit control port (Port C) is used for control and status for the 8-bit, bi-directional bus port (Port A).

The three modes MODE0, MODE1 and MODE2 are operating modes in I/O mode, which is selected by setting D7 = 1 in control word. However there is another mode of operation called BSR Mode which selected by making D7 = 0 in control word as given in single Bit/Reset feature.

THE BSR MODE FEATURES

- Using this mode individual bits of port C can be set or reset by writting BSR control word in control word register.
- BSR control word affects only one bit at a time.
- BSR Mode does not affect the I/O Mode Operation.

6.3 8255 INTERFACING

6.3.1 TEMPERATURE MEASUREMENT

A very general purpose temperature measurement system based on 8051 is shown in Fig. 6.6. The main blocks of this system are 8255 PPI, ADC 0808 and sensor and clock circuitry.

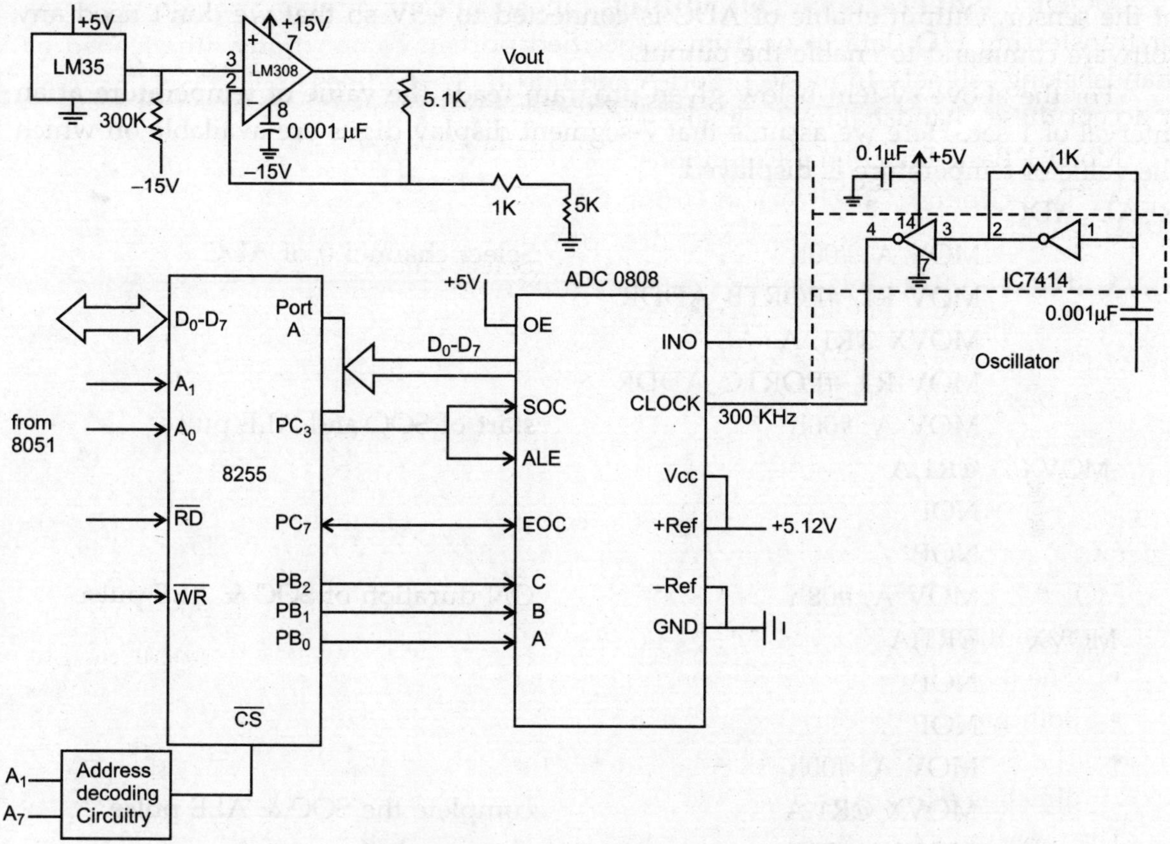

Figure 6.6 Temperature measurement

The power supply block is not included for simplicity and clarity. The temperature sensing element in the circuit is an LM35 precision celsius temperature sensor. The voltage between the output pin and the ground pin of this device will be 0V at 0°C and will increase by 10 mV for each increase of 1°C. The 300 kΩ (Kilo-ohm) resistor connecting the output of the LM35 to –15V allows the output to go negative for temperatures below 0°C. To measure temperatures over the range of –55 to +150°C. An LM308 buffers and amplifies the signal from the sensor by 2 so that the signal uses a greater part of the input range of the A/D converter. Some Schmitt-trigger inverters in a IC7414 are connected as an oscillator to produce a 300 KHz clock for the ADC. With 5.12 V Vcc and V_{ref} the ADC will have a resolution of 20 mV, i.e. a change of 20 mV will cause 1 bit increment in digital output.

Since the temperature sensor signal is amplified by 2, each degree celsius of temperature change will produce an output-change of 20 mV, or one step on the A/D converter. This gives us a resolution of 1°C, which is about equal to the typical accuracy of the sensor. Output enable of ADC is connected to +5V so that we don't need any software command to enable the output.

For the above system below given program reads the value of temperature at an interval of 1 sec. Here we assume that 7-segment display digits are available on which the value of temperature is displayed.

```
READ_ADC:
            MOV A, #00h                ;Select channel 0 of ADC
            MOV R1, #PORTB_ADDR
            MOVX @R1, A
            MOV R1, #PORTC_ADDR
            MOV A, #00h                ;start of SOC and ALE pulse
    MOVX    @R1,A
            NOP
            NOP
            MOV A, #08h                ;ON duration of SOC & ALE pulse
    MOVX    @R1,A
            NOP
            NOP
            MOV A, #00h
            MOVX @R1,A                 ;complete the SOC & ALE pulse
            MOVX A,@R1                 ;check end of conversion
CHECK_EOC:RLC A
            JNC CHECK_EOC
            MOV R1, #PORTA_ADDR
    MOVX    A,@R1                      ;Conversion is completed
    RET     ;read the data in ACC
MAIN:
            MOV A, #98h                ;command word to configure 8255
            MOV R1, #CWR_ADDR          ;CWR address in R1
            MOVX @R1, A                ;write command word at CWR
AGAIN:      ACALL READ_ADC             ;read temp in accumulator
            ACALL DISPLAY_TEMP         ;Display the temp
            ACALL ONE_SEC_SUB          ;Wait for 1 sec
            LJMP AGAIN
```

6.3.2 ADC INTERFACING TO 8255

The figure 6.7 shows interfacing of ADC 0808/0809 to microcontroller through 8255.

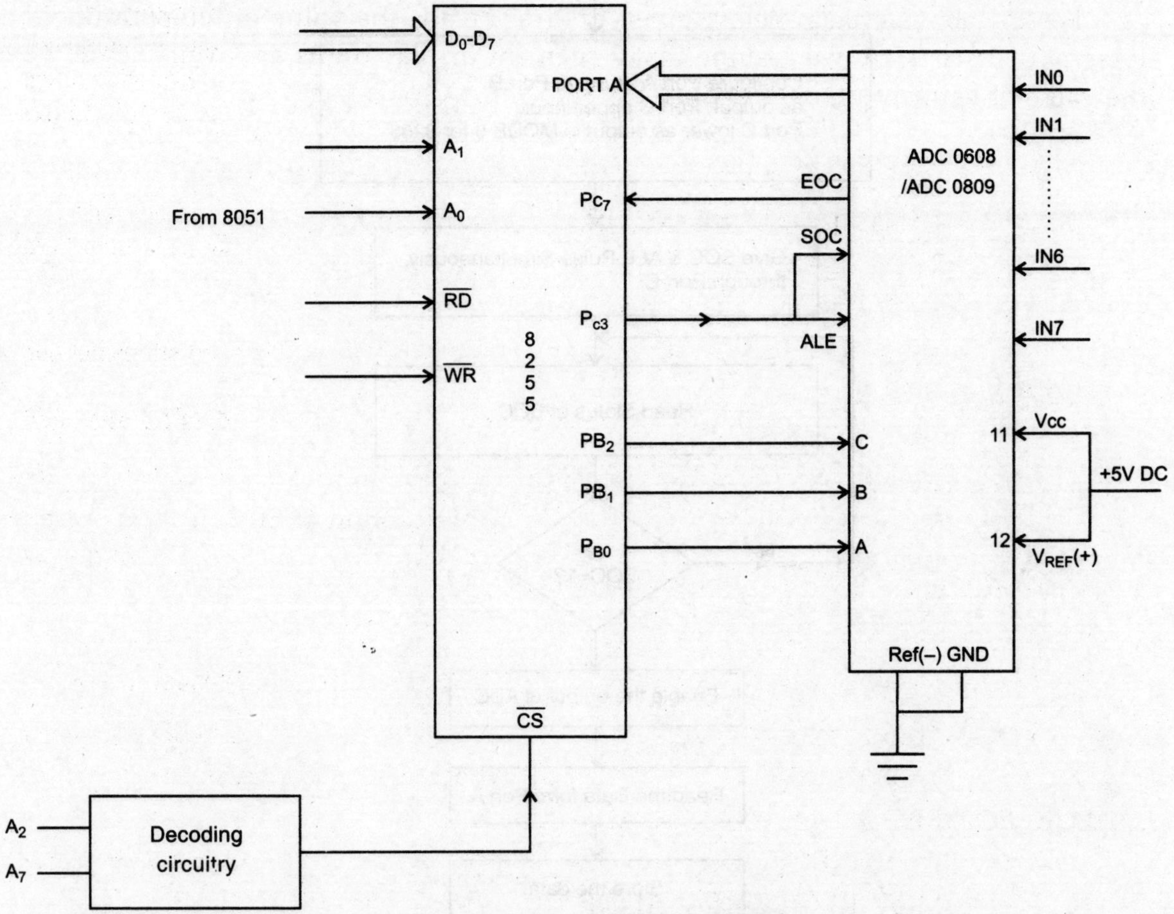

Figure 6.7 ADC connection to 8255

Control word for 8255 for above configuration CW = 10010000 = 90h.

Data table for above configuration for digital output for a given analog input for 0 to 5V analog input.

Analog input voltage (mV)	Digital O/P of ADC (in hex)
0	00
1	34
2	6D
3	9A
4	CE
5	FF

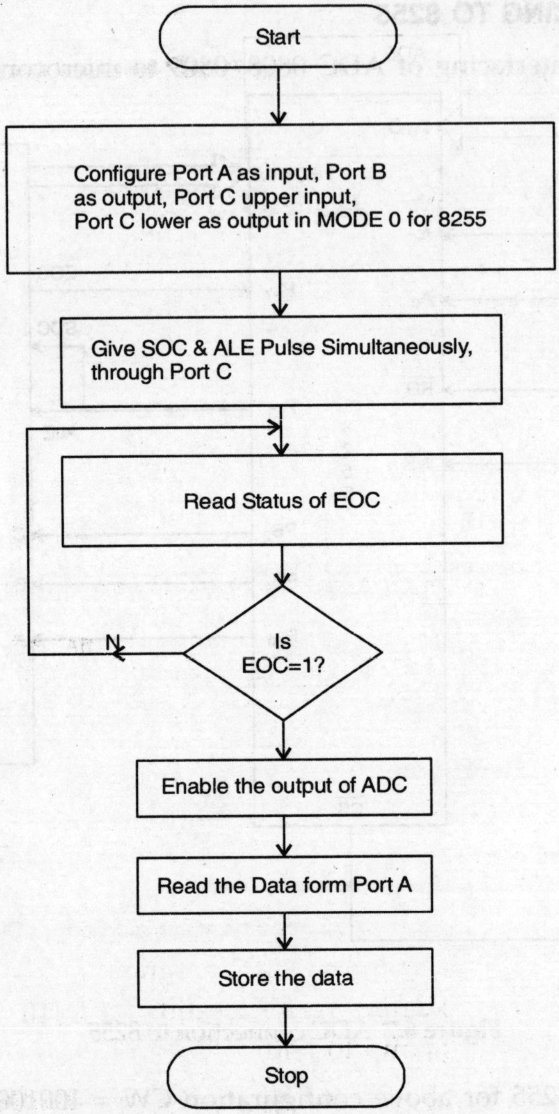

Figure 6.8 Flowchart for ADC interface

The flowchart of Fig. 6.8 show ADC interfacing. On the basis of this flowchart one can write program (ALP) for 8051. It is left as an excercise for reader.

Example: A simple 8-bit analog to digital converter device as shown in Fig. 6.9(a) is to be interfaced to an 8051 microcontroller. The READY line goes low when conversion data is available. The READY line should be used to interrupt the 8051 microcontroller.

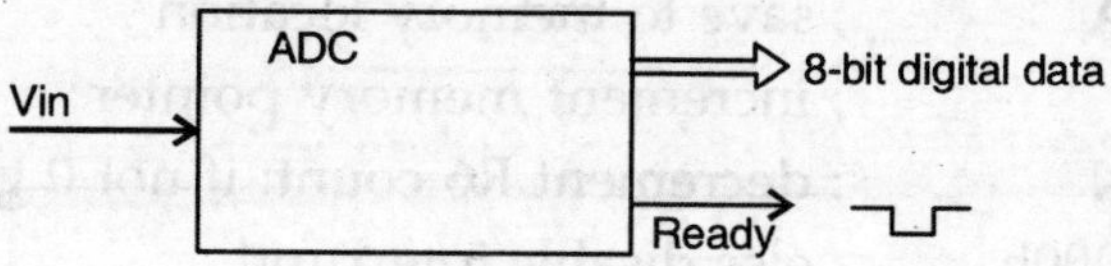

Figure 6.9 (a)

Write an ALP which will capture 250 data samples from the A/D converter and store this data in external data memory. The program is to be interrupt driven.

Solution: Interfacing of ADC is given in figure 6.9(b).

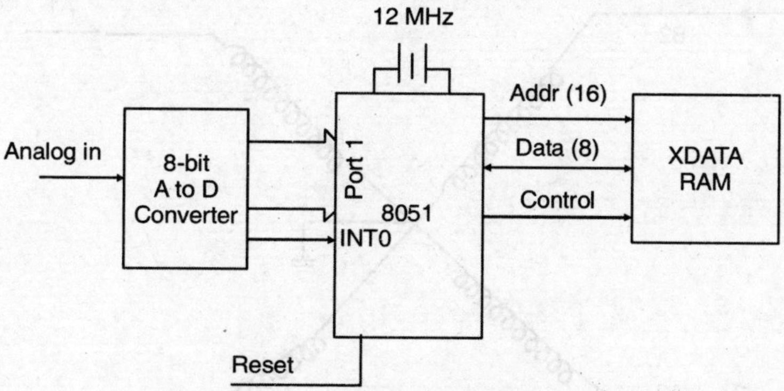

Figure 6.9(b) Interfacing block diagram

The given ALP capture 250 samples from ADC. When a sample is ready the 8051 is interrupted. This ALP uses External interrupt 0 and ADC is connected to Port 1.

```
    ORG 0000h               ; define memory start address 0000h
    LJMP MAIN               ; jump to MAIN program
    ORG 0003h               ; define vector location for INT0
    LJMP ISR0               ; jump to ISR0
MAIN:
    MOV P1, #0FFh           ; initialise Port 1 for use as input
    MOV DPTR, #2000h        ; set up memory pointer
    MOV R6, #250d           ; use R6 to count
    SETB IT0                ; define negative edge trigger for int 0
    MOV IE, #10000001b      ; enable Interrupt 0
LOOP:
    LJMP LOOP               ; just loop around!
ISR0:
    MOV A, P1               ; read the ADC
```

```
    MOVX @DPTR, A          ; save to memory location
    INC DPTR               ; increment memory pointer
    DJNZ R6, AGAIN         ; decrement R6 count: if not 0 go again
    MOV IE, #00000000b     ; else disable interrupt!
AGAIN:
    RETI                   ; return from interrupt
```

6.3.3 STEPPER MOTOR CONTROL

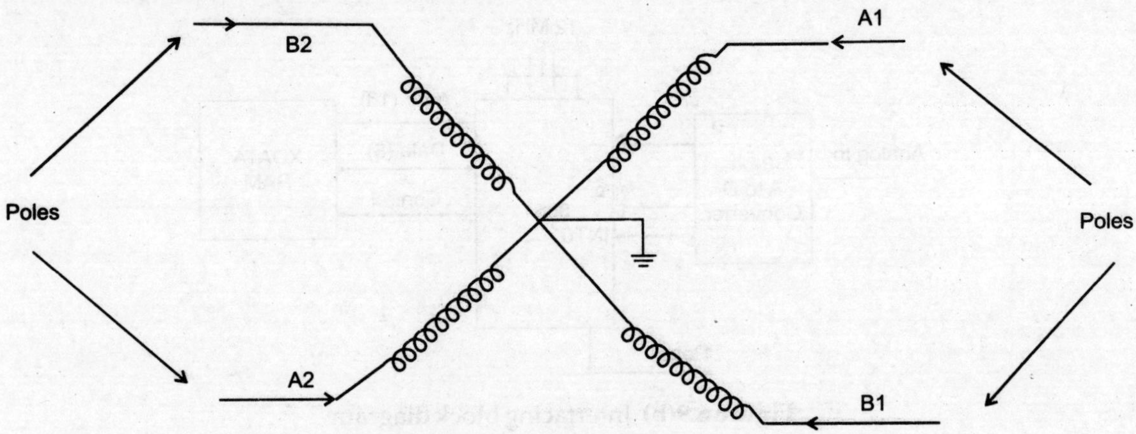

Figure 6.10 4-Pole stepper motor

Figure 6.10 shows simple representation of a stepper motor having 4 poles. To energize a pole, winding of the pole must be connected to a rated (for ex 12V) DC supply. Simply by connecting and disconnecting the supply to coils, motor can be rotated in any direction. In a microcontroller based system, these coils are connected to supply whenever controller sends pulses to switch on supply. The supply remains connected for some times (i.e. time delay) and then they are disconnected. This time delay controls the speed of motor.

To rotate the motor two poles must be energized at time. The sequence in which the poles are energized decides the direction of rotation. Below tables specifies the energising set, and sequence that must be used for rotation in clockwise or anticlockwise.

For Clockwise

Poles	A_1	B_1	A_2	B_2
	1	1	0	0
	0	1	1	0
	0	0	1	1
	1	0	0	1
	1	1	0	0

Anticlockwise

Poles	A_1	B_1	A_2	B_2
	1	1	0	0
	1	0	0	1
	0	0	1	1
	0	1	1	0
	1	1	0	0

The below Fig. 6.11 shows interfacing diagram for stepper motor control using 8255 ports.

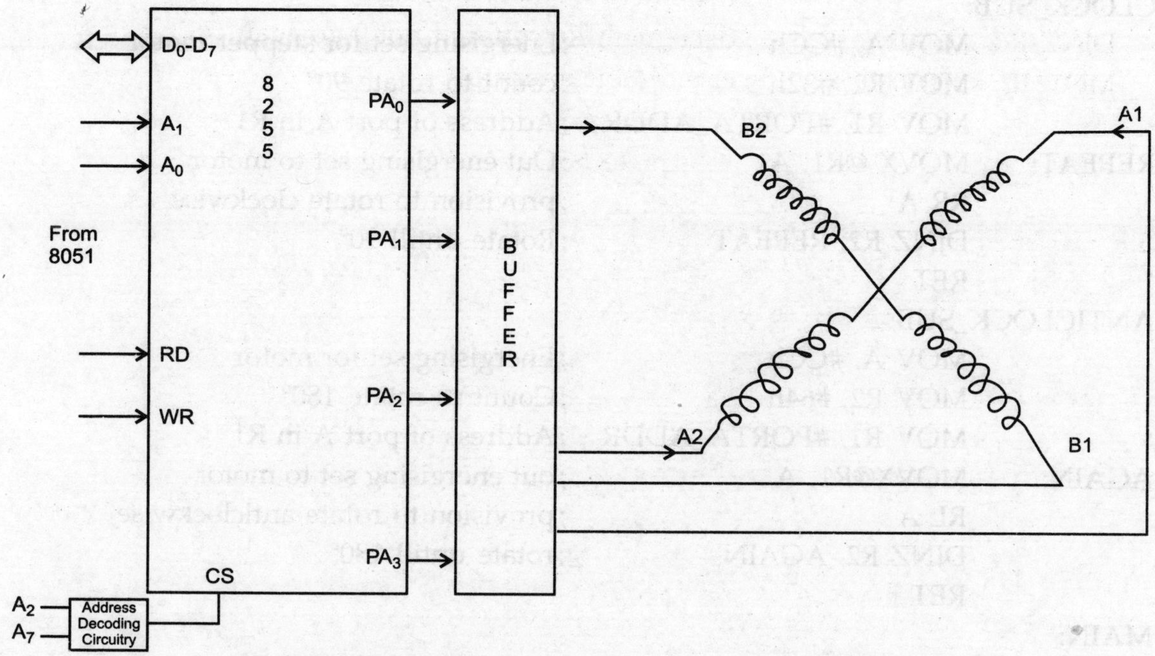

Figure 6.11 Interfacing stepper motor through 8255

Example: Rotate a stepper motor through 90° in clockwise direction and then by 180° in anticlockwise direction. Step angle of this motor is 1.8°. Show hardware connection and write software to meet the requirement.

Solution: The interfacing diagram is same as shown in Fig. 6.11.

Step angle is the angular movement corresponding to one step. So no. of steps (or count) to rotate the motor by θ° can be given as

$$\text{Count to rotate } \theta° \Rightarrow N = \frac{\theta}{\text{Step angle}}$$

(i) For θ = 90°

$$N_1 = \frac{90}{1.8} = 50 = 32h$$

(ii) For θ = 180°

$$N_2 = \frac{180}{1.8} = 100 = 64h$$

As shown earlier, the energising set for poles of motor start from A_1 B_1 A_2 B_2 = 1100 = Ch. By rotating this sequence to left we move motor in counter clockwise direction and by rotating right we move the motor in clockwise direction. Since registers of 8051 are 8 bit registers we load CCh in the register instead of Ch.

```
CLOCK_SUB:
           MOV A, #CCh               ;Energising set for stepper motor
           MOV R2, #32h              ;count to rotate 90°
           MOV R1, #PORTA_ADDR       ;Address of port A in R1
REPEAT:    MOVX @R1, A               ;Out energising set to motor
           RR A                      ;provision to rotate clockwise
           DJNZ R2, REPEAT           ;Rotate untill 90°
           RET
ANTICLOCK_SUB:
           MOV A, #CCh               ;Energising set for motor
           MOV R2, #64h              ;Count to rotate 180°
           MOV R1, #PORTA_ADDR       ;Address of port A in R1
AGAIN:     MOVX@R1, A                ;out energising set to motor
           RL A                      ;provision to rotate anticlockwise
           DJNZ R2, AGAIN            ;rotate untill 180°
           RET
MAIN:
           MOV A, #80h               ;command word to configure port A as
                                      output port
           MOV R1, #CWR_ADDR         ;CWR address in R1
           MOVX @R1, A               ;write command word at CWR
           ACALL CLOCK_SUB           ;rotate the motor in clockwise direction by
                                      90°
           ACALL ANTICLOCK_SUB       ;rotate the motor in anticlockwise direction
                                      by 180°
```

The Fig. 6.11 shows the interfacing of stepper motor using 8255. The 8051 can be directly control the stepper motor operation, the connection for this is shown in Fig. 6.12.

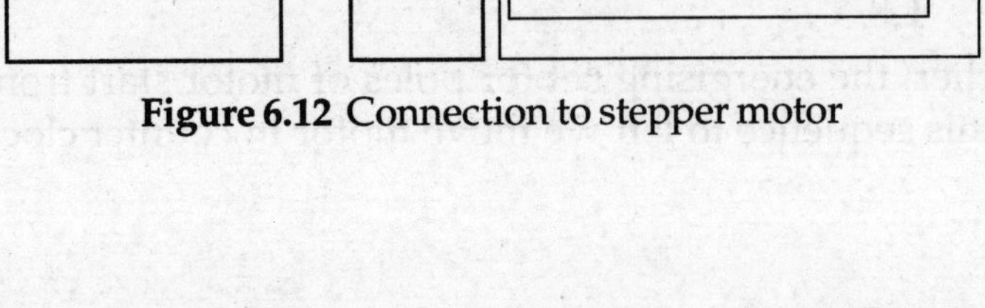

Figure 6.12 Connection to stepper motor

Buffer is simply river such as ULN 2003 to drive motor winding since the 8051 have not sufficient current to drive the motor.

Example: For the stepper motor connection of Fig. 6.12. Write program to rotate it continuously by 90º in clockwise direction step angle is given as 1.8º.

Solution: For 90º rotation, θ = 90º

$$N = \frac{\theta}{\text{step angle}} = \frac{90}{1.8} = 50 = 32h$$

```
        MOV A, #CCh         ; Energising set for stepper motor
        MOV R2, #32h        ; Count to rotate 90°
REPEAT: MOV P1, A           ; Issue step sequence to motor
        RR A                ; provision to rotate clockwise
        DJNZ R2, REPEAT     ; rotate untill 90°
        RET
```

6.4 PROBLEMS

1. Write the basic operations performed by 8255.
2. What are the function of Read / Write control logic register? Give the status of , $\overline{RD}$, $\overline{WR}$, $\overline{CS}$, A0 & A1 for basic operations of 8255.
3. Describe the control word register of 8255.
4. Discuss single bit set/reset feature of 8255.
5. How many pins of 8255 are used for ports and how they are categorized?
6. What are the features of BSR mode?
7. Write a program to get data from port C and send it to ports A and B.
8. Write a program for stepper motor control using 8255 and also using 8051.
9. Discuss the operation of stepper motor. How it is controlled by 8051?
10. Discuss the mechanism for temperature measurement through 8051.

Chapter 7

Microcontroller Applications

7.1 INTRODUCTION

In the chapters 5 and 6, we have seen how 8051 microcontroller can be interfaced with different electrical and electromechanical devices. Fundamentals of interrupts, timer/counter operation and serial communication along with interfacing techniques of microcontroller's are used in different real life application. This chapter deals with application of microcontroller's in generation of different waveforms and pulse generation, application in frequency counting, measurement and automation and controller application. In this chapter main emphasis is on explanation of different applications with the help of examples for the better understanding.

7.2 WAVEFORM GENERATION

7.2.1 SQUARE WAVE GENERATION

It is the simplest type of waveform that can be generated through programmable devices such as microcontrollers. The waveform generation involves making an output line HIGH (i.e. logic 1) for t_{ON} time and then making the output line low for t_{OFF} time. The ratio of on time period (t_{ON}) to total time (t_{ON} + t_{OFF}) is referred as "on-time duty cycle" or simply the *Duty Cycle*. For 50% duty cycle, the output wave is called as *Square Wave*. When duty cycle is not 50% the output wave is called *Rectangular Wave*, which is discussed in article 7.2.2.

The following two examples show how to generate square waves using 8051. In 8051 square waveform can be generated with the help of timer's.

Example: Write a program to generate a square wave of 2 KHz frequency on pin P1.5. Assuming crystal frequency 11.0592 MHz.

Solution:

```
         MOV TMOD,#10h     ;timer 1, mode 1(16-bit)
REPEAT:  MOV TL1,#1Ah      ;TL1 = 1A,low byte of timer
         MOV TH1,#0FFh     ;TH1 = FF,high byte
         SETB TR1          ;start the timer 1
```

```
RETURN:   JNB TF1,RETURN      ;stay until timer rolls over
          CLR TR1             ;stop timer 1
          CPL P1.5            ;comp. p1.5 to get high, low
          CLR TF1             ;clear timer flag 1
          SJMP REPEAT         ;reload timer since mode 1 is not auto-reload
```

Example: Write a program to generate a square wave of 50 Hz frequency on pin P1.5. Assuming crystal frequency 11.0592 MHz.

Solution:

```
          MOV TMOD,#10h       ;timer 1, mode 1 (16-bit)
REPEAT:   MOV TL1,#00         ;TL1=00, low byte of timer
          MOV TH1,#0DCh       ;TH1=DC, High byte of timer
          SETB TR1            ;start the timer 1
RETURN:   JNB TF1,RETURN      ;stay until timer rolls over
          CLR TR1             ;stop timer 1
          CPL P2.3            ;comp. p2.3 to get hi, lo
          CLR TF1             ;clear timer flag 1
          SJMP REPEAT         ;reload timer since mode 1 is not auto-reload
```

7.2.2 RECTANGULAR WAVE GENERATION

As we have already seen in previous article that when duty cycle is not 50% the output wave is called *Rectangular Wave*. Now with the example we see how to generate rectangular waveform using 8051.

Example: Write a program to generate a rectangular wave of duty cycle 40% on pin P 1.5. Assuming crystal frequency 11.0592 MHz.

Solution:

Duty cycle = 40%

$$40 = \frac{T_{ON}}{T_{ON} + T_{OFF}} \times 100$$

Therefore $\frac{T_{ON}}{T_{OFF}} = \frac{2}{3}$

selecting $T_{ON} = .2$ ms

$T_{OFF} = .3$ ms

For on-delay, $\frac{.2\text{ms}}{1.085\mu\text{s}} = 184$ and $65536 - 184 = 65352$

In hexadecimal it is equal to FF48.

Therefore for on-delay, timer 1 in mode 1 (16-bit) must be loaded with TL = 48H, TH = FFH.

Similarly for off-delay: $\frac{.3\text{ ms}}{1.085\ \mu\text{s}} = 276$ and $65536 - 276 = 65260$

In hexadecimal it is equal to FEEC.

Therefore, for off delay, timer 1 must be loaded with
TL=ECH, TH=FEH.

The ALP for the generation of rectangular waveform of 40% duty cycle is

```
            ORG                 0000h
            SJMP                MAIN
            ORG                 001Bh
            AJMP                INT_T1
MAIN:
            MOV TMOD, #10h      ; timer 1, mode 1 (16-bit)
            SETB ET1            ; Enable timer 1 interrupt
            SETB EA             ; Enable interrupt
            SETB TR1            ; Start the timer 1
LOOP:       SJMP LOOP           ; Wait
INT_T1:     CLR TR1             ; Stop timer
            CLR EA              ; Disable interrupts
            CPL P1.5
            JNB P1.5, OFF_DELAY
ON_DELAY:   MOV TH1, #FFh       ; For on-time=200 microsecond
            MOV TL1, #48h       ;
OFF_DELAY:  MOV TH1, FEh;       For off-time = 300 microsecond
            MOV TL1, #ECh       ;
            SETB TR1            ; Start the timer 1
            SETB EA             ; Enable interrupt
```

7.2.3 STAIR-STEP RAMP WAVE GENERATION

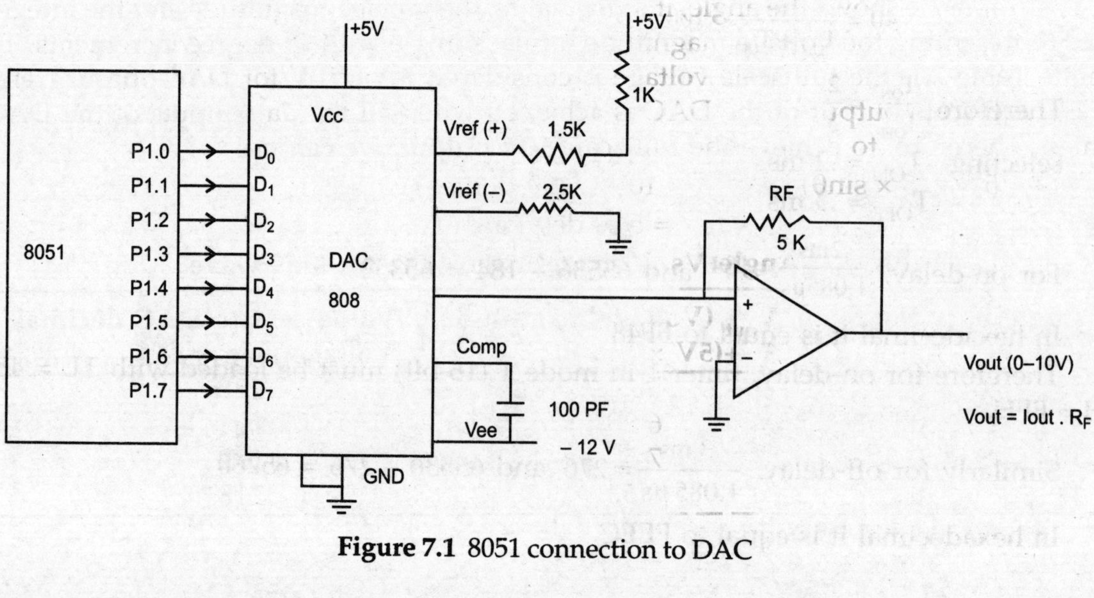

Figure 7.1 8051 connection to DAC

The stair-step ramp waveform can be generated using 8051 microcontroller. To generate stair-step ramp the 8051 can be connected as shown in Fig. 7.1.

The program to generate a stair-step ramp is as follow:

```
                CLR A
REPEAT:         MOV P1, A               ; data is send to DAC
                INC A
                ACALL ONE_MILLI_SUB     ; To let DAC to recover
                SJMP REPEAT
ONE_MILLI_SUB:
                PUSH 07h
                MOV R7, #250d
LOOP_1_MILLI:
                NOP
                NOP
                DJNZ R7, LOOP_1_MILLI
                POP 07h
                RET
```

7.2.4 SINE WAVE GENERATION

The sinewave can be generated by the circuit shown in Fig. 7.1. To generate a sinewave we first generate a table representing the magnitude of the sine of angle between 0 and 360 degrees. Since the value of sine function vary from –1.0 to +1.0 for 0 to 360 degree angles. Therefore the table values are integer numbers representing the voltage magnitude for the sine of theta. This is ensure that only integer numbers are output to the DAC by the 8051.

This Table 7.1 shows the angle, it's sine value, the voltage magnitude and the integer values representing the voltage magnitude for each angle with 15 degree increments. To generate Table 7.1, the full scale voltage is considered to be 10V for DAC output (refer fig). The full-scale output of the DAC is achieved when all the data inputs of the DAC are high. Therefore, to achieve the full-scale 10V output, we can use

$V_{out} = 5V + (5 \times \sin\theta)$ i.e. $V_{out} = 10V$ (90 degree)

$= 5$ (0 degree)

Table 7.1: Angle Vs. Voltage magnitude for sine wave

Angle θ (degrees)	Sin θ	V_{out} (Voltage magnitude) 5V+(5V × Sin θ)	Value sent to DAC decimal Voltage mag × 25.6
0	0	5	128
15	0.258	6.29	161
30	0.5	7.5	192
45	0.707	8.53	218

60	0.866	9.33	238
75	0.965	9.82	251
90	1.0	10	255
105	0.965	9.82	251
120	0.866	9.33	238
135	0.707	8.53	218
150	0.5	7.5	192
165	0.258	6.29	161
180	0	5	128
195	–0.258	3.71	95
210	–0.5	2.5	64
225	–0.707	1.47	37
240	–8.66	0.669	17
255	–0.965	0.18	4
270	–1.0	0	0
285	–0.965	0.18	4
300	–0.866	0.669	17
315	–0.707	1.47	37
330	–0.5	2.5	64
345	–0.258	3.71	95
360	0	5	128

To find the value sent to DAC for various angles, multiply the V_{out} voltage by 25.60 because there are (2^8) 256 steps and full-scale V_{out} is 10 volts. Therefore, 256 steps/10V=25.6 steps per volt.

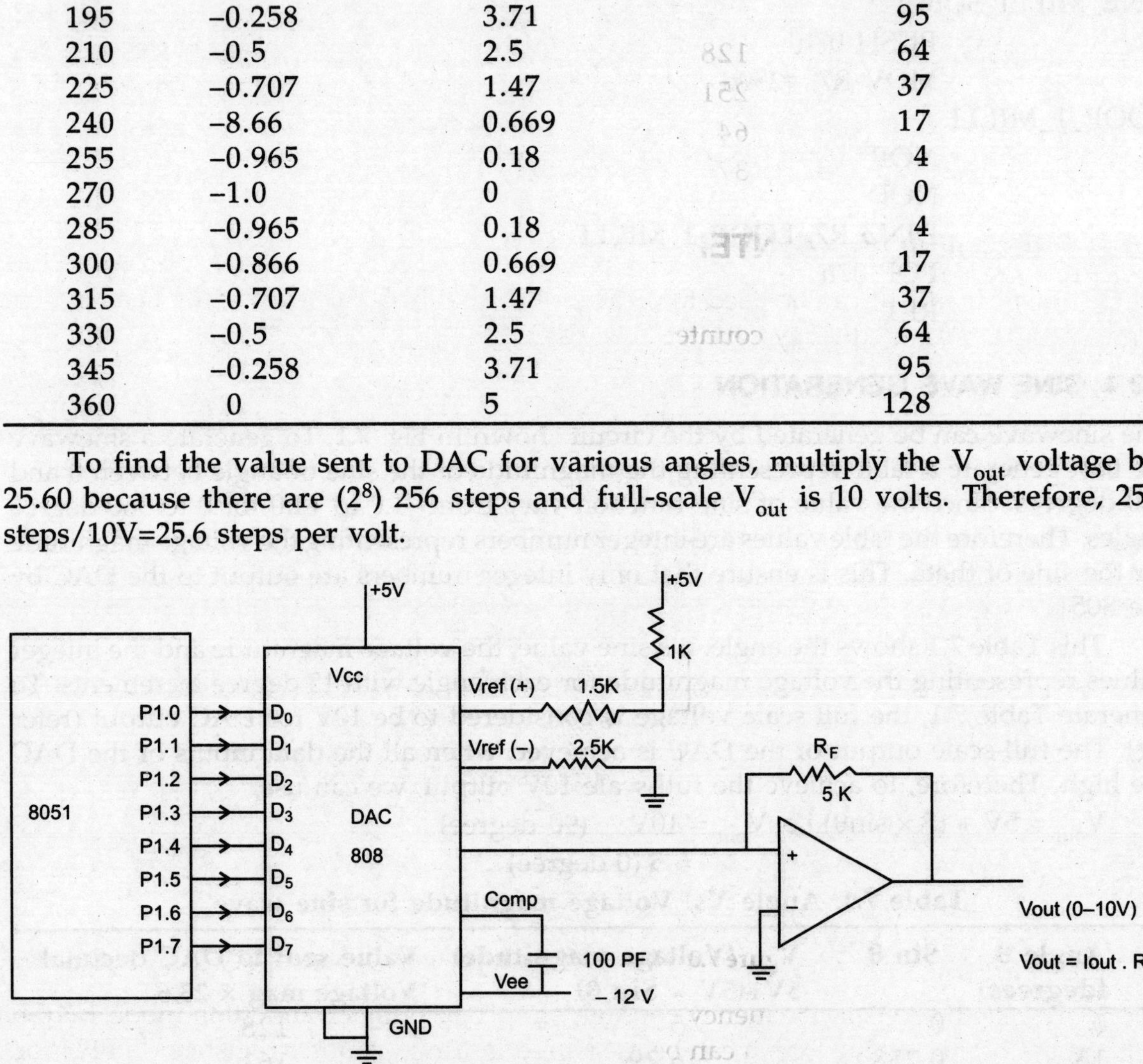

Figure 7.2 8051 connection to DAC 808

To produce the sinewave these values of table 7.1 to be send to DAC continuously. The program to generate sinewave using 8051 will be

```
REPEAT:         MOV DPTR, #Lookup_table
                MOV R2, #25                           ; Since 25 values are taken
BACK:           CLR A                                 ;therefore count will be 25
                MOVC        A, @A+DPTR
                MOV         P1, A
                INC         DPTR
                DJNZ        R2, BACK
                SJMP        REPEAT
                ORG         300
Lookup_table:   DB    128   161   192   218   238   251   255
                DB    251   238   218   192   161   128   95
                DB    64    37    17    4     0     4     17
                DB    37    64    95    128
```

7.3 FREQUENCY COUNTER

The timer T0 and T1 can be used to measure external frequencies in 8051. The flow chart and program for frequency counter is as follows.

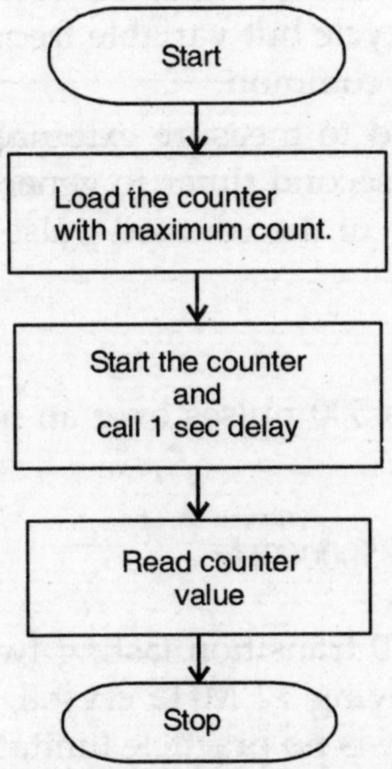

Figure 7.3 Flowchart for frequency counter

To use the 8051 as frequency counter, simply use timer1/timer0 in mode 1 (16-bit). Load the highest value which can be measured in timer/counter registers (FFFFH for 16 bit counter). Wait for 1 sec and read the counter value. This value directly gives the frequency of system.

```
MOV TMOD, #10h          ;Timer 1, mode1 (16-bit)
MOV TL1, #FFh           ;load the counter with
MOV TH1, #FFh           ;maximum count
SETB TR1                ;Start the timer 1
ACALL ONE_SEC_SUB       ;Introduce 1 sec delay stop the timer
CLR TR1                 ;Read the counter value
MOV R0, TL1
MOV R1, TH1
```

Note: We have already introduced delay routines in chapter 8. Here we used 1sec subroutine to introduce 1 sec delay. Since the no. of count per second is frequency. It directly gives the frequency count. We read the frequency count through R0 and R1 register.

7.4 MEASUREMENT APPLICATIONS

7.4.1 FREQUENCY COUNTER

In industrial and commercial control applications sensors are used to produce pulses that contains information about the quantity sensed. By varying the sensor output frequency using a constant duty cycle but variable frequency pulses to indicate changes in the measured variable, is most common.

Timer T0 and T1 can be used to measure external frequencies by configuring one timer as a counter and using the second timer to generate a timing interval over which the first can count. The frequency of the counted pulse train is then

$$\text{Unknown frequency} = \frac{\text{Counter}}{\text{Timer}}$$

for example, if the counter counts 500 pulses over an interval of 1 ms generated by the timer, the frequency will be

$$\text{Frequency measured} = \frac{500}{1\times10^{-3}} = 500000\text{Hz}$$

An input pulse make a 1 to 0 transition lasting two machine cycles, of f/24, to be counted. Therefore using 8051 having 12 MHz crystal, the maximum frequency of 500 KHz can be measured. While there is no practicle limitation on the lowest frequency that can be counted.

The following program Freq-Count measure an unknown frequency on port 3, pin 4 that is P3.4(T0).

The unknown frequency is counted in T0 configured as a 16-bit counter. T0 is reset and begins counting the unknown frequency.

It is left as an exercise for reader to write program Freq-Count to measure unknown frequency.

7.4.2 PULSE WIDTH MEASUREMENT

We have seen that frequency output of sensors used in controllers and industrial applications. One way is to use variable frequency pulses of constant duty cycle while the other is of constant frequency but variable duty cycle. The constant frequency pulses are generated by varying the duration of pulse width.

If the input pulse is square wave, then the pulse frequency can be measured by finding the time the wave is high (T_H). The pulse frequency is given by

$$\text{frequency} = \frac{1}{T_H \times 2}.$$

If T_H 100 microseconds, the pulse frequency will be 5000 Hz.

Both timers (T0 and T1) may be configured so that the internal clock is counted only when the corresponding $\overline{\text{INT0}}/\overline{\text{INT1}}$ pin is high by setting the GATE0/GATE1 bit in TMOD.

The width of an unknown pulse is measured by enabling a timer when the pulse generates an programmed to occur on a high-to-low edge on the $\overline{\text{INT0}}/\overline{\text{INT1}}$ pin. The interrupt is programmed to occur on a high-to-low edge on the $\overline{\text{INT0}}/\overline{\text{INT1}}$. The counter starts counting when the unknown pulse goes high, enabling the counter to count when $\overline{\text{INT0}}/\overline{\text{INT1}}$ goes high. The next pulse edge stops the counter. The counter will contain the width of the pulse to the nearest microsecond for a 12 MHz crystal.

The following program pulse_width measure the width of the pulse applied to port3 pin2 that is P3.2($\overline{\text{INT0}}$). Timer T0 is enabled to count on the first pulse edge, counts when the pulse is high, and stops on the second edge. The ports P1(LSB) and P2 (MSB) show the width of the pulse in microseconds.

```
        EQE Wflag, 00h          ;bit flag used to notify main program
        ORG 0000h
        SJMP MAIN               ;jump over INT0 interrupt
        ORG 03h                 ;INT0 interrupt at this program location
        JBC TR0, STOP           ;If T0 is running then stop it
        SETB TR0                ;If T0 is not running then start it
STOP:
        SETB Wflag
        CLR EX0                 ;Disable INT0 until next measurement
        RET1                    ;return with T0 stopped are Wflag set
MAIN:
        MOV TMOD, #09h          ;To count when INT0 pin high
        SETB IT0                ;INT0 interrupt on negative edge
        MOV TL0, #00h           ;Reset T0 to 004
        MOV TH0, #00h           ;
        MOV IE, #80h            ;Enable interrupts
```

```
TEST:
    JBC Wflag, Pwidth        ;test flag until measurement made
    SJMP TEST
Pwidth:
    MOV P1, TL0              ;display LSB on P1
    MOV P2, TH0              ;display MSB on P2
    SJMP MAIN                ;get next width measurement
    END
```

7.5 AUTOMATION AND CONTROLLER APPLICATION

7.5.1 OVERVIEW OF INDUSTRIAL PROCESS CONTROL

One of the major application of microcontrollers are in industrial process control. Process control involves first measuring system variables such as motor speed, temperature the level of a liquid in a tank etc. The output of the controller than adjusts the value of each variables until it is equal to a predetermined value called a set point. The system controller must maintain each variable as close as possible to its set-point value. A simple example will show the traditional approach to control of a process variable and explain terminology used in control system.

The circuit of Fig. 7.4 shows an analog approach to controlling the speed of a dc motor.

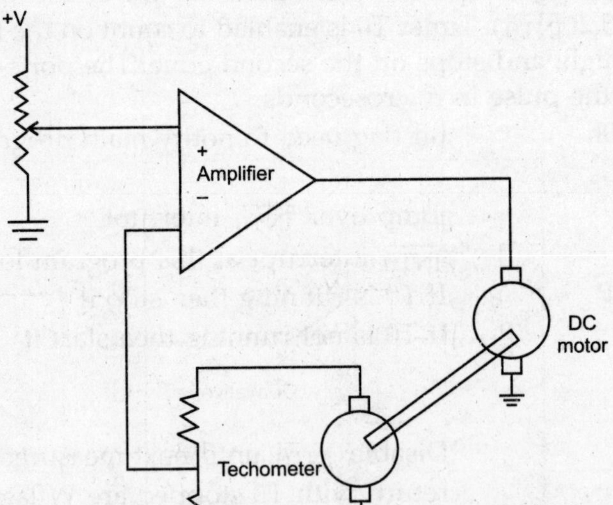

Figure 7.4 Circuit for controlling speed of a dc motor using feedback from techometer

A dc generator, or techometer is attached to the shaft of the motor which generate output voltage proportional to the speed of the motor. A fraction of the output voltage is fed back to the inverting input of the power amplifier. A positive voltage is applied to the noniverting input of the amplifier as a set point. When the power turned on, the motor accelerates until the voltage fed back from the techometer to the inverting input of the amplifier is nearly equal to the set-point voltage.

If the load on the motor is increased the motor will initially slow down and the voltage output from the techometer will decrease. This will increase the difference in voltage between the inputs of the amplifier and cause it to drive more current to the motor. The increased current will increase the speed of motor to nearly the speed it had before the increased load was added. The same thing occurs if the load on the motor is decreased.

Using negative feedback to control a system such as this is often calted servo control. A control loop of this type keeps the motor keeped quite constant for applications where the load on the motor does not change much.

The circuit of Fig. 7.4 have many limitations such as overshoot, undershoot and residual error. To overcome these problems circuits with more complex feedback are used. The circuit of figure 7.5 implement proportional, integral and derivative feedback control.

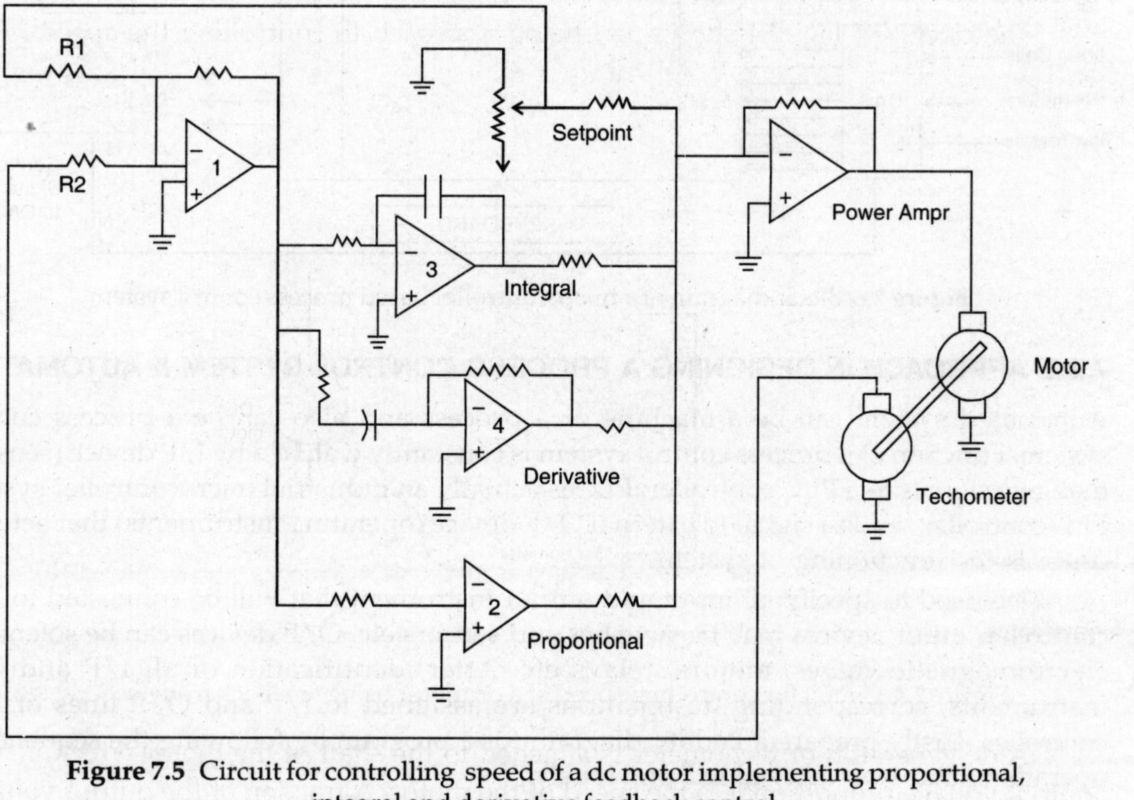

Figure 7.5 Circuit for controlling speed of a dc motor implementing proportional, integral and derivative feedback control.

Amplifier 1 produces simple dc feedback proportional to the difference between the set point and the techometer output. This is exactly the same effect as the voltage divider on the techometer output in figure 7.4.

The effect of the increased load is corrected by proportional feedback while the residual error by integral feedback. To improve the response time of the system derivative feedback is used. Process control loops that use all three types of feedback are called PID proportional integral derivative control loops. Because process variables changes much slowly than the response of microcontrollers, a microcontroller can perform all the functions of the analog circuits of Fig. 7.5.

Figure 7.6 shows a block diagram of a microcontroller based process control system.

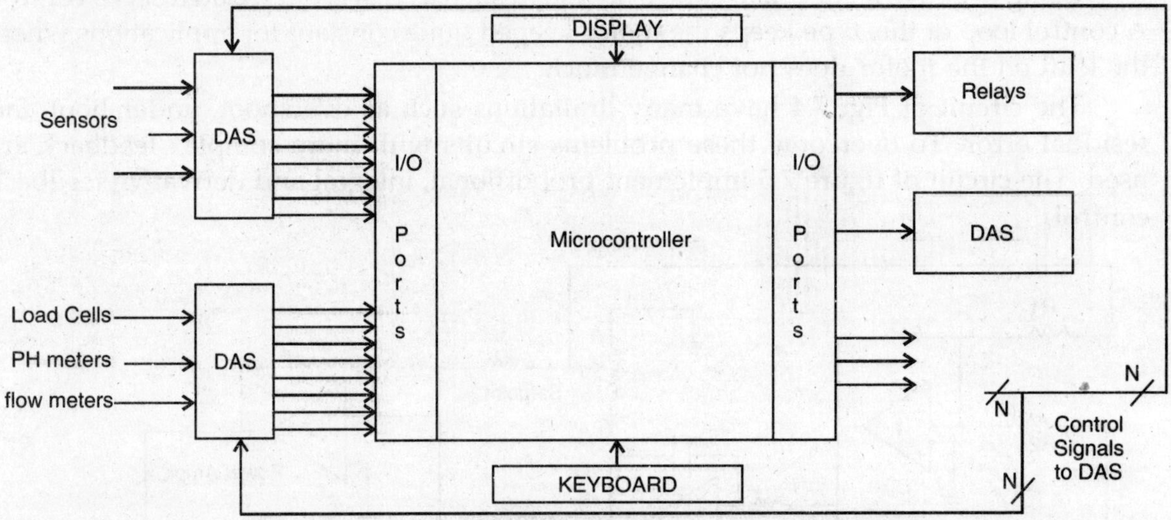

Figure 7.6 Block-diagram of a microcontroller based process control system

7.5.2 APPROACH IN DESIGNING A PROCESS CONTROL SYSTEM & AUTOMATION

Automated system can be a machine or a process and also can be a process control system. Function of a process control system is constantly watched by I/P device (sensors) that give signals to a PLC controller. PLC is actually an industrial microcontroller system. PLC controller sends a signal to external O/P device (operating instruments) that actually controls the functioning of system.

One need to specify all input and output instrument that will be connected to PLC controller. Input devices may be switches and sensors etc. O/P devices can be solenoids, electromagnetic valves, motors, relays etc. After identification of all I/P and O/P instruments, corresponding designations are assigned to I/P and O/P lines of PLC controller. Lastly prepare a Ladder diagram for a program by following the sequence of operations that was determined previously.

7.5.2.1 PLC Controller Components

PLC is actually an industrial microcontroller system, which have hardware and software specifically adapted to industrial environment. Block schema with typical components that PLC consists is shown in Fig. 7.7.

Protection needed in isolating a CPU blocks from damaging influences that industrial environment can bring to a CPU via input lines. Program unit is usually a computer used for writing a program (often in ladder diagram) or a hand-held Programming device.

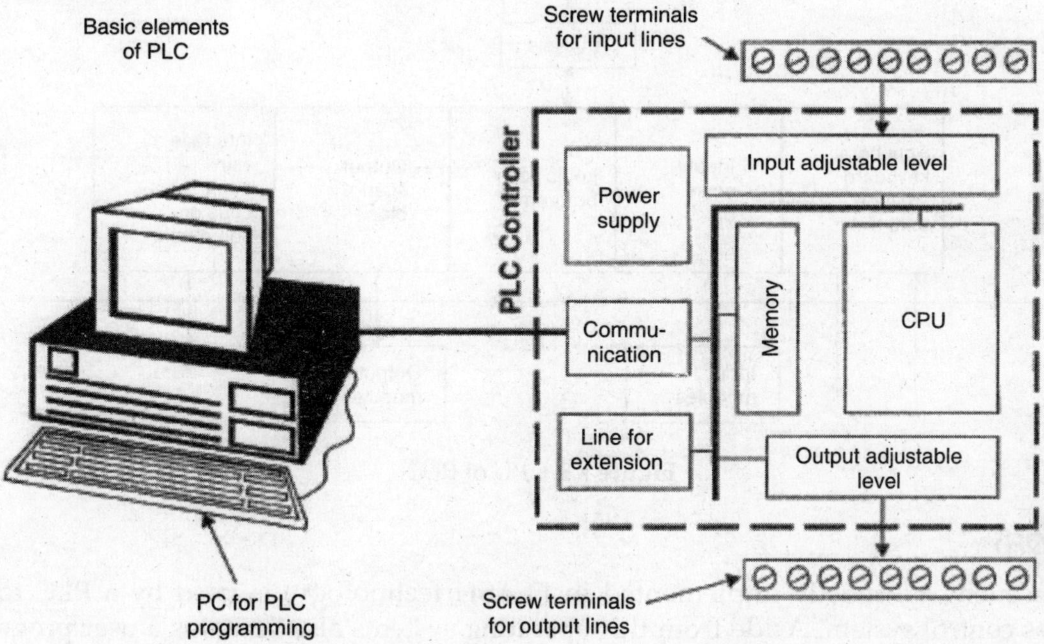

Figure 7.7 Basic elements of PLC controller

CENTRAL PROCESSING UNIT - CPU

Central processing unit (CPU) is the brain of a PLC controller. CPU itself is usually one of the microcontrollers. A foretime these were 8-bit microcontrollers such as 8051, and now these are 16- and 32- bit microcontrollers. CPU also takes care of communication, interconnection among other parts of PLC controller, program execution, memory operation, overseeing input and setting up of an output. PLC controllers have complex routines for memory checkup in order to ensure that PLC memory was not corrupted. Generally speaking, CPU unit makes a great number of check-ups of the PLC controller itself so eventually errors would be discovered early. You can simply look at any PLC controller and see that there are several indicators in the form of light diodes for error signalization. The CPU is shown in figure 7.8.

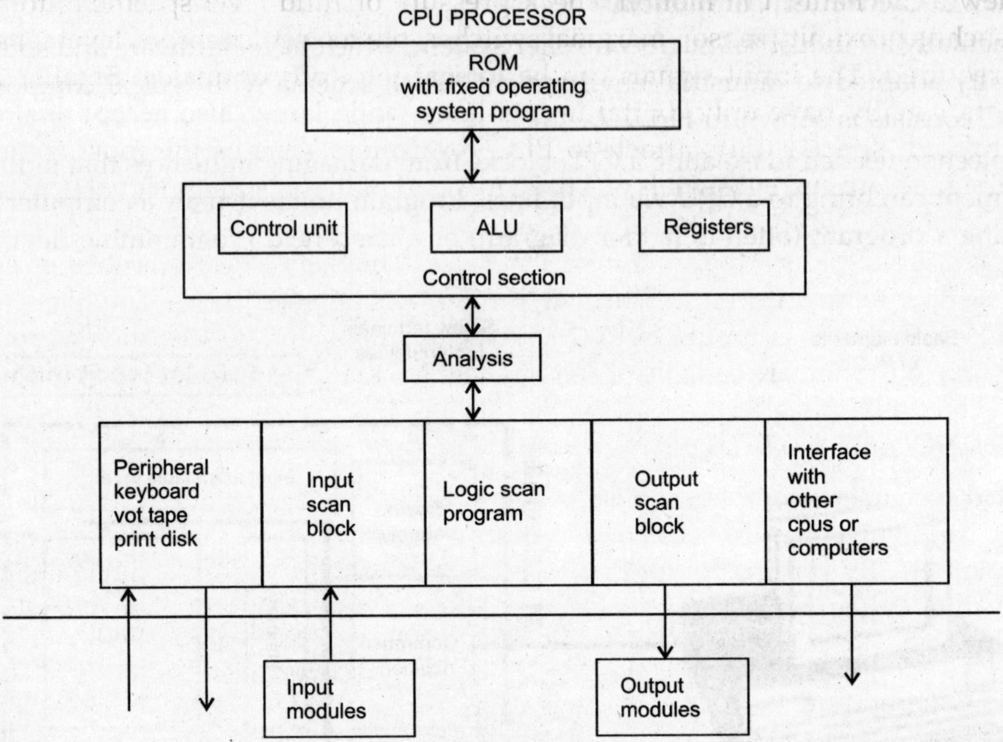

Figure 7.8 CPU of PLC

MEMORY

System memory (mostly implemented in FLASH technology) is used by a PLC for a process control system. Aside from this operating systems also contains a user program translated from a ladder diagram to a binary from. FLASH memory contents can be changed only in case where user program is being changed. PLC controllers were used earlier have EPROM memory instead of FLASH memory which had to be erased with UV lamp and to be reprogrammed. With the use of FLASH technology this process was greatly shortened. Reprogramming a program memory is done through a serial cable in a program for application development.

User memory is divided into blocks having special functions. Some parts of a memory are used for storing input and output status. The real status of input is stored either as "1" or as "0" in a specific memory bit. Each input or output has one corresponding bit in memory. Other parts of memory are used to store variable contents for variables used in user program.

PLC CONTROLLER INPUTS

Intelligence of an automated system depends largely on the ability of a PLC controller to read signals from different types of sensors and inputs devices. In order to detect a working piece, view a mechanism in motion, check pressure or fluid level specific automatic devices such as proximity sensor, marginal switches, photoelectric sensors, level sensors, etc. are required. The input signals can be logical (on /off) or analog. Smaller PLC Controllers usually have only digital inputs lines while larger also accept analogue inputs through special units attach to PLC controllers. One of the most frequent analogue signals are current signals of 4 to 20 mA and millivolt voltage signal generated by various sensors.

Sensors are usually used as inputs for PLCs. They can sense presence of some parts, measures temperature, pressure, or some other physical dimension, etc. Other devices also can serve as inputs to PLC controller. Intelligent devices such as robots, video system, etc. often are capable of sending signals to PLC controller input modules.

PLC CONTROLLER OUTPUT

Automated system is incomplete if it is not connected with some output devices. Some of the most frequently used devices are motors, solenoids, relays, indicators, sound signalization etc. By starting a motor, or a relay, PLC can manage or control a simple system such as system for positioning head of CNC machine. Output can be of analog or digital type.

7.5.2.2 PLC Operation

Let us consider the typical operation of a PLC. Programmer should always keep in mind that, the operation is not simultaneous for the entire ladder diagram and is not continuous as it is for relay sequencers. This is of great significance and can have significant impact if not taken into consideration during logic design. Operation of the programmable controller can be considered in two modes

- The I/O scan mode
- The Execution mode.

I/O SCAN MODE

During the I/O scan mode, the processor updates all outputs and inputs state of the system taking one input at a time. The time required for updation of I/O depends on the speed of the processor.

EXECUTION MODE

During execution mode, the processor evaluates each rung of the ladder diagram program that is being executed sequentially, starting from the first rung and proceeding to the last rung. As a rung is evaluated, the last known state of each of the input and/or output elements in the rung is considered, and if any true path to the output device is detected, then that output is indicated to be energized- that is, set to ON.

At the end of the ladder diagram, the I/P mode is entered again, and all output device are provided with the on or off state determined from execution of the ladder diagram program. All inputs are sampled, and the execution mode starts again.

SCAN TIME

An important characteristic of the programmable controller is, how much time is required for one complete cycle of I/O scan and execution. Of course, this depends on how many inputs and output channels are involved and on the length of the ladder diagram program.

The speed of the programmable controller depends on the clock frequency of the processor. The higher the clock frequency, the greater the speed and faster the scan/execution time.

The length of time for one scan consists of three parts:

- Input scan time
- Execution time
- Output scan time

Most of the scan time comes from the execution phase. The scan time may have an impact on the ability of the PLC to detect events that occur on the inputs.

7.5.2.3 PLC Programming

PLC can programmed (reprogrammed) through a computer, if the software needed for programming is available or through manual programmers (consoles). Through regular checking of programs in PLC, execution only of good programs can be insured.

Almost every program for programming a PLC controller possesses various useful options such as: Forced switching on and off of the systems inputs/outputs (I/O lines), program follow up in real time as well as documenting a diagram. There are some special considerations in programming which includes the availability of special functions and the relation between external I/O devices and their programmed representations.

LADDER DIAGRAM INTERPRETATION

There is an important difference between the interpretation of physical ladder diagram and a programmed ladder diagram. This difference arises from the fact that the programmed diagram bases the state of a rung on a logical interpretation of the symbol rather than its physical state.

In a programmed diagram rung, the ON or OFF state of the output of the rung is determined by testing the elements of the rung for a TRUE or FALSE condition. If a complete TRUE element path to output exists in the rung, then the output will be made TRUE or ON.

ADDRESSING

The programmable controller identifies the different elements such as inputs, outputs, flags etc. with some unique number called as address. The addresses are used to identify both the physical and software devices according to the following categories:

- Physical input devices- ON or OFF
- Physical output devices- energized (ON) or de-energized (OFF)
- Programmed control relay coils and contacts
- Programmed time-delay relay coils and contacts
- Programmed counters and contacts
- Special Functions

The address designation depends on the type of programmable controller. Some controllers may reserve certain addresses for physical I/O devices, other addresses for software control relays, and yet others for special function.

PLC SOFTWARE FUNCTIONS

A PLC has many functions implemented in the software associated with the processor. In this section, some of the common function of PLCs are described. Individual PLC manufacturers will have their own details on actual implementation.

CONTROL RELAY

The software control relay is denoted by a circle (or using parentheses *-( )-*) with an identification number. It can have any number of NO or NC contacts, which are identified by the same number as the relay. The relay state can be shown as follows:

Normally Open Contact

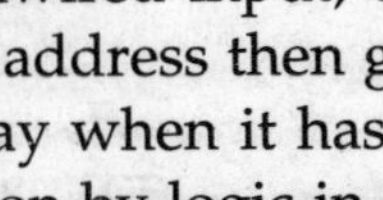

The symbol far a NO contact indicates a normally open contact through which current cannot flow unless the contact has been closed. If it is the contact of a relay, then the relay coil must be energized.

When used with a hardwired input, this instruction is off until there is a voltage applied to the Input. The bit address then goes high, or on, and the instruction becomes "true." It works the same way when it has the same address as an internal coil, except that the coil must be turned on by logic in the program.

In a ladder diagram, the symbol for a NO contact indicates that the device should be interpreted as FALSE if the contact is tested and found to be open, and TRUE if it is found to be closed.

Normally Closed Contact

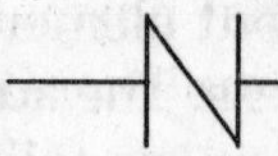

For the NC contact, the idea is that current will flow until the contact has been opened. If it is a push –button switch, then someone must open the contact and stop the current flow by pushing. If it is the contact of a relay, then the relay must be energized to open the contact and stop current flow through the contacts.

This is an inverted normally open contact. When used with a hardwired input, this instruction is "true" until there is a voltage applied to the input. It then goes low, or off, and becomes "false."

Consider the programmed NC symbol. This means if it is tested and found to be closed, then it is FALSE, and if tested and found open, it is ON. This is not like the physical.

COUNTER

A counter is a programmed function that counts (increments/decrements) every time the input changes from false to true. This means that, if in one scan the input is false and in the next scan the input is true, the counter changes. No further counts will occur until the inputs goes false again and then true.

There are also counters that start with some preset value and count down to zero, at which time the counter becomes true. Different PLC manufacturers have their individual ways of addressing and describing the counter function.

The counter function used to count events. It could be used to keep track of machine cycles, count parts, etc. It can be programmed with a preset value that triggers another event when the count is reached.

Some PLCs also provide a counter that can count either up or down depending upon the state of an input.

TIMERS

The programmed timer function plays an important role in PLC application. It provide delays in some manufacturing sequence and to specify the period of time that some operation is to last. Timers are of two type:

- On delay type
- Off delay type

The timer will have an address and the preset number of ticks to count. The amount of time per tick is a function of the type of PLC being used. Typical values are 10 ms and 100 ms. The timer only counts while it has a true input. If the inputs become false and then true again, the timer will reset to zero and start to count again.

SPECIAL FUNCTION

In this section some other functions are described that normally available in most PLCs. The one-shot is an output that will go true for only one scan when its input path is true. This device is normally used for initialization and other instances when an event is to occur only once, but the conditions that make it true may occur again.

A shift-register is used to remember a certain number of previous states of a rung (ladder-diagram). A two-event shift register could be used to remember that state of a rung for the latest two scans.

Nowadays PLCs are able to handle multi-digit number as well as single-bit, binary numbers. Thus, it is possible for a PLC to accept input from an 8-bit ADC and store the result in a known memory location or register. These PLCs have the ability to perform a variety of math operations like simple addition, subtraction, multiplication, and division and trigonometric operations etc.

SCAN-TIME/TIMER RELATIONSHIP

Depending upon the size of the program and the type of PLC, a scan time can range from 5 ms to 20 ms or more. Care must be taken not to design timer functions with reactions less than a scan time. Suppose a software timer with time base .001 sec and PLC scan time of 10 ms, than if some one is using 5 ms preset value of timer and the output of timer is used to control a process, the result will be inconsistent. For example: If a programmer is programmed to on a hooter with above value, the hooter should be ON after 5 ms but the result will be inconsistent although theoretically it should be alright. In practice due to scanning one should avoid using software timer when the scanning time will comparable or less than PLC scan time, in that case it is advisable to use hardware timer in place of software timer.

7.5.3 TEMPERATURE CONTROL

Figure 7.9 shows an temperature control system where a heating oven, as part of a manufacturing process, is to be controlled within the temperature range, between 190°C and 200°C. An 8051 microcomputer based system is used to control the temperature. The oven has two built-in temperature sensors. The low threshold sensor outputs a logic 0 if the temperature is below 190°C, otherwise it outputs a logic high level (say 5 volts). The high threshold sensor outputs a logic low level if the temperature exceeds 200°C, otherwise it outputs a logic high level. The temperature sensors are connected to the 8051's interrupt inputs, INT0 and INT1, as shown in the diagram. Both of these interrupt inputs are set to trigger at negative voltage transitions. The microcomputer outputs a logic 1 on the P1.0 output pin to turn on the heater element and it outputs a logic 0 to turn off the heating element. Assume the necessary hardware driver circuitry, to switch power to the oven, is included in the oven.

The program is written so that an interrupt from the low threshold sensor will cause the heating element to turn on and interrupt from the high threshold sensor will cause the heating element to turn off.

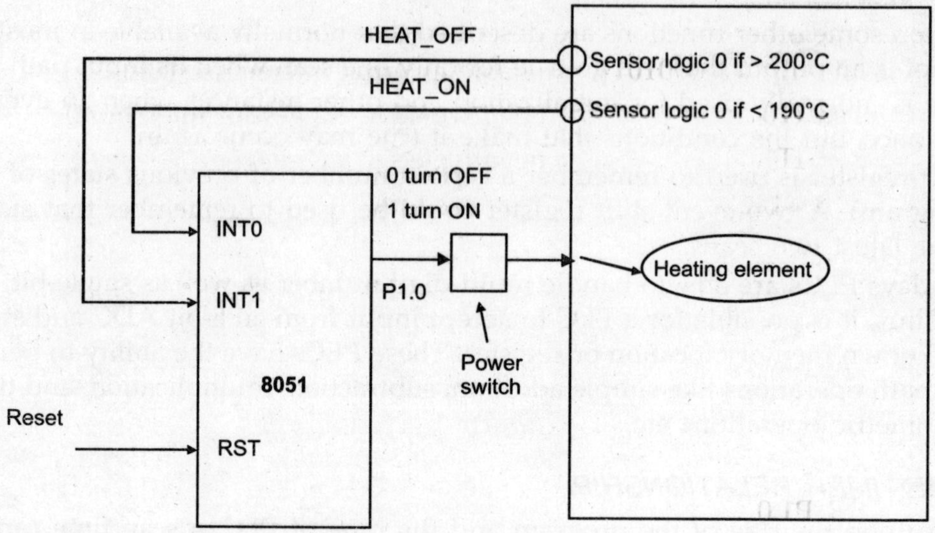

Figure 7.9 Temperature controlled heating oven

The ALP to control the oven is given below. Since the ISR routines (Interrupt Service Routines) are very short they could have been positioned within the 8 bytes of memory available at the respective vector locations. However, the ISR routines are located higher up in memory to show the memory positioning structure which would be used for larger ISR routines. Three vector locations are defined at the beginning of the program. The RESET vector, at address 0000h, contains a jump instruction to the MAIN program. Location 0003h is the vector location for external interrupt 0, and this contains a jump instruction to the relevant ISR routine, ISR0. External interrupt 1 uses the vector location 0013h which contains a jump instruction to the ISR routine, ISR1. In this oven control program example the main program just loops around doing nothing. When an interrupt occurs, the required action is carried out by the relevant ISR routine.

```
ORG 0000h          ; entry address for 8051 RESET
LJMP MAIN          ; MAIN starts beyond interrupt vector space
ORG 0003h          ; vector address for interrupt 0
LJMP ISR0          ; jump to start of ISR0
ORG 0013h          ; vector address for interrupt 1
LJMP ISR1          ; jump to start of ISR1
ORG 0100h          ; Beginning of MAIN
```

```
MAIN:
        MOV IE, #10000101B   ; enable external interrupts IE0, IE1
        SETB IT0             ; negative edge trigger for interrupt 0
        SETB IT1             ; negative edge trigger for interrupt 1
        SETB P1.0            ; heater is ON
I_WAIT:
        LJMP I_WAIT          ; wait for interrupt
ISR0:
        SETB P1.0            ; turn ON heater
        RETI                 ; return from interrupt
ISR1:
        CLR P1.0             ; turn OFF heater
        RETI                 ; return from interrupt
        END                  ; end of program
```

7.6 PROBLEMS

1. Write a program to generate square wave of 1KHz on port1, pin4 of 8051. Assume crystal frequency to 11.0592 MHz.
2. Modify the program of problem 1 so that it generate a rectangular wave of 60% duty cycle.
3. Write a program for generating stair-step ramp waveform. Also show connections of 8051 for generating the stair-step ramp.
4. How we generate sine wave form using microcontroller. Write an program using lookup table to generate the sine wave.
5. How 8051 can be used for
   (I) Frequency counter
   (II) Pulse width measurement
6. Describe the basic block of PLC used in automation application.
7. With the schematic show how 8051 can be used for temperature controller operation. Also write a program to maintain temperature to heater between 100°C to 150°C.

Chapter 8

8096 Microcontroller

8.1 INTRODUCTION

High speed digital signals are frequently encountered in modern control applications. In addition there is often a requirement for high speed 16-bit and 32-bit precision in calculations. The MCS-96 generically referred to as the 8096 is designed to be used in applications which require high speed calculations and fast I/O operations.

The 8096 is a 16-bit microcontroller with dedicated I/O subsystems and a complete set of 16-bit arithmetic instructions including multiply and divide operations.

8.2 8096 OVERVIEW

8.2.1 GENERAL DESCRIPTION

Unlike microprocessors microcontrollers are generally optimized for specific applications. Intels 8048 was optimized for general control tasks while the 8051 was optimized for 8-bit math and single bit boolean operations. The 8096 has been designed for high speed high performance control applications. Because it has been designed for these applications the 8096 architecture is different from that of the 8048 or 8051.

The features of 8096 microcontroller are:

- 232 Byte resister file.
- Resister to resister architecture.
- 10 bit A/D converter with S/H.
- Five 8 bit I/0 ports.
- 20 Interrupt sources.
- Pulse width modulation output.
- High speed I/0 subsystem.
- Dedicated band rate generator.

- Full Duplex Serial port.
- 16 bit watchdog timer.

There are two major sections of the 8096 the CPU section and the I/O section. Each of these sections can be subdivided into functional blocks as shown in Fig. 8.1 (a) and block diagram of resister file, RALU, memory controller and interrupt controller shown in figure 8.1(b).

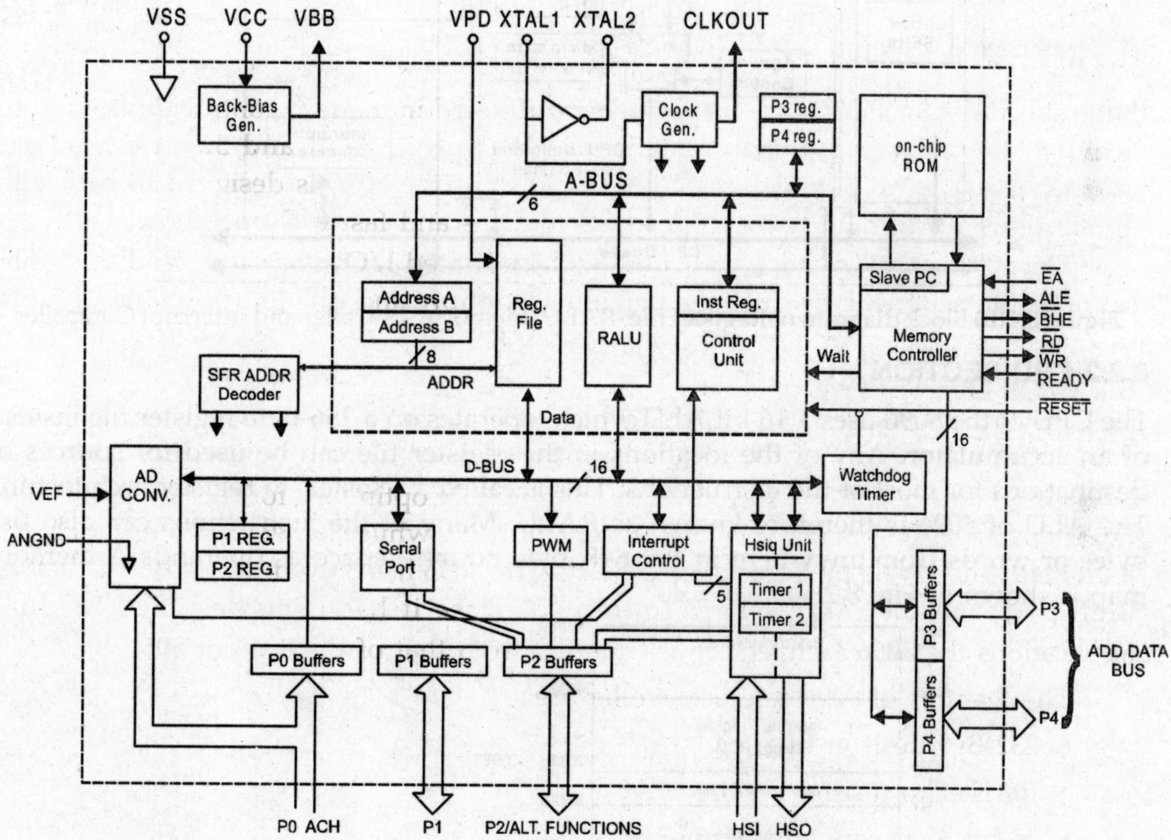

Figure 8.1(a) 8096 Block diagram

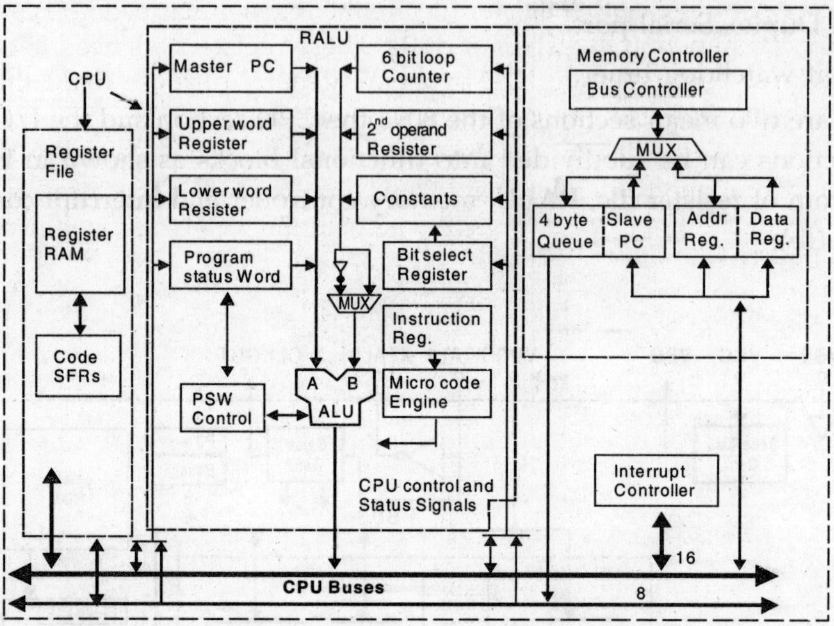

Figure 8.1(b) Block diagram of Register file, RALU, Memory Controller and Interrupt Controller

8.2.2 CPU SECTION

The CPU of the 8096 uses a 16-bit ALU which operates on a 256-byte register file instead of an accumulator. Any of the locations in the register file can be used for sources or destinations for most of the instructions. This is called a register to register architecture. The ALU of 8096 is therefore known as RALU. Many of the instructions can also use bytes or words from anywhere in the 64K byte address space as operands A memory map is shown in Fig. 8.2.

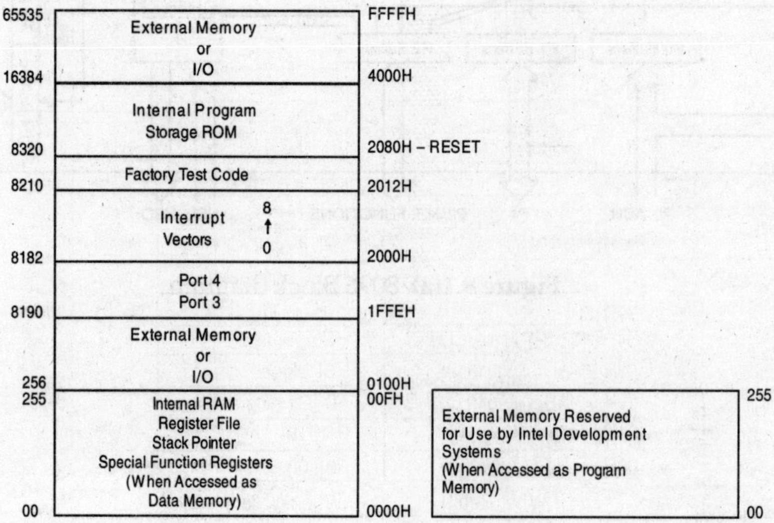

Figure 8.2 8096 Memory map

In the lower 24 bytes of the register file are the register mapped I/O control locations also called Special Function Registers or SFRs. These registers are used to control the on-chip I/O features. The remaining 232 bytes are general purpose RAM the upper 16 of which can be kept alive using a low current power-down mode.

Figure 8.3 shows the layout of the register mapped I/O. Some of these registers serve two functions one if they are read from and another if they are written to. More information about the use of these registers is included in the description of the features which they control.

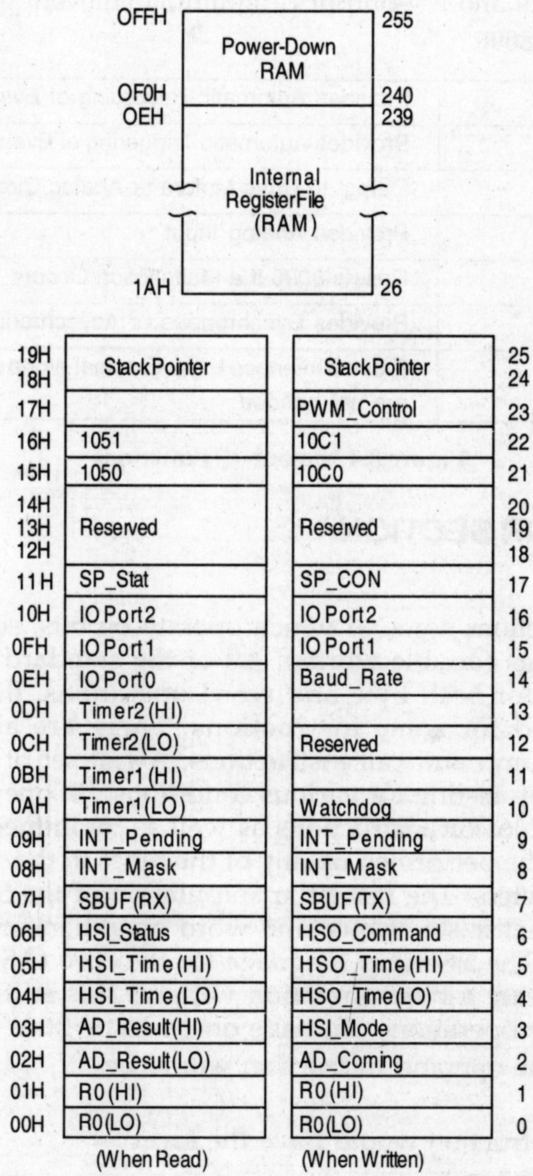

Figure 8.3 SFR layouts

8.2.3 I/O FEATURES

Many of the I/O features on the 8096 are designed to operate with little CPU intervention. A list of the major I/O functions is shown in Fig. 8.4. The Watchdog Timer is an internal timer which can be used to reset the system if the software fails to operate properly. The Pulse-Width-Modulation (PWM) output can be used as a D to A, a motor driver or for many other purposes. The A to D converter (ADC) has 8 multiplexed inputs and 10-bit resolution. The serial port has several modes and its own baud rate generator. The High Speed I/O section includes a 16-bit timer, a 16-bit counter, a 4-input programmable edge detector, 4 software timers and a 6-output programmable event generator.

Major I/O Functions of 8096

High Speed Input Unit	Provides Automatic Recording of Events
High Speed Output Unit	Provides Automatic Triggering of Events and Real-Time Interrupts
Pulse Width Modulation	Output to Drive Motors or Analog Circuits
A to D Converter	Provides Analog Input
Watchdog Timer	Resets 8096 if a Malfunction Occurs
Serial Port	Provides Synchronous or Asynchronous Link
Standard I/O Lines	Provide Interface to the External World when other Special Features are not needed

Figure 8.4 Major I/O Functions

8.3 THE PROCESSOR SECTION

8.3.1 OPERATIONS

The 8096 has 100 instructions some of which operate on bits, some on bytes, some on words and some on longs (double words). All of the standard logical and arithmetic functions are available for both byte and word operations. Bit operations and long operations are provided for some instructions. There are also flag manipulation instructions as well as jump and call instructions. A full set of conditional jumps has been included to speed up testing for various conditions. Bit operations are provided by the Jump Bit and Jump Not Bit instructions as well as by immediate masking of bytes. These bit operations can be performed on any of the bytes in the register file or on any of the special function registers. The fast bit manipulation of the SFRs can provide rapid I/O operations. A symmetric set of byte and word operations make up the majority of the 8096 instruction set. The assembly language for the 8096 (ASM-96) uses a "B" suffix on a mnemonic to indicate a byte operation without this suffix a word operation is indicated. Many of these operations can have one, two or three operands.

An example of a one operand instruction would be

NOT Value 1

A two operand instruction would have the form

ADD Value 2, Value 1

A three operand instruction might look like

MUL Value 3, Value 2, Value 1

The three operand instructions combined with the register to register architecture almost eliminate the necessity of using temporary registers. This results in a faster processing time than machines that have equivalent instruction execution times but use a standard architecture.

Long (32-bit) operations include shifts, normalize and multiply and divide. The word divide is a 32-bit by 16-bit operation with a 16-bit quotient and 16-bit remainder. The word multiply is a word by word multiply with a long result. Both of these operations can be done in either the signed or unsigned mode. The direct unsigned modes of these instructions take only 6.5 microseconds. A normalize instruction and bit flag have been included in the instruction set to provide hardware support for the software floating point.

8.3.2 ADDRESSING MODES

One operand of most of the instructions can be used with any one of six addressing modes. These modes increase the flexibility and overall execution speed of the 8096. The addressing modes are :

- Register-direct addressing
- Immediate addressing
- Indirect addressing
- Indirect with auto-increment addressing
- Long indexed addressing
- Short indexed addressing

The fastest instruction execution is gained by using either register direct or immediate addressing. Register-direct addressing is similar to normal direct addressing except that only addresses in the register file or SFRs can be addressed. The indexed mode is used to directly address the remainder of the 64K address space. Immediate addressing operates as would be expected using the data following the opcode as the operand. Both of the indirect addressing modes use the value in a word register as the address of the operand. If the indirect auto-increment mode is used then the word register is incremented by one after a byte access or by two after a word access. This mode is particularly useful for accessing lookup tables. Access to any of the locations in the 64K address space can be obtained by using the long indexed addressing mode. In this mode a 16-bit 2's complement value is added to the contents of a word register to form the address of the operand. By using the zero register as the index the assembler can accept "direct" addressing to any location. The zero register is located at 0000H and always has a value of zero. A short indexed mode is also available to save some time and code. This mode uses an 8-bit 2's complement number as the offset instead of a 16-bit number.

8.3.3 ASSEMBLY LANGUAGE

The multiple addressing modes of the 8096 make it easy to program in assembly language and provide an excellent interface to high level languages. The instructions accepted by the assembler consist of mnemonics followed by either addresses or data. The addresses or data are given in different formats depending on the addressing mode. These modes and formats are shown in Fig. 8.5.

Mnem	Dest or Src 1	; One operand direct
Mnem	Dest, Src 1	; Two operand direct
Mnem	Dest, Src 1, Src 2	; Three operand direct
Mnem	#Src 1	; One operand immediate
Mnem	Dest, #Src 1	; Two operand immediate
Mnem	Dest, Src 1, Src 2	; Three operand immediate
Mnem	[addr]	; One operand indirect
Mnem	[addr]+	; One operand indirect auto-increment
Mnem	Dest, [addr]	; Two operand indirect
Mnem	Dest, [addr]+	; Two operand indirect auto-increment
Mnem	Dest, Src 1, [addr]	; Three operand indirect
Mnem	Dest, Src 1, [addr]+	; Three operand indirect auto-increment
Mnem	Dest, offs [addr]	; Two operand indexed (short or long)
Mnem	Dest, Src 1, offs [addr]	; Three operand indexed (short or long)

where; "Mnem" is the instruction mnemonic
"Dest" is the destination register
"Src1", "Src2" are the source registers
"addr" is a register containing a value to be used in computing the address of an operand
"offs" is an offset used in computing the address of an operand

Figure 8.5 Instruction format

8.3.4 INTERRUPTS

The flexibility of the instruction set is carried through into the interrupt system. There are 20 different interrupt sources that can be used on the 8096. The 20 sources vector through 8 locations or interrupt vectors. The vector names and their sources are shown in Fig. 8.6 with their locations listed in Fig. 8.7. Control of the interrupts is handled through the Interrupt Pending Register (INT- PENDING), the Interrupt Mask Register (INT- MASK) and the I bit in the PSW (PSW.9). Figure 8.8 shows a block diagram of the interrupt structure.

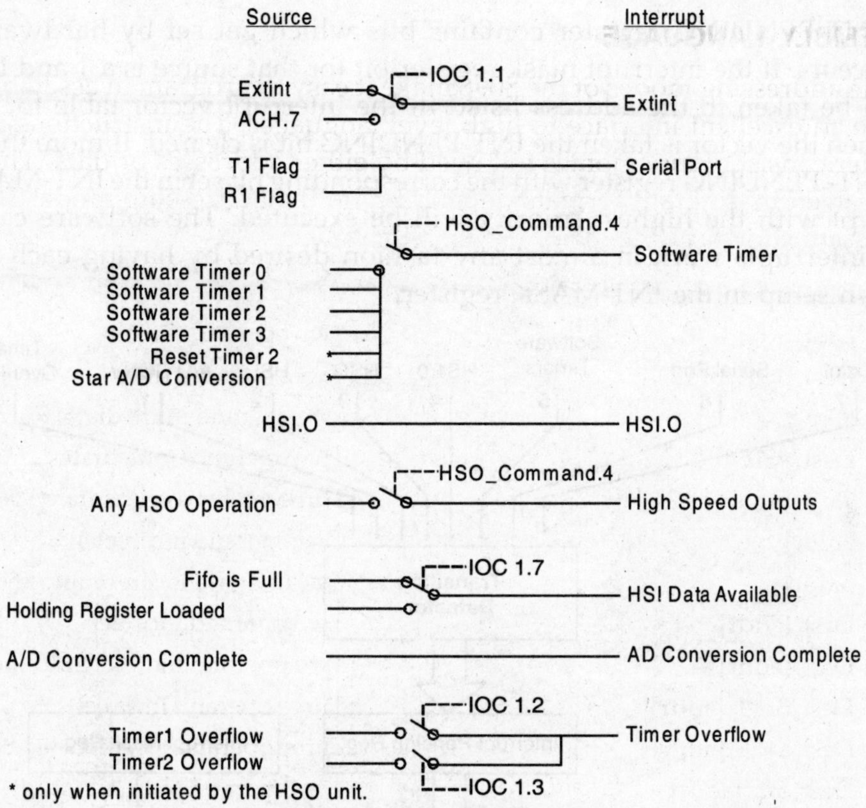

Figure 8.6 Interrupt sources

Source	Vector Location		Priority
	(High Byte)	(Low Byte)	
Software	2011 H	2010H	Not Applicable
Extint	200 FH	200EH	7 (Highest)
Serial Port	200 DH	200 CH	6
Software Timers	200 BH	200 AH	5
HIS.0	2009 H	2008 H	4
High Speed Outputs	2007 H	2006 H	3
HIS Data Available	2005 H	2004 H	2
A/D Conversion Complete	2003 H	2003 H	1
Timer Overflow	2001 H	200 H	0 (Lowest)

Figure 8.7 Interrupt Vectors and Priorities

The INT-PENDING register contains bits which get set by hardware when an interrupt occurs. If the interrupt mask register bit for that source is a 1 and PSW.9 = 1, a vector will be taken to the address listed in the interrupt vector table for that Vector Source. When the vector is taken the INT-PENDING bit is cleared. If more than one bit is set in the INT- PENDING register with the corresponding bit set in the INT-MASK register, the Interrupt with the highest priority will be executed. The software can make the hardware interrupts work in almost any fashion desired by having each routine run with its own setup in the INT-MASK register.

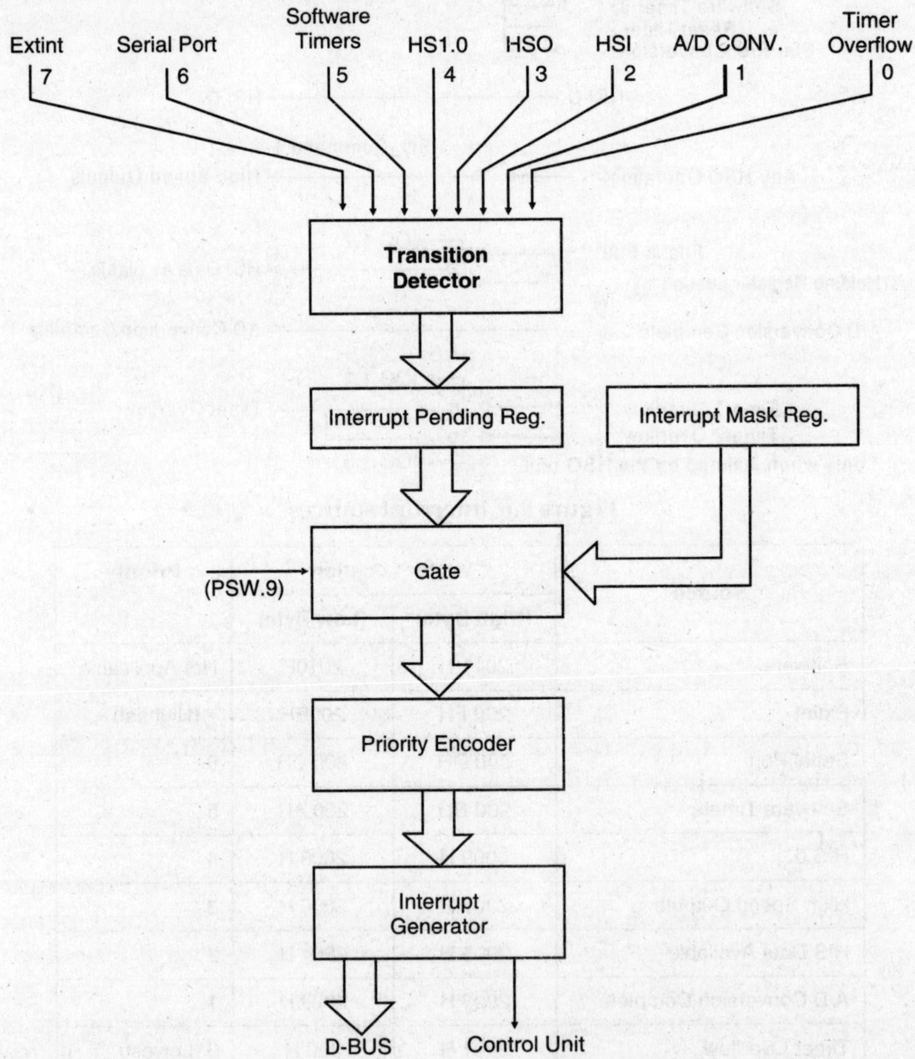

Figure 8.8 Interrupt structure

PROGRAM STATUS WORD

15	14	13	12	11	10	09	08	07	06	05	04	03	02	01	00
Z	N	V	VT	C	–	I	ST	INT_MASK							

WHERE:

Z is the zero flag. It is set when the result of an operation is zero.

N is the negative flag. It is set to the algebraically correct sign of the result regardless of overflows.

V is the overflow flag. It is set if an overflow occurs.

VT is the overflow trap flag. It is set when the VT flag is set and cleared ny JVT, JNVT, or CLRVT.

C is the carry flag. It is set if a carry was generated by the prior operation.

I is the global interrupt enable bit.

ST is the sticky bit. It is set during a right shift if a one was shifted into and then out of the carry flag.

INT_MASK is the interrupt mask register and contains bits which individually enable the 8 interrupt vectors.

Figure 8.9 PSW register

PSW (shown in Fig. 8.9), stores the INT-MASK register in its lower byte so that the mask register can be pushed and popped along with the machine status when moving in and out of routines. The action of pushing flags clears the PSW which includes PSW.9, the interrupt enable bit. Therefore, after a PUSHF instruction interrupts are disabled.

The PUSHF instruction saves the PSW including the old INT-MASK register. The PSW including the interrupt enable bit are left cleared. If some interrupts need to be enabled while the service routine runs, the INT-MASK is loaded with a new value and interrupts are globally enabled before the service routine continues. At the end of the service routine a POPF instruction is executed to restore the old PSW. The RET instruction is executed and the code returns to the desired location. Although the POPF instruction can enable the interrupts the next instruction will always execute. This prevents unnecessary building of the stack by ensuring that the RET always executes before another interrupt vector is taken.

8.4 ON-CHIP I/O SECTION

All of the on-chip I/O features of the 8096 can be accessed through the special function registers as shown in Fig. 8.3. The advantage of using register-mapped I/O is that these registers can be used as the sources or destinations of CPU operations. There are seven major I/O functions as shown in Fig. 8.4.

8.4.1 TIMER/COUNTERS

The 8096 has two time bases, Timer 1 and Timer 2. Timer 1 is a 16-bit free running timer which is incremented every 8 state times (A state time is 3 oscillator periods or 0.25 microseconds with a 12 MHz crystal). Its value can be read at any time and used as a reference for both the HSI section and the HSO section. Timer 1 can cause an interrupt when it overflows, and cannot be modified or stopped without resetting the entire chip. Timer 2 is really an event counter since it uses an external clock source. Like Timer 1, it is 16-bits wide, can be read at any time, can be used with the HSO section and can generate an interrupt when it overflows. Control of Timer 2 is limited to incrementing it and resetting it. Specific values cannot be written to it.

Although the 8096 has only two timers the timer flexibility is equal to a unit with many timers because of the HSIO unit. The HSI enables one to measure times of external events on up to four lines using Timer 1 as a timer base. The HSO unit can schedule and execute internal events and up to six external events based on the values in either Timer 1 or Timer 2. The 8096 also includes separate dedicated timers for the baud rate generator and watchdog timer.

8.4.2 HSI

The HSI unit can be thought of as a message taker which records the line which had an event and the time at which the event occurred. Four types of events can trigger the HSI unit as shown in the HSI block diagram in Fig. 8.10.

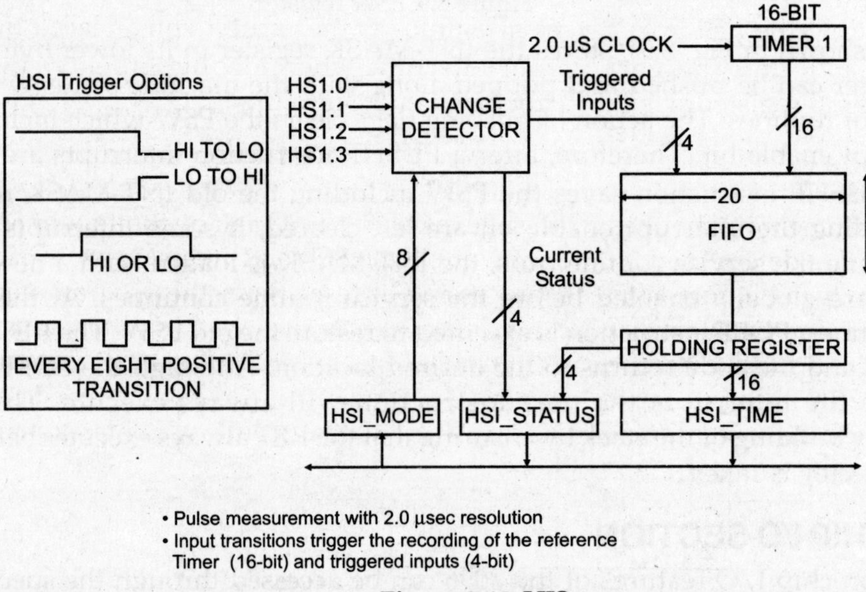

Figure 8.10 HIS

The HSI unit can measure pulse widths and record times of events with a 2 microsecond resolution. It can look for one of four events on each of four lines simultaneously based on the information in the HSI Mode register shown in Fig. 8.11.

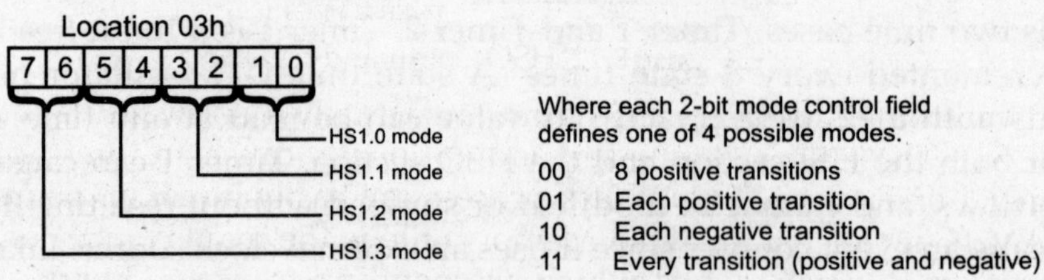

Figure 8.11 HSI mode register

The information is then stored in a seven level FIFO for later retrieval. Whenever the FIFO contains information the earliest entry is placed in the holding register. When the holding register is read the next valid piece of information is loaded into it. Interrupts can be generated by the HSI unit at the time the holding register is loaded or when the FIFO has six or more entries.

The function of HIS can be summarized as:

- The 8096 HIS unit can record times of external events with a 9 state time resolution. It can monitor four independently configurable HSI lines and captures the value of timer 1 when events take place.
- The four types of events that can trigger captures include: rising edge only, falling edge only, rising or falling edges, or every eight rising edge.
- The HSI unit can store up to 8 entries (Timer 1 values).
- Reading the HSI holding register unloads the earliest entry placed in the FIFO.
- The HSI unit can generate an interrupt when loading an entry into the HSI holding register or loading the sixth entry into the FIFO.

8.4.3 HSO

As the HSI can be thought of as a message taker, the HSO can be thought of as a message sender. At times determined by the software, the HSO sends messages to various devices to have them turn on, turn off, start processing or reset. Since the programmed times can be referenced to either Timer 1 or Timer 2, the HSO makes the two timers look like many. For example if several events have to occur at specific times the HSO unit can schedule all of the events based on a single timer. The events that can be scheduled to occur and the format of the command written to the HSO Command register are shown in Fig. 8.12.

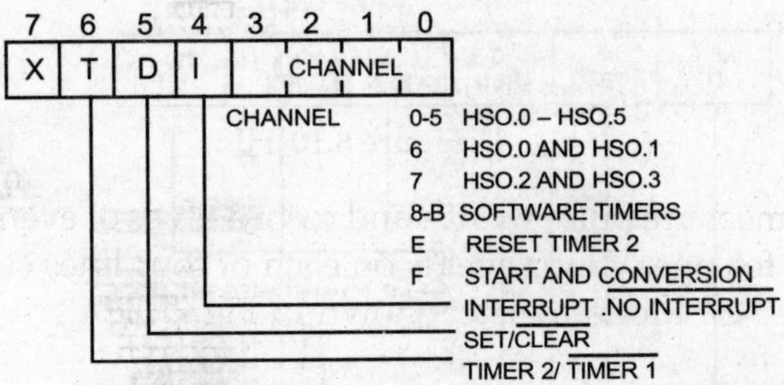

Figure 8.12 HSO Command register

The software timers listed in the figure are actually 4 software flags in I/O Status Register 1 (IOS1). These flags can be set, and optionally cause an interrupt, at any time based on Timer 1 or Timer 2. A multitask process can easily be set up using the software timers. A CAM (Content Addressable Memory) file is the main component of the HSO. This file stores up to eight events which are pending to occur. Every state time one location of the CAM is compared with the two timers. After 8 state times (two microseconds with a 12 MHz clock) the entire CAM has been searched for time matches.

If a match occurs the specified event will be triggered and that location of the CAM will be made available for another pending event.

The function of HSO can be summarized as:

- The 8096 HSO unit can trigger events at specified times based on Timer 1 or Timer 2.
- These programmable events include: starting an A/D conversion, resetting Timer 2, generating up to four software time delays, and setting or cleaing one or more of the six HSO output lines.
- The HSO unit stores pending event and specified times in a Content Addressable Memory (CAM) file. This file stores up to 8 commands.
- Each command specifies the action time, the nature of the action, whether an interrupt is to occur, and whether timer 1 or timer 2 is the reference timer.
- Every 8 state times the HSO compares the CAM locations for time matches. The HSO unit triggers the specified event when it find a time match.
- A Command is cleared from the CAM as soon as it executes.

8.4.4 SERIAL PORT

The 8096 has an on-chip serial port similar to that on the 8051. It has one synchronous and three asynchronous modes. In the asynchronous modes baud rates of up to 187.5 Kbaud can be used, while in the synchronous mode rates up to 1.5 Mbaud are available. The chip has a baud rate generator which is independent of Timer 1 and Timer 2, so using the serial port does not affect any of the HIS, HSO or timer flexibility or functionality. Control of the serial port is provided through the SPCON/SPSTAT (Serial Port CONtrol/Serial Port STATus) register.

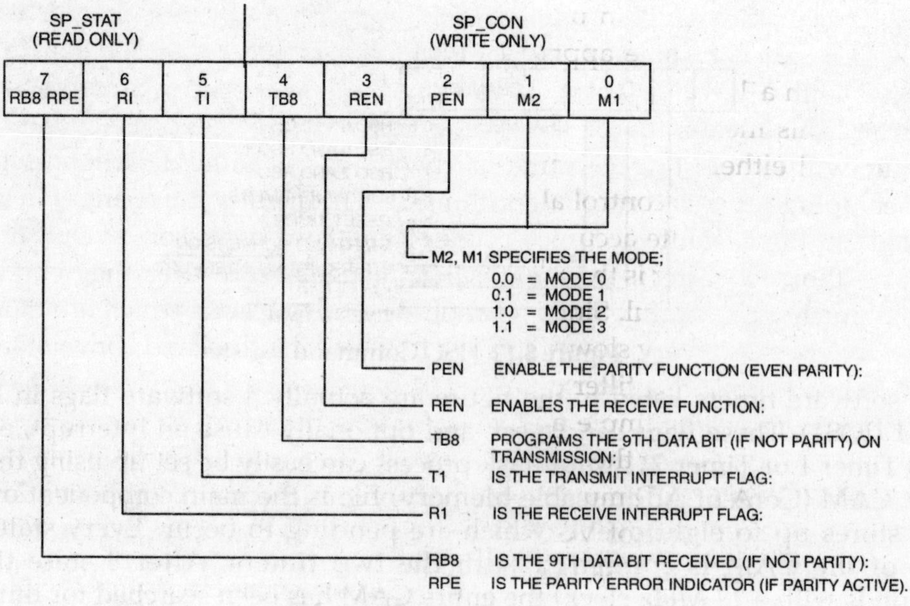

Figure 8.13 SPCON/SPSTAT register

This register shown in Fig. 8.13 has some bits which are read only and others which are write only. Although the functionality of the port is similar to that of the 8051 the names of some of the modes and control bits are different. The way in which the port is used from a software standpoint is also slightly different since RI and TI are cleared after each read of the register.

The four modes of the serial port are referred to as modes 0 ,1, 2 and 3. Mode 0 is the synchronous mode and is commonly used to interface to shift registers for I/O expansion. In this mode the port outputs a pulse train on the TXD pin and either transmits or receives data on the RXD pin. Mode 1 is the standard asynchronous mode, 8 bits plus a stop and start bit are sent or received. Modes 2 and 3 handle 9 bits plus a stop and start bit. The difference between the two is, that in Mode 2 the serial port interrupt will not be activated unless the ninth data bit is a one; in Mode 3 the interrupt is activated whenever a byte is received. These two modes are commonly used for interprocessor communication.

Baud rates for all of the modes are controlled through the Baud Rate register. This is a byte wide register which is loaded sequentially with two bytes and internally stores the value as a word. The least significant byte is loaded to the register followed by the most significant. The most significant bit of the baud value determines the clock source for the baud rate generator.

Serial port Mode 1 is the easiest mode to use as there is little to worry about except initialization and loading and unloading SBUF, the Serial port buffer.

8.4.5 A TO D CONVERTER

Analog inputs are frequently required in a microcontroller application. The 8097 has a 10-bit A to D converter that can use any one of eight input channels. The conversions are done using the successive approximation method and require 168 state times (42 microseconds with a 12 MHz clock). The results are guaranteed monotonic by design of the converter. This means that if the analog input voltage changes, even slightly, the digital value will either stay the same or change in the same direction as the analog input. When doing process control algorithms, it is frequently the changes in inputs that are required not the absolute accuracy of the value. For this reason, even if the absolute accuracy of a 10-bit converter is the same as that of an 8-bit converter, the 10-bit monotonic converter is much more useful. Since most of the analog inputs which are monitored by a microcontroller change very slowly relative to the 42 microsecond conversion time, it is acceptable to use a capacitive filter on each input instead of a sample and hold. The 8097 does not have an internal sample and hold, so it is necessary to ensure that the input signal does not change during the conversion time. The input to the A/D must be between ANGND and VREF. ANGND must be within a few millivolts of VSS and VREF must be within a few tenths of a volt of VCC. Using the A to D converter on the 8097 can be a very low software overhead task because of the interrupt and HSO unit structure.

The A to D can be started by the HSO unit at a preset time. When the conversion is complete it is possible to generate an interrupt. By using these features the A to D can be run under complete interrupt control. The A to D can also be directly16 controlled by software flags which are located in the AD_RESULT/AD_COMMAND Register.

8.4.6 PWM REGISTER

True digital to analog converters are difficult to make on a microprocessor because of all of the digital noise and the necessity of providing an on chip, relatively high current, rail to rail driver. They also take up a fair amount of silicon area which can be better used for other features. The A to D converter does use a D to A but the currents involved are very small.

For many applications an analog output signal can be replaced by a Pulse Width Modulated (PWM) signal. This signal can be easily generated in hardware and takes up much less silicon area than a true D to A. The signal is a variable duty cycle, fixed frequency waveform that can be integrated to provide an approximation to an analog output. The frequency is fixed at a period of 64 microseconds for a 12 MHz clock speed. Controlling the PWM simply requires writing the desired duty cycle value (an 8-bit value) to the PWM Register.

Converting the PWM signal to an analog signal varies in difficulty, depending upon the requirements of the system. Some systems, such as motors or switching power supplies actually require a PWM signal not a true analog one. For many other cases it is necessary only to amplify the signal so that it switches rail-to-rail, and then filter it. Switching rail-to-rail means that the output of the amplifier will be a reference value when the input is a logical one, and the output will be zero when the input is a logical zero. The filter can be a simple RC network or an active filter. If a large amount of current is needed a buffer is also required.

8.4.7 STANDARD I/O PORTS

The 8096 has five 8 bit I/O ports.

- Port 0 is an input port that is also the analog input for the A/D converter.
- Port 1 is a quasi-bidirectional port.
- Port 2 contains three types of port lines.
- Quasi-Bidirectional, input and output. Other functions on the 8096 share the input and output lines with port 2.
- Port 3 and 4 are open-drain bidirectional ports that share their pins with the address/data bus.

8.5 CONCLUSION

An overview of the MCS-96 family has been presented in this chapter. The additional information on the 8096 can be found in the Microcontroller Intel Handbook.

8.6 PROBLEMS

1. Why is the ALU of the 8096 is called RALU?
2. Discuss the features of 8096 family of microcontrollers.
3. Write short notes on following 8096 family microcontroller features:
    - High Speed Input Unit
    - High Speed Output Unit
    - Input/Output
    - A to D Converter
4. Explain memory mapping of 8096.
5. Distinguish between 8096 and 8051.
6. Intel 8096 is of ________ bit microcontroller family called as ________.
    (a) 8, MCS51 (b) 16, MCS51
    (c) 8, MCS96 (d) 16, MCS96.
7. 8096 has following features fill up the following.
    (i) ____________ Resgister file.
    (ii) ____________ I/O Ports
    (iii) ____________ architecture.
    (a) 256 byte, five 8 bit, register to register
    (b) 256 byte, four 8 bit, register to register
    (c) 232 byte, five 8 bit, register to register
    (d) 232 byte, six 8 bit, register to register
8. How many synchronous and asynchronous modes are there in serial port of 8096?
    (a) 2, 2 respectively (b) 3, 1 respectively
    (c) 1, 3 respectively (d) 1, 2 respectively
9. In 8096 has ____ interrupt sources and ________ interrupt vectors.
    (a) 18, 8 (b) 21, 6
    (c) 21, 8 (d) 16, 8
10. 8096 has ________ general purpose I/O ports, Port 2 includes ________ of the following:
    (i) two-quasi-bidirectional I/O lines (ii) two output lines
    (iii) four input lines (iv) oepn drain outputs
    (a) 4, i, iv
    (b) 6, ii, iii
    (c) 4, i, ii, iii
    (d) 6, i, ii, iv

Chapter 9

MC 68HC11 Microcontrollers

9.1 INTRODUCTION

The 68HC11 is a powerful 8-bit data, 16-bit address microcontroller from Motorola with an instruction set that is similar to the previous 68xx (6801, 6805, 6809) microcontrollers. Depending on the variety, the 68HC11 has built-in EEPROM/OTPROM, RAM, digital I/O, timers, A/D converter, PWM generator and synchronous and asynchronous communications channels (RS232 and Serial Peripheral Interface (SPI)). Typical current draw is less than 20 ma.

9.2 68HC11 SERIES OF MICROCONTROLLERS

The MC68HC11 family has many versions described as follows:

HC11A series microcontrollers

8K ROM (A8), ROMless (A0, A1), 256 RAM, 512 EEPROM (A1, A8), SPI, SCI, 3 IC 5 OC, 8 channel 8 bit A/D

HC11C0 microcontrollers

ROMless, on chip bank switching to support memory maps up to 256. Chip selects on board, on chip Read Enable and Write Enable signals, 256 RAM, 8 channel 8 bit A/D.

HC11D series microcontrollers

Smallest and cheapest member of the hc11 Family. ROMless (D0), 4K ROM (D3), 4K EPROM (711D3)—No A/D or EEPROM, but has standard timers and serial ports.

HC11E series microcontrollers

Same as A series except 512 bytes RAM and 512 EEPROM (2048 for E2). Pin compatible, only difference is one timer pin (PA4) can be used for IC or OC instead of just OC. Also have EPROM devices and larger memory—hc711e9 (12K OTP), hc711e20 (20K OTP).

HC11F series microcontrollers

ROMless, non-multiplexed address/data bus with 4 chip selects built in. 1K RAM, 512 bytes EEPROM, same peripherals as E series.

HC11G series microcontrollers

16K ROM/EPROM. Non multiplexed address/data bus, 512 RAM, 4 channel PWM, 10 Bit A/D converter, 2 separate 16 bit timers.

HC11K4 microcontroller

24K ROM/EPROM, 1Mb addressing using on chip memory mapping. Non-multiplexed address and data bus. 4 programmable chip selects, 8 channel 8 bit A/D, 4 channel PWM, 768 bytes RAM.

Several of the microcontrollers within the M68HC11 family have 'x1' and 'x0' versions. These are identical to the main member of the series but have some of their on-chip functions disabled. For example, MC68HC11A1 is identical to the MC 68HC11A8 except that its ROM is disabled. An MC68HC11A0 has disabled EPROM and EEPROM arrays.

Normally all series within the M68HC11 family have both a ROM version and an EPROM version. Any device in the M68HC11 family that has a 7 preceding the 11 is a device containing EPROM instead of ROM (e.g., MC68HC711E9). These devices operate exactly as the ROM-based version (e.g., MC68HC11E9) but can be programmed by the user. EPROM-based devices in a windowed package can be erased and reprogrammed. While EPROM-based devices in standard packages are one-time-programmable (OTP). The Figure 9.1 summaries the MC68HC11 family devices.

Microcontroller	RAM	ROM	EPROM	EEPROM	COMMENTS
MC68HC11A8	256	8K	0	512	16-bit timer; 8 channel 8-bit A/D, SCI, SPI
MC68HC11A7	256	8K	0	0	
MC68HC11A1	256	0	0	512	
MC68HC11A0	256	0	0	0	
MC68HC11D3	192	4K	0	0	16-bit timer; SCI, SPI
MC68HC711D3	192	0	4K	0	
MC68HC11D0	192	0	0	0	
MC68HC11ED0	512	0	0	0	
MC68HC11ED0	512	0	0	0	16-bit timer; SCL, SPI
MC68HC11E9	512	12K	0	512	16-bit timer; SCI, SPI, 8 channel 8-bit A/D
MC68H711E9	512	0	12K	512	
MC68HC11E8	512	12K	0	0	
MC68HC11E1	512	0	0	512	
MC68HC11E0	512	0	0	0	
MC68HC811E2	256	0	0	2048	16-bit timer; SCI, SPI, 8 channel 8-bit A/D, 2K EEPROM

Contd...

MC68HC811E2	256	0	0	2048	16-bit timer; SCI, SPI, 8 channel 8-bit A/D, 2K EEPROM
MC68HC11E20	768	20K	0	512	16-bit timer; SCI, SPI, 8 channel 8-bit A/D, 20K ROM/EPROM
MC68HC711E20	768	0	20K	512	
MC68HC11F1	1024	0	0	512	non-multiplexed bus, 8 channel 8-bit A/D, 4 chip selects, SCI, SPI
MC68HC11G7	512	24K	0	0	non-muliplexed bus, 8 channel 10-bit A/D, 4 channel PWM.
MC68HC11G5	412	16K	0	0	SCI, SPI, 66I/O pins
MC68HC811G5	512	0	16K	0	
MC68HC11G0	512	0	0	0	
MC68HC11K4	768	24K	0	640	non-multiplexed bus, memory expansion to 1MB, 8 channel 8-bit A/D, 4 channel PWM, 4 chip selects
MC68HC711K4	768	0	24K	640	
MC68HC11K3	768	0	0	0	
MC68HC11K1	768	0	0	640	
MC68HC11K0	768	0	0	0	
MC68HC811KA4	768	0	24K	640	non-multiplexed bus, 8 channel 8-bit A/D, SCI, SPI, 4 channel PWM
MC68HC711KA4	768	0	24K	640	
MC68HC11KA2	1024	32K	0	640	
MC68HC7111KA2	1024	0	32K	640	
MC68HC11L6	512	16K	0	512	multiplexed bus, 16-bit timer; 8 channel 8-bit A/D, SCI, SPI
MC68HC711L6	512	0	16K	512	
MC68HC11L5	512	16K	0	0	
MC68HC11L1	512	0	0	512	
MC68HC11L0	512	0	0	0	
MC68HC11M2	1280	32K	0	640	non-multiplexed bus, 8 channel 8-bit A/D, 4 channel PWM,
MC68HC711M2	1280	0	32K	640	DMA, on-chip math coprocessor, SCI, 2 SPI
MC68HC11N4	768	24K	0	640	non-multiplexed bus, 12 channel 8-bit A/D, 2 channel 8-bit D/A,
MC68HC711N4	768	0	24K	640	6 channel PWM, on-chip math coprocessor, SCI, SPI
MC68HC11P2	1024	32K	0	640	non-multiplexed bus, PLL, 8channel 8-bit A/D, 4 channel PWM,
MC68HC711P2	1024	0	32K	640	3 SCI (2 with MI bus), SPI, 62 I/O pins

Figure 9.1 The MC68HC11 Family Microcontrollers

9.3 ARCHITECTURE

The 68HC11 CPU has two 8 bit accumulators (A & B) that can be concatenated to provide a 16 bit double accumulator (D). Two 16 bit index registers (X, Y) are available to provide indexing to anywhere in the memory map. Having the two index registers means the 68HC11 is very good for processing data. Although an eight bit processor, the 68HC11 has some 16 bit instructions (add, subtract, 16 * 16 divide, 8 * 8 multiply, shift, and rotates). A 16 bit stack pointer is also present and instructions are provided for stack manipulation and multiplexed address and data bus.

The MC68HC11 family have many versions but all are built around MC68H C11A8. The Figure 9.2 shows the block diagram of MC68HC11A8.

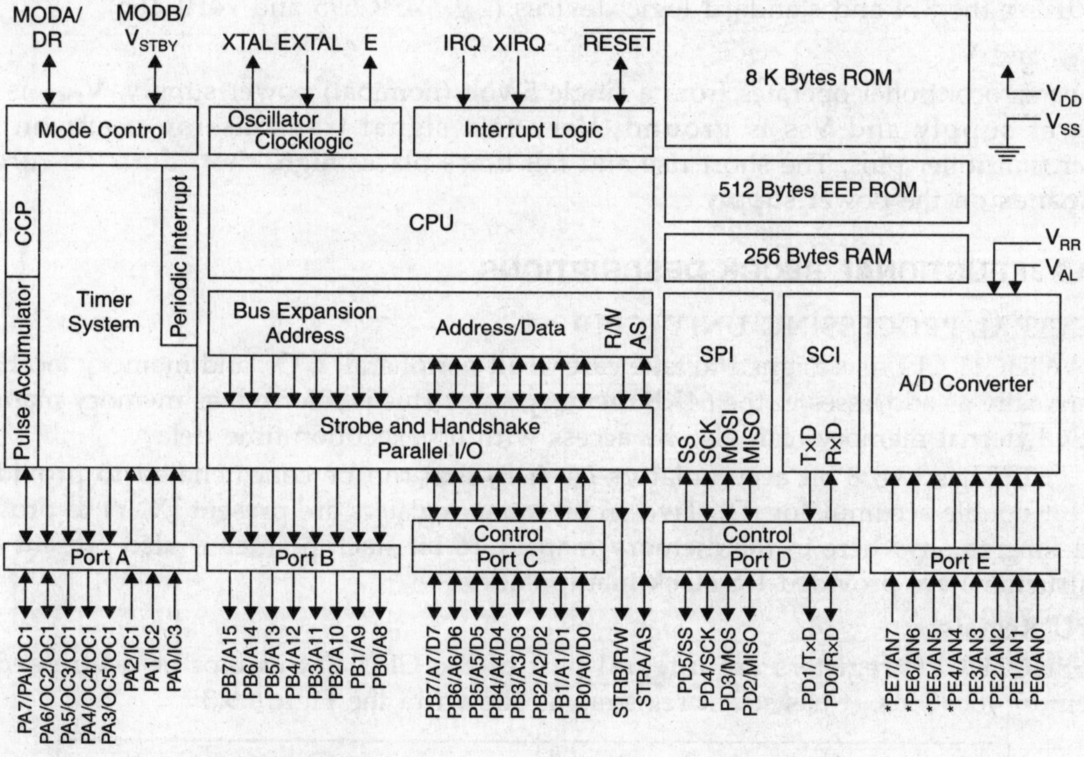

Figure 9.2 The Block Diagram of MC68HC11A8

9.3.1 ONBOARD SUBSYSTEMS

TIMER

The 68HC11 timer system comprises of a single 16 bit counter, clocked at the E clock (2, 3, or 4 Mhz). There is a programmable prescaler to slow it down if required this single counter run a number of input capture and output compare registers (3-4 IC, 5-4OC). The Input Capture and Output capture functions are very versatile, and pulses as short as 1 E clock can be generated.

A-D CONVERTOR

The 68HC11 has typically 8 channel 8 bit A/D, although the G5 has a 10 bit A/D.

SERIAL COMMUNICATIONS INTERFACE (SCI)

Asynchronous serial communications; Data format—1 Start, 8 or 9 data, and one stop bit.

DATA RATE

The 68HC11 data rate varies from 50 - 312500 Baud (312500 is using 4 mhz E clock).

SERIAL PERIPHERAL INTERFACE (SPI)

Synchronous serial communications comprises CLK, DATA IN, DATA OUT and optionally chip selects. As well as using specific SPI devices, it is very easy to expand IO using the SPI and standard logic devices (e.g. 74HC595 and 74HC165).

V_{DD} and V_{SS}

The microcontroller operates from a single 5-volt (nominal) power supply. V_{DD} is the power supply and Vss is ground. Very fast signal transmission occur on the microcontroller pins. The short rise and fall times places high, short duration current demands on the power supply.

9.3.2 FUNCTIONAL BLOCK DESCRIPTIONS

CENTRAL PROCESSING UNIT (CPU)

The 68HC11 CPU is designed to take care of all peripheral, I/O , and memory locations identically as addresses in the 64KB memory map. This is referred, as memory-mapped I/O. External memory can also be access with no execution-time delay.

CPU has two 8 bit accumulators (A & B) that can be concatenated to provide a 16 bit double accumulator (D). Two 16 bit index registers are present (X, Y) to provide indexing to anywhere in the memory map. A 16 bit stack pointer is also present and instructions are provided for stack manipulation.

CPU Registers:

M68HC11 CPU registers are integral part of the CPU but cannot be addressed as memory locations. It has seven registers as shown in the Figure 9.3.

ACCUMULATOR A	ACCUMULATOR B
DOUBLE ACCUMULATOR D	
INDEX REGISTER X	
INDEX REGISTER Y	
STACK POINTER	
PROGRAM COUNTER	

Figure 9.3 CPU Registers

ACCUMULATORS A, B AND D

Accumulators A, B are general purpose accumulator of 8 bit used for arithmetic calculations or data manipulation.

D is also accumulator (combination of A and B) but of 16 bit so called double accumulator.

INDEX REGISTER X (IX)

IX provides a 16-bit indexing value that can be added to the 8-bit offset provided in an instruction to create an effective address. The IX register can be used as a counter or as a temporary storage register.

INDEX REGISTER Y (IY)

IY is 16-bit register same as IX but require an extra byte of machine code and an extra cycle of execution time because of the way the opcode map is implemented.

STACK POINTER (SP)

The stack pointer (SP) is a 16-bit register that contains the address of the next free location on the stack. The stack is configured as a sequence of LIFO read/write registers which allow data to be stored during interrupts and subroutine calls. Each time a new byte is added to the stack (a push instruction), the SP is decrement; whereas, each time a byte is removed from the stack (a pull instruction) the SP is incremented.

PROGRAM COUNTER (PC)

The program counter is a 16-bit register that contains the address of the next instruction to be executed.

CONDITION CODE REGISTER (CCR)

This 8-bit register contains five condition code indicators (C, V, Z, H and N), two interrupt masking bit (IRQ and XIRQ) and a stop disable bit (S). Each bit of CCR signifies the results of the instruction just executed. The CCR have 8 bits as shown in the Figure 9.4.

S	X	H	I	N	Z	V	C

Figure 9.4 Condition Code Register

The function of each CCR bit is as follows:

CARRY/BORROW (C)

The C bit is set if there is a carry or borrow out of the arithmetic logic unit (ALU) after execution of last arithmetic operation. The C bit is also affected during shift and rotate instructions.

OVERFLOW (V)

The overflow bit is set if there is an arithmetic overflow as a result of the operation; otherwise, the V bit is cleared.

ZERO (Z)

The zero bit is set if the result after execution of arithmetic, logic, or data manipu- lation operation is zero; otherwise, the Z bit is cleared.

NEGATIVE (N)

The negative bit is set if the result of the last arithmetic, logic, or data manipulation operation is negative; otherwise, the N bit is cleared. A result is said to be negative if its most significant bit is a one.

INTERRUPT MASK (I)

The I interrupt mask bit is set either by hardware or program instruction to disable (mask), all maskable interrupt sources (both external and internal).

HALF CARRY (H)

The H bit is set when a carry occurs between bit-3 and 4 of the arithmetic logic unit during an ADD, ABA or ADC instruction. Otherwise, H bit is cleared; half carry is used during BCD operations.

X INTERRUPT MASK (X)

After any reset, X is set by default and must be cleared by software instruction. The X -interrupt mask bit is set only by hardware (RESET or XIRQ acknowledge), and it is cleared only by program instruction (TAP, where the associated bit of A is 0; or RTI, where bit 6 of the value loaded into the CCR from the stale has been cleared). There is no hardware action for clearing the X.

I/O PORTS

There are five I/O ports discussed as follows:

Port A

In all operating modes, port A can be configured for four timer input capture (IC) functions and four timer output compare (OC) functions or for four OC and three IC function, and either a pulse accumulator input (PAI), or a fifth DC function.

Port B

During single chip-operation mode, all port B pins are general purpose O/P pins. Port B can also be used in a simple strobed output mode where an output pulse appeared at the STRB signal each time data is written to port B.

In expanded multiplexed operating mode, all port B pins act as high order address output signals (A8—A15). The Port B register is treated as an external address in expanded modes.

Port C

In single-chip operating mode, all port C pins are general purpose I/O pins. Port C can also be used in full handshake modes of parallel I/O where the STRA input and STRB output act as handshake control lines.

In expanded multiplexed modes, all port C pin act as multiplexed address/data signals. During the data portion of microcontroller cycle these pins act as bidirectional data signal line. The direction of data at the port C pins is indicated by R/W signal.

Port D

Pins PD5-0 used as general purpose I/O signals. These pins alternatively serve as SCI (serial communication interface) and SPI (serial peripheral interface) signal when those subsystems are disabled.

Pin PD-0: Receive data input (RxD) signal for the SCI.

Pin PD1: Transmit data output (TxD) signal for SCI.

Pins PD 5-2: Used for SPI.

PD-2: Master in slave out (MISO) signal.

PD-3: Master out slave in (MOSI) signal.

PD-4: Serial clock ($\overline{\text{SCK}}$).

PD-5: Slave select (SS) input.

Port E:

Use for general purpose or A/D Inputs. Reading port E should be avoided during sampling for high accuracy of A/D conversion.

9.4 MEMORY MAP

Memory map for single-chip, expanded multiplexed, special bootstrap, and special test are shown in the Figure 9.5. Memory locations are the same for single-chip and expanded multiplexed modes.

The first 256 bytes from 0000 to 00FF constitute internal RAM. The 64 byte register block is mapped to $1000 after next and also corresponds to SFR of 8096. It can be placed at any other 4k boundry ($x000) by writing an value to the INIT register the 512 bytes of EEPROM be from B600H to B7FFH. The 8K internal ROM lies from F000H to FFFFH.

The special bootstrap operating mode memory locations are similar to the single-chip operating mode memory locations except that a bootstrap program at memory locations $BF40 through $BFFF is enabled. The reset and interrupt vectors are addressed at $BFC0-$BFFF while in the special bootstrap operating mode. These vector addresses are within the 192 byte memory used for the bootstrap program.

The special test operating mode memory map is the same as the expanded multiplexed operating mode memory map except that the reset and interrupt vectors are located at external memory locations $BFC0-$BFFF.

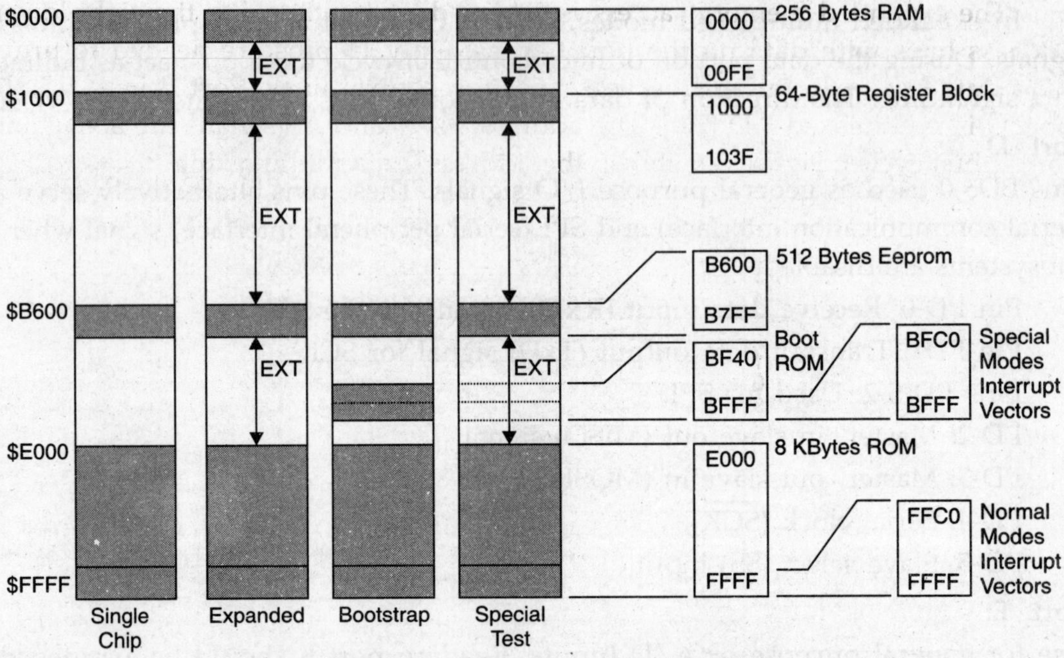

Figure 9.5 Memory Mapping of 68HC11

9.5 OPERATING MODES

For the MC68HC11 there are four operating modes: single-chip operating mode, expanded multiplexed operating mode, special bootstrap operating mode, and special test operating mode.

The operating mode determined by the MODB and MODA mode select inputs during reset.

Single-chip and expanded multiplexed are the normal mode. With Single—chip mode only on-board memory is available. Expanded multiplexed mode, however, allows access to external memory. Each of these modes is paired with a special mode.

Bootstrap, a variation of the single—chip mode that executes a boot loader program in an internal bootstrap ROM. Test, is a special mode that allows privileged access to internal resources.

SINGLE—CHIP OPERATING MODE

In this mode MC68HC11 has no external address or data bus. Port B, C, strobe A (STRA) and strobe B (STRB) are available for general purpose parallel I/O.

EXPANDED MULTIPLEXED OPERATING MODE

In this mode microcontroller can access a 64 Kbytes address space using multiplexed external address and data bus.

The expanded memory access is achieved by multiplexing the eight lower-order address lines with data on the port C pins. Only 18 pins are needed to provide an 8-bit data bus, a 16-bit address bus and two control lines. Port B is A [15:8], while port C is multiplexed AD [7:0]. The address, R/W and AS signals are active and valid for all bus cycles. Figure 9.6 shows the address/data multiplexing.

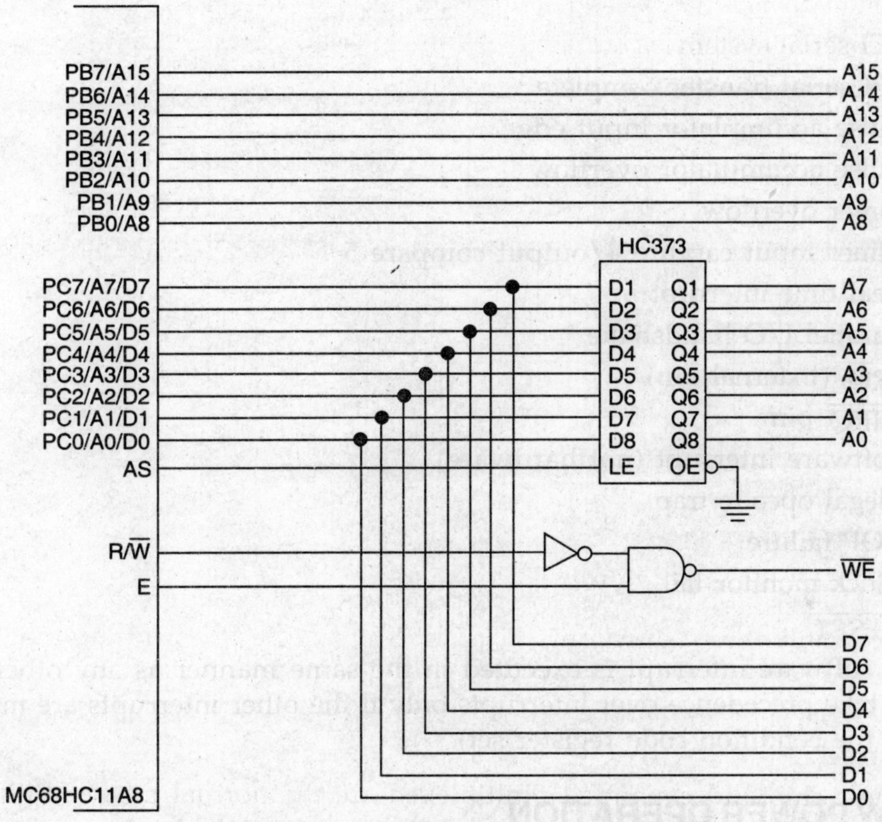

Figure 9.6 The Address/Data multiplexing

SPECIAL TEST MODE

It is used during Motorola's internal production testing, however, it is accessible for programming the CONFIG register, programming calibration data into EEPROM, and debugging during development.

SPECIAL BOOTSTRAP MODE

When the microcontroller is reset in the special bootstrap mode, a small on-chip ROM is enabled at address $BF40–$BFFF. This is a mask-programmed 192 byte ROM. The ROM contains a reset vector and a bootloader program. The microcontroller fetches the reset vector and then executes the bootloader.

9.6 INTERRUPTS

The microcontroller has 18 interrupt vectors, in which 15 maskable interrupt vectors are generated by on-chip peripheral systems when global interrupt mask bit (I) in the condition code register (CCR) is clear. The 3 nonmaskable interrupt sources are illegal opcode trap, software interrupt, and $\overline{\text{XIRQ}}$ pin. The hardware interrupt corresponds to

- SCI serial system
- SPI serial transfer complete
- Pulse accumulator input edge
- Pulse accumulator overflow
- Timer overflow
- Timer input capture 4/output compare 5
- Real time interrupt
- Parallel I/O handshake
- $\overline{\text{IRQ}}$ (External pin)
- $\overline{\text{XIRQ}}$ pin
- Software interrupt (not hardware)
- Illegal opcode trap
- COP failure
- Clock monitor fail
- $\overline{\text{RESET}}$

The software interrupt is executed in the same manner as any other instruction and will take precedence over interrupts only if the other interrupts are masked (I and X bits in the condition code register set).

9.7 LOW POWER OPERATION

In MC68HC11 there are two programmable low power modes:

- STOP
- WAIT

STOP

Stop occurs when S bit (Stop disable) in the CCR (Condition code register) become zero. If the S bit is not zero (set), the stop opcode is treated as a no-operation (NOP) instruction. The stop condition offers minimum power consumption because all clocks, including the crystal oscillator, are stopped while in this mode. To exit STOP and resume normal processing, logic low level must be applied to one of the external interrupts ($\overline{\text{IRQ}}$ or $\overline{\text{XIRQ}}$) or to the $\overline{\text{RESET}}$ pin. A pending edge-triggered $\overline{\text{IRQ}}$ can also bring the CPU out of STOP.

WAIT

The wait condition suspends processing and reduces power consumption to an intermediate level. During WAIT, the CPU register are stacked and CPU processing is suspended until a qualified interrupt is detected. The interrupt can be an external $\overline{IRQ}$ or $\overline{XIRQ}$ or internal interrupts such as the timer or serial interrupts. The on-chip crystal oscillator remain active throughout WAIT standby period.

9.8 SERIAL COMMUNICATION INTERFACE (SCI)

It is a universal asynchronous receiver transmitter (UART) serial communi- cations interface with standard NRZ format (one start bit, eight or nine data bits, and one stop bit), which communicates with other device. For SCI several baud rates are available. The TXD and RXD pins are in port D, in which TXD is used for transmission and RXD is used for receiving operation. SIP is separated from SCI in 68HC11.

The functionality of SCI can be understood with the block diagram of the SCI shown in Figure 9.7. The user has option bits in serial communications control register 1 (SCCR1) to determine the "wake-up" mode and data word length of the SCI. Serial communications control register 2 (SCCR2) provides control bits which individually enable/disable the transmitter or receiver (TE and RE, respectively), enable system interrupts (TIE, TCIE, ILIE) and provide the wake-up enable bit (RWU) and the send break code bit (SBK). The baud rate register (BAUD) bits allow the user to select different baud rates that may be used as the rate control for the transmitter and receiver.

Data transmission is initiated by a write to the serial communications data register (SCDR). Provided the transmitter is enabled, data stored in the SCDR is transferred to the transmit data shift register. This transfer of data sets the TDRE bit of the SCI status register (SCSR) and generate an interrupt if the transmit interrupt is enabled. The transfer of data to the transmit data shift register is synchronized with the bit rate clock. All data is transmitted LSB first. Upon completion of data transmission, the transmission complete (TC) bit of the SCSR is set (provided no pending data, preamble, or break is to be sent), and an interrupt generated if the transmit complete interrupt is enabled. If the transmitter is disabled, and the data, preamble, or break (in the transmit shift register) has been sent, the TC bit will also be set. This will also generate an interrupt if the TCIE bit is set. If the transmitter is disabled in the middle of a transmission, that character will be completed before the transmitter gives up control of the TxD pin. When the SCDR is read, it contains the last data byte received, provided that the receiver is enabled. The RDRF bit of the SCSR is set to indicate that a data byte has been transferred from the input serial shift register to the SCDR, which can cause an interrupt if the receiver interrupt is enabled. The data transfer from the input serial shift register to the SCDR is synchronized by the receiver bit rate clock. The OR (over-run), NF (noise), or FE (framing) error bits of the SCSR may be set if data reception errors occurred.

An idle line interrupt is generated if the idle line interrupt is enabled and the IDLE bit (which detects idle line transmission) of SCSR is set. This allows a receiver that is not in the wake-up mode to detect the end of a message, the preamble of a new message, or to resynchronize with the transmitter. A valid character must be received before the idle line condition or the IDLE bit will not be set and an idle line interrupt will not be generated.

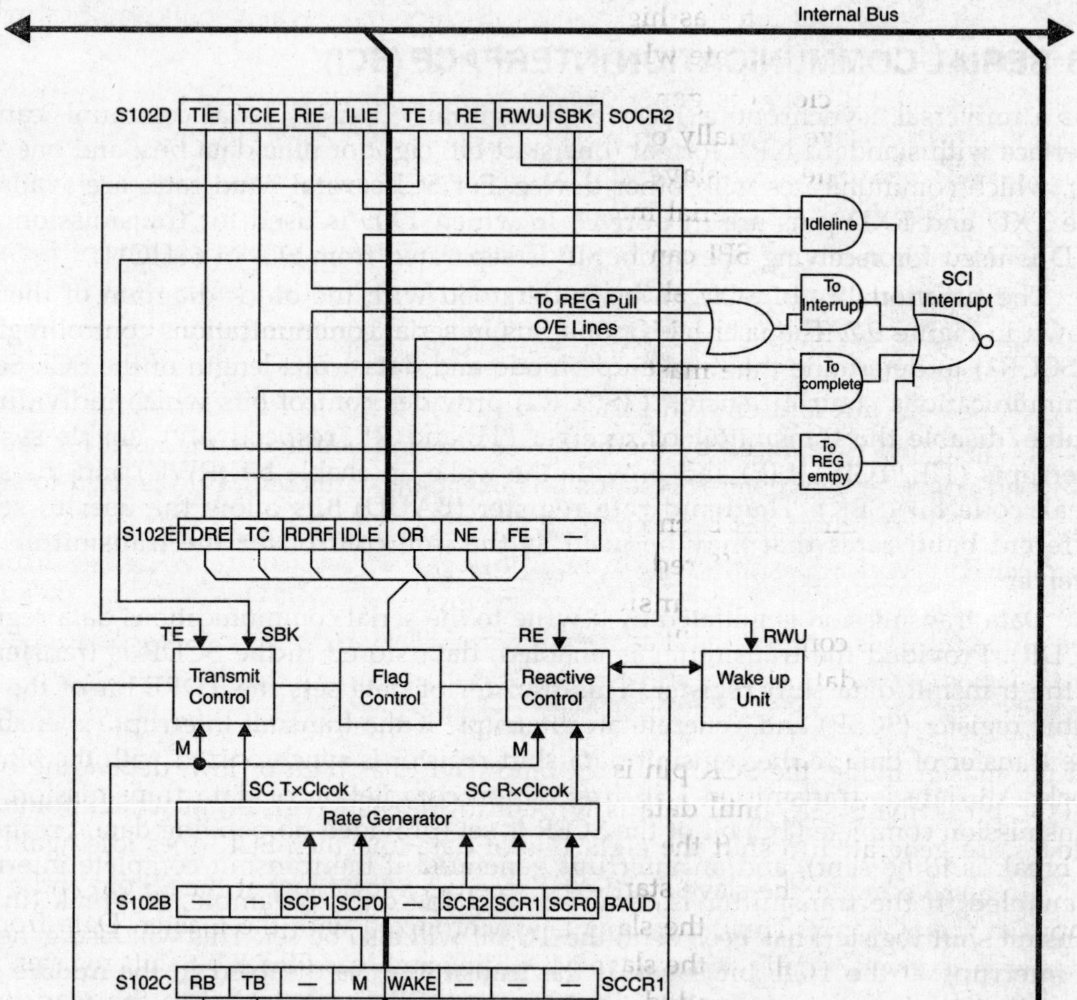

Figure 9.7 Block Diagram of Serial Communications Interface

9.9 SERIAL PERIPHERAL INTERFACE (SPI)

It is independent of SCI, allows the microcontroller to communicate synchronously with peripheral devices such as TTL shift register, LCD driver, A/D converter system and other microprocessor. The SPI is also capable of interprocessor communication in a multiple master system. The SPI system can be configured as either a master or a slave device with data rates as high as 1/2 E clock rates when configured as master, and as fast as the E clock rate when configured as slave.

A SCK (serial clock) is generated by the master device and synchronizes data transmitted or received serially on master out slave in (MOSI) pins or master in slave out (MISO) pin. The $\overline{SS}$ (slave select) pin selects the slave device. In 8096 this corresponds to mode 0 of serial interface.

The functionality of SPI can be understood with the block diagram of the serial peripheral interface circuitry shown in Figure 9.8. When a master device transmits data to a slave device via the MOSI line, the slave device responds by sending data to the master device via the master's MISO line. This implies full duplex transmission with both data out and data in synchronized with the same clock signal. Thus, the byte transmitted is replaced by the byte received and eliminates the need for separate transmit-empty and receiver-full status bits. A single status bit (SPIF) is used to signify that the I/O operation has been completed.

The SPI is double buffered on read, but not on write. If a write is performed during data transfer, the transfer occurs uninterrupted, and the write will be unsuccessful. This condition will cause the write collision (WCOL) status bit in the SPSR to be set. After a data byte is shifted, the SPIF flag of the SPSR is set.

DWOM

In the master mode, the SCK pin is an output. It idles high or low, depending on the CPOL bit in the SPCR, until data is written to the shift register, at which point eight clocks are generated to shift the eight bits of data and then SCK goes idle again.

In a slave mode, the slave start logic receives a logic low at the SS pin and a clock input at the SCK pin. Thus, the slave is synchronized with the master. Data from the master is received serially at the slave MOSI line and loads the 8-bit shift register. After the 8-bit shift register is loaded, its data is parallel transferred to the read buffer. During a write cycle, data is written into the shift register, then the slave waits for a clock train from the master to shift the data out on the slave's MISO line.

Due to data direction register control of SPI outputs and the port D wire-OR mode (DWOM) option, the SPI system can be configured in a variety of ways. Systems with a single bidirectional data path rather than separate MISO and MOSI paths can be accommodated.

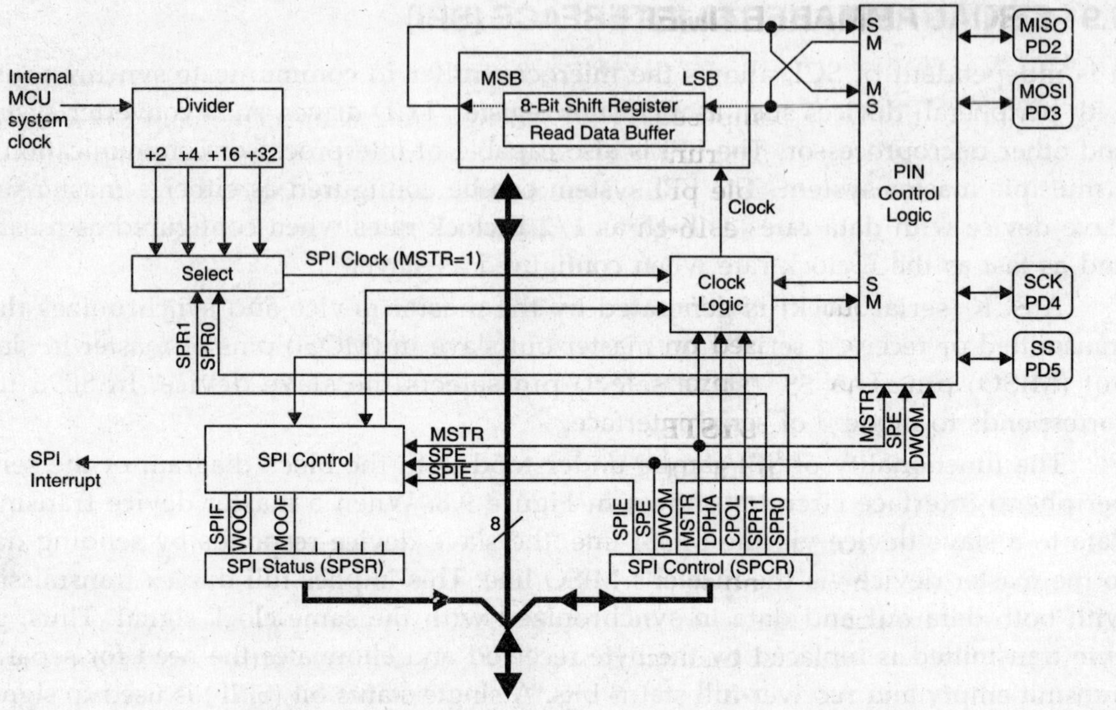

Figure 9.8 Block Diagram of Serial Peripheral Interface

9.10 ANALOG TO DIGITAL CONVERTER

The A/D system is an 8-channel, 8-bit, multiplexed-input converter, successive approximation, analog-to-digital (A/D) converter with sample and hold to minimize conversion errors caused by rapidly changing input signals accurate to ±1 least significant bit (LSB) which includes ± 1/2 LSB of quantization error.

It does not require external sample and hold circuit because of the type of charge redistribution technique used. A/D converter timing can be synchronized to the system E clock, or to an internal resister capacitor (RC) oscillator. The A/D converter system consists of four parts or functional blocks, multiplexer, analog converter, digital control and result storage. Its conversion time is 32 E clock if the E clock rate is greater than 750 kHz. For systems that operate at clock rates less than 750 kHz, an internal R-C oscillator must be used to clock the A/D system. E clock is an O/P corresponding to ¼ of oscillator frequency. This is same as 8096 A/D converter except A/D converter of 8096 is of 10 bits. The O/P of A/D converter is obtained on port E.

9.11 PROGRAMMABLETIMER

TIMING SYSTEM

The M68HC11 timing is composed of five clock divider chain. The main clock divider chain includes a 16-bit free-running counter, which is driven by programmable prescaler. The programmable prescaler on the main timer provide one of the four clocking rates to derive the 16-bit counter. Two prescaler control bits select the prescaler rate.

The prescaler output dividing the system clock by 1,4,8 or 16. The clock circuitry generate the slower clock used by the pulse accumulator, the real time interrupt (RTI), and the computer operating properly (COP) watchdog subsystem.

WORKING OF TIMING SYSTEM

The 16-bit counter counts from $0000 to (as the microcontroller comes out of reset) and continues to max count, $FFFF. At max count, the counter rolls over to $0000, sets an overflow flag, and continues to increment. As long microcontroller running in normal operating mode, there is no way to reset, change, or interrupt the counting. The capture/compare subsystem features three I/P capture channels, four output compare channels, and one channel that can be selected to perform either input capture or output compare.

9.12 CONCLUSION

Advantages realized in implementing control applications on this family of microcontrollers are:

- **Traditional architecture**
  A more traditional architecture than other competing products (such as the 8051 and PIC) makes it easier to learn and develop on (especially well-suited for teaching microcontrollers)
- **More features**
  A 68HC11 is typically a "one-chip" solution since it often includes such items as A/D. PWM, and many I/O lines
- **Popular**
  Widely used since it is very inexpensive and has a wide range of development tools available.

An overview of the M68HC11 family has been presented in this chapter. However for the interested readers programming aid is provided in Appendix A. The additional information on the M68HC11 can be referenced from MOTOROLA "M68HC11 Reference Manual".

9.13 PROBLEMS

1. Describe Low Power Operation of 68HC11 microcontrollers.
2. Discuss the features of 68HC11 series of microcontrollers.
3. Write short notes on following 68HC11 microcontrollers features:
   - Serial Communications Interface
   - Serial Peripheral Interface
   - Low Power Modes
   - A to D Converter
4. Explain memory mapping of 68HC11 microcontrollers.
5. Write about Operating Modes of 68HC11 microcontrollers.

Appendix

Motorola MC68HC11 Microcontroller Programming Aid

MC68HC11 INSTRUCTIONS WITH EXAMPLES

aba	**Add register B to register A** aba	*Similar commands are* abx aby add the value in register B to the value in register A and store in register A
anda	**Logical and with register A** anda #label	Similar command is andb Differs from bita in that the contents of register A is changed perform a logical AND between the value stored at memory location *label* and register A and store the result in register A
asr	**Arithmetic Shift Right** asr	Similar commands are asra asrb asl asla aslb Preserves signed numbers by retaining the leading bit. Use lsr and related commands with unsigned numbers. A right shift divides by 2, a left shift multiplies by 2
bcc	**Branch if C-bit is clear** bcc	Similar command is bcs (branch if C-bit set) branches if the C-bit is clear. The C-bit indicates a carry or borrow
bclr	**Clear Bit(s)** bclr #label $F0	Similar command is bset this example zeros the first four bits of the value stored at memory location label. $F0 is the mask in binary it is 11110000; the 1's correspond to the bits that will be cleared.

beq	**Branch on Equal or Zero, i.e. if CCR Z-bit is 1** cmpa #20 beq label tsta beq label	 compares the value in register A to decimal 20 by subtracting 20 from A. if the last value in memory was a zero (checks the CCR Z-bit) then go to program location label. test the value in register A if the value in register A is zero (i.e. the Z-bit is set) then we branch to the memory location label.
bita	**Logical and with register A** bita #%10000000	Similar commands are bita, bitb Differs from anda in that register A remains unchanged. The result affects only the CCR. this example checks bit 7 in register A and set the CCR accordingly. This could be follow with the beq or bne instruction to branch based on the result of the bit test. Another way to test bit 7 is to simply tsta and then branch based on the N-bit since bit 7 = 1 is characteristic of a signed negative number and will set the N-bit of the CCR.
ble	**Branch if Lower or Equal**	Compares **signed** numbers. Similar commands: blt (branch if lower), bgt (branch if greater than), bge (branch if greater or equal). See bls for comparable unsigned number commands with examples.
bls	**Branch if Lower or Same** cba bls label ldd Num1 cpd #1000 bls label	Compares **unsigned** numbers. Similar commands: blo (branch if lower), bhi (branch if higher), bhs (branch if higher or same). May not work properly if there is an overflow. first compare the value in register B to the value in register A (A-B) branch to location label if A is less than or equal to B **16-Bit Version:** first load the value stored at Num1 into register D compare the value in D to 1000 branch to location label if D is less than or equal to 1000

Contd...

bmi	**Branch on Minus** Tsta bmi label	Similar command is bpl (branch on positive) test the value in register A if the value in register A is negative (i.e. the N-bit is set) then we branch to the memory location label.
bne	**Branch if Not Equal or Zero**	Opposite of beq
bra	**bra Branch** bra label	go to program location label and continue execution (don't return).
brclr	**Branch if Bit(s) Clear** brclr label 1 #%11100000 label2	go to program location label2 if the first three bits of the value stored at label1 are zeros (clear).
bsr	**Branch to Subroutine** bsr label	go to the subroutine at program location label and return here when done
bvs	**Branch if Overflow bit is set** bvs label	go to the program location label if the v bit is set in the CCR. The V-bit indicates a two' s-complement overflow.
cba	**Compare B to A** cba	Similar commands are cmpa cmpb cpd cpx cpy; see example at bls compare the value in register B to the value in register A by subtraction (A-B) and set the CCR accordingly. If A=B then Z®1. Can be used before beq, ble, blt, bgt, bge, bls, blo, bhi, bhs, etc.
clr	**Replace Contents with Zeros** clr Ddrc clra	Similar commands are clra clrb this example causes Port C to be an input port (all pins). This would go near the beginning of the program after the lds command. this example places zeros in register A.
cmpa	Compare to A cmpa #$04	Similar commands are cba cmpb cpd cpx cpy; see example at bls this example compares the value in register A to $04 by subtracting $04 from

Contd...

	cmpa #EOT cmpa #end-3 cmpa 0,x	register A. If the result is zero then they are equal and the CCR bit Z is set to 1. $04 is EOT or end of string. Often used before beq. this example compares the character in register A to the end of string character. "end" must be a constant, not a label. The subtraction of end-3 is performed and the value in register A is compared to the result. compare the value in register A to the value in the byte pointed to by register X.
coma	**Complement of A** coma	Similar commands are com comb complement the value in register A and store the result in register A.
dec	**Decrement by 1** dec label deca des dec 0,x	Similar commands are deca decb des dex dey decrement the value stored at memory location label by 1. decrement the value stored in register A by 1. decrement the stack pointer; may be used to **allocate** stack space decrement the value stored at the top of the stack
end	**End Program end**	last program instruction
eora	**Exclusive OR with reg A** eora label	Similar command is eorb an exclusive OR is performed with the contents of register A and the value at address label with the result stored in register A.
equ	**Equate a Label to a Value** label equ 3	the assembler substitutes the value 3 wherever it sees label in the code. This does not use any memory space. The purpose is to facilitate code maintenance by permitting a single change of value here to result in multiple changes throughout the code wherever label appears. The line should be placed toward the beginning of the program or section of code before the first use of label.

Contd...

fcb	**Form Constant Byte**	see SUBROUTINE LIBRARIES
fcc	**Form Constant Character String**	see SUBROUTINE LIBRARIES
fdb	**Form Double Byte Constant** fdb main label fdb 5,8,465,17,89	This particular example is common to all our programs. By appearing after the org $FFFE instruction near the end of the program, this code loads the starting address of the program (represented by the label main) into the last two bytes of ROM. The cpu looks in the last two bytes of ROM to obtain the address for the beginning of the program when power is applied or in the event of a reset. 5 is stored in a 2-byte block at mem location label, 8 is stored in a 2-byte block at location label+2, etc.
fdiv	**Fractional Divide D/X** ldd #2 ldx #3 f f div	Related commands are fdiv, mul 2 is loaded into register D (numerator) 3 is loaded into register X (denominator) the numerator is multiplied by 65536 before being divided by the denominator, quotient (43690) goes in register X, remainder (2) in register D
inc	**Increment by 1** inc label inca ins	Similar commands are inca incb ins inx iny increment the value stored at memory location label by 1 increment the value stored in register A by 1. increment the stack pointer; used to **deallocate** space on the stack
idiv	**Integer Divide D/X** ldd #9 ldx #4 idiv	Related commands are fdiv, mul 9 is loaded into register D (numerator) 4 is loaded into register X (denominator) division takes place, quotient (2) goes in register X, remainder (1) in register D
jmp	**Jump to Another Location** jmp label	go to program location label. You can use this if you are not planning on returning to the current location.

Contd...

jsr	**Jump to Subroutine** jsr InString jsr InitSCI	go to a subroutine. This is used with the libraries because they are too far away to be accessed with the branch instructions which use relative addressing. Program execution returns to this point following the subroutine. this example initializes the serial port and appears once in the program right after *main*. InitSCI is in subroutine library.

ldaa	**Load Register A**
	ldd 10
	
	ldaa #10
	ldaa #$B
	ldaa #'B
	ldaa #%10011001
	ldd #label
	ldaa label
	ldaa Porte
	const equ 2
	ldaa #const
	ldaa const,x
	ldaa 4,X
		Similar commands are ldab ldd lds ldx ldy
		load the value at address $000A into register D
		load the decimal value 10 into register A
		load the hex value B into register A
		load the ASCII character code for B into register A
		load the binary value 10011001 into register A
		load the **address** value of *label* into register D
		load the **data** value of *label* into register A
		load the **data** from input Port E into register A
		create a constant
		load the **data** value 2 into register A
		load the **data** that is 2 bytes past the address in register X into register A
		load the **data** located 4 bytes past the location stored in register X into register A

lds	**Load Stack Pointer** lds #$00FF	this example initializes the stack pointer; required if the stack is to be used; same value is normally used; goes near the top of the program after org $E000
lsr	**Logical Shift Right**	Similar commands are lsra lsrb lsrd and for left shift: lsl lsla etc. For use with unsigned numbers. See asr and related commands for use with signed values. A right shift divides by 2, a left shift multiplies by 2.

Contd...

	lsr label lsra	divide the value pointed to by *label* by 2 the contents of register A are shifted to he right one bit and bit 7 becomes zero.
mul	**Multiply A × B = D** ldaa #10 ldab #5 mul	Related commands are idiv fdiv load 10 into register A load 5 into register B the values are multiplied, result goes in register D (unsigned values only, no overflow is possible).
org	**Sets the Program Counter, which specifies the address of the next byte to be loaded** org 0 org $E000 org $FFFE	 first program instruction follows global variables; moves to the beginning of the program area third from last command; makes room for a 2-byte reset address. The address stored here tells the CPU where to look for the beginning of the program when it is powered up.
psha	**Push Register A onto Stack** psha	Similar *commands are* pshb pshx pshy put the contents of register A on the stack and decrement the stack pointer; used for saving the contents of a register at the start of a subroutine, the registers are restored near the end of the subroutine using pula pulb pulx puly
pula	**Pull from Stack to Register A** pula	Similar commands are pulb pulx puly pull the value from the top of the stack and store in register A; increment the stack pointer; used for restoring the contents of a register at the end of a subroutine, the registers are saved near the beginning of the subroutine using psha pshb pshx pshy
rmb	**Reserve Memory Bytes** label rmb 2	creates a global variable or array, goes near the top of the program after org 0. Consists of the label name to be used for the memory location followed by rmb following by the number of bytes

Contd...

rts	**Return from Subroutine** rts	Similar command is rti goes at the end of a subroutine, pulls the return address from the stack
rti	**Return from Interrupt** rti	Similar command is rts goes at the end of an interrupt routine, pulls all registers and the return address from the stack
sev	**Set the V-bit** sev	sets the V-bit to 1 in the condition code register (CCR)
staa	**Store the value that is in Register A into...** staa label	Similar commands are stab std sts stx sty store the value that is in register A in the memory location label
stop	**Stop Program Execution** stop	stops the program at this point
suba	**Subtract from register A** suba label suba #12	Similar commands are subb subd subtract the value stored at label from register A and store in register A subtract decimal 12 from register A and store in register A
tab	**Transfer A to B**	transfers the value in register A to register B, leaving A intact
tcnt	**Timer Counter Register**	a 2-byte register that increments once with each program instruction during execution
tsx	**Transfer Stack Pointer to Register X** tsx	Similar command txs stores the address of the last value saved on the stack into register X. The stack pointer continues to point to the next empty byte, i.e. SP + 1 = X.
xgdx	**Exchange D and X**	exchanges values in registers D and X. Commonly used to permit 16-bit arithmetic to be done on a register address.

Contd...

Memory Locations

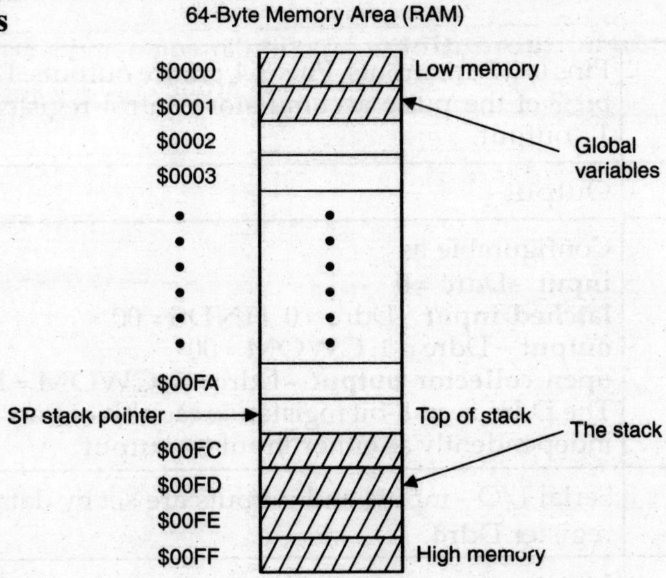

$0000 - $00FF	RAM, 256 bytes. Globals and the Stack reside here. Globals are loaded at the **low** end, i.e. $0000, $0001, etc. The Stack is builds from the **high** end also referred to as the **bottom** of the stack, i.e. $00FF. The stack pointer points to the **top** of the stack, which is the first unused stack location, i.e. if $00FC contains the last stored data then the stack pointer points to $00FB.
$1000 - $103F	Control registers, status registers and ports are mapped to this area
$1040 - $B5FF	Unused addresses
$B600 - $B7FF	Internal EEPROM,512 bytes for short programs
$B800 - $DFFF	Unused addresses
$E000 - $FFFF	ROM, 8192 bytes. Object code and libraries go here. Libraries begin at $FE00 (a convention in this class) and interrupt vectors begin at $FFF6. Interrupt vectors are pointers to code to be implemented in the event of an interrupt. For example, the reset interrupt consists of the bytes $FFFE and $FFFF so this is where we put the address that tells the CPU where to begin program execution on power-up.

Contd...

PORTS

PortA ($1000)	Pins 0, 1, 2 are inputs. Pins 3, 4, 5, 6 are outputs. Pin 7 is selectable by bit 7 of the pulse accumulator control register (Pact1) 0 = input, 1 = output.
PortB ($1004)	Output
PortC ($1003)	Configurable as **input** - Ddrc = 0 **latched input** - Ddrc = 0, HNDS = 00 **output** - Ddrc = 1, CWOM = 00 **open collector output** - Ddrc = 1, CWOM = 1 The Ddrc is an 8-bit register so each bit of Port C can be set independently as either input or output.
PortD ($1008)	Serial I/O - inputs and outputs are set by data direction register Ddrc
PortE ($100A)	Input ADPU bit = 1 - A/D conversion. ADPU bit = 0 - parallel input

SUBROUTINE LIBRARIES

InCh	accepts input from the keyboard. When a key is pressed, the ASCII value is loaded in **register A** and the routine returns to the main program.
InDec	accepts input from the keyboard. Returns an unsigned 16-bit number in **register D**. V-bit isset if illegal character is typed.
InHex	accepts input from the keyboard as hex (must be 0-9, A-F, or a-f; ignored are space, tab and $). Result goes in **register D**
InitSCI	initializes the serial communications interface. Gets executed once near the beginning of the program.
InString	accepts input from the keyboard. Before calling this routine, **register X** must point to a memory array and **register B** must contain the maximum length of the string. The string is inputted to the SCI window and stored in the array pointed to by register X; the last character is EOT=$04. The string array may be created as a global as follows: **Str rmb 20 String variable**
OutCh	places the character in **register A** on the screen in the SCI window
OutDec	outputs a 16-bit number in **register D** to the SCI window

Contd...

OutHex	outputs the contents of **register D** to the SCI window in unsigned hex format
OutString	displays a string in the SCI window. Before calling this routine, **register X** must point to a memory array containing the string, ending with EOT=$04.

PARALLEL I/O CONTROL REGISTER (PIOC)

7	6	5	4	3	2	1	0
STAF	STAI	CWOM	HNDS	OIN	PLS	EGA	INVB

STAF	**Strobe A Flag**	Set in response to STRA pin change of state, selectable rising or falling edge according to how the EGA bit is set. How the STAF is cleared depends on the selected handshake mode: **Simple Strobe Mode (HNDS=0)** - clears when PORTCL is read **Full-Input Handshake Mode (HNDS=1, OIN=0)** - clears when PORTCL is read **Full-Output Handshake Mode (HNDS=1, OIN=1)** - clears when PORTCL is written to
STAI	**Strobe A Interrupt Enable**	0 - STAF interrupts are inhibited. 1 - A hardware interrupt request is generated whenever the STAF bit is set
CWOM	**Port C Wired-OR Mode**	0 - Port C outputs are active push-pull drivers. 1 - Port C outputs are open-drain drivers.
HNDS	**Handshake/Simple Strobe Mode Select**	0 - Simple Strobe mode is selected; STRB is pulsed for 2 clock cycles after each write to port B (no handshaking). 1 - .either full-input or full-output handshake mode is selected; Port C is used.
OIN	**Output/Input Handshake Select**	HNDS must be 1 or there is no effect. 0 - full-input handshake is selected. 1 - full-output handshake is selected

Contd...

PLS	**Strobe B Pulse Mode Select**	Controls the configuration of the STRB pin. HNDS must be 1 or else STRB will default to pulsed mode. 0 - Interlocked mode; (HNDS must be 1) STRB will remain active until an edge is detected at the STRA pin. 1 - Pulsed mode; STRB is active for 2 clock cycles when triggered.
EGA	**Edge Select for Strobe A**	0 - falling edges are detected at the STRA input pin. 1 - rising edges are detected at the STRA input pin.
INVB	**Invert Strobe B**	0 - Negative logic; STRB signals are active low. 1 - Positive logic; STRB signals are active high.

Index